MW01595520

THE OPEN ROAD

Autobiography of
GEORGE A. HORMEL

Copyright © 2017 Thomas D. Hormel & James C. Hormel

All rights reserved. Printed in the United States of America.
No part of this publication may be reproduced, stored in a retrieval system, or
transmitted in any form or by any means, electronic, mechanical, photocopying,
recording, or otherwise, without the written permission of the publisher.

ISBN: 978-09976-8581-7 (Trade paper)
ISBN: 978-09976-8580-0 (Hardcover)
Library of Congress Control Number: 2016945072

Hormel Historic Home
208 4th Avenue NW
Austin, Minnesota 55912

Table of Contents

Foreword

By James C. Hormel

In the early 1970's, during the time I was a member of the board of directors of Hormel Foods, I received a cardboard box sent to me from Jim Holton, who had recently become the company's CEO. The box contained old, typewritten pages—a manuscript I did not know existed—the unpublished autobiography written by the company's founder, my grandfather, George A. Hormel.

I read the manuscript and was fascinated. This was my grandfather, a man who was already in his seventies when I was born and with whom I had never had a substantive conversation. I was thirteen when he died and he epitomized a generation of elderly people of no particular interest to me.

But here he was, with keen insights and visionary philosophies, sharing his observations on a whole era of American history—how we went from gaslight and buggies to television and airplanes in three generations. George A., as he was known, put into vivid context the transformation of a United States that, almost tearing itself asunder when he was a tiny boy, became recognized as the most powerful country on earth at the time of his death. The U.S. wasn't even as old as I am now (84 years) when George A. was born.

Many years later, I was delighted when my brother Thomas decided to publish our grandfather's text. My reaction was personal. I wasn't thinking about how his story might affect the world; I was thinking more in terms of how members of our family would have something wonderful on which to reflect.

My grandfather was guided by a social conscience. It took precedence in his personal philosophy, politics and reflex reactions to his surroundings, and caused him to give great consideration to the world around him and how people are affected by the actions of others.

In an industry that is often nasty, hard, brutish, and backbiting, it is this quality of George A. Hormel as a human being that made him a champion and a pioneer.

Preface

By Thomas D. Hormel

A stunning description of the tired, old horses in the tannery yard opens this book, dispelling any doubt as to the author's skill with words.

It was after my second reading of my grandfather's manuscript that I resolved to see it published. In his lifetime, George A. had witnessed great changes in the American lifestyle. His viewpoint has a unique value. His humanity and subtle wit makes this autobiography priceless.

In his 86 years, George A. saw Lincoln on his way to his second inauguration. He observed the industrial age as it effected a huge change in the way of life in the western world. He described the development of public sanitation as it began to support the needs of a fast-growing population. He put into perspective the changes that grew out of communication and transportation, as energy became converted from manpower to electric and mechanical. He lived through the horrors of two world wars. He founded what would become a major, international food corporation. I hope you will agree that his unique perspective of the world in this period of dynamic transformation should be preserved and treasured as part of our American history.

I called my brother Jim to solicit his thoughts about the editing task in preparing this manuscript for publication. We asked Sandra Weinrib Stanfield to lead the process. Sandy and I began by studying the writing styles of biographers of Benjamin Franklin, Thomas Jefferson, George Washington, the Marquis de Lafayette, and Mark Twain. In addition, Jim and I studied our grandfather's writing and speculated on the best way to edit it.

We would like to acknowledge Sandy's astute assessment of what Jim and I agree was our grandfather's moral focus. Sandy understood and felt the respectful connection that George A. had to his workers and to his community. She prepared the manuscript, organized the posse and rode shotgun on all the little parts of the research that had to be done to turn this project into a published book.

George A. last worked on *The Open Road* in 1946, the year of his passing. We question whether he considered the manuscript complete. We all felt there was a special power in the original version, *The Open Road*, that should not be compromised. Although this book is based on that original manuscript, a later, edited version entitled *Three Men and a Business*, was bound and privately distributed in 1994 to members of the Hormel family and other interested parties. That version removed some passages that captured the social conditions of the times. We have elected to retain those passages.

We followed some other basic rules in preparing the final manuscript for this publication. Wherever we encountered differences between the two manuscripts, we would opt for *The Open Road* version, which seemed to more authentically display George A.'s unique way of thinking things through and expressing himself. We decided that a few passages from *Three Men and a Business*, which contained informative aspects of the story missing from *The Open Road*, would be incorporated into this text. The book that follows is true to what we (my brother Jim and I) consider our grandfather's original intent in writing about his life's work.

This is a glimpse inside the humble, caring mind of a great man with an extraordinary work ethic. His dreams and accomplishments purposefully benefitted his entire community.

Sandra Weinrib Stanfield

CHAPTER ONE

My World of Yesterday

Every rib showing in their poor, uncared-for coats, the half-starved horses tethered in my father's tannery yard hungrily neighed and pawed the ground as I began filling their nose bags with oats.

"Give them good measure, George," Father said. "The Lord knows the poor scarecrows need it." He sighed as he examined the thin sides of the latest arrivals among them. "It's going to cost more to get them in condition than the price they will bring."

Besides the horses, butchers' carts, meat blocks, counters and other market equipment littered the yard and sheds.

"What are you going to do with these things?" I asked.

"I don't know," Father answered. "What can I do with them when people are going out of business every day, all over the country?"

Even at thirteen, I knew that I had asked my troubled father a needlessly foolish question. What, indeed, could anyone do with anything at a time like this? A mysterious something called a "panic" had swept out of a vague place called "Wall Street." I thought it must resemble a tornado, for I had heard my father say to his partner,

Heyer, "When the storm blows down the big trees, the little trees in their path go down too. Remember how it was in '57?"

My father and his partner were evidently "little trees," as were the butchers whose poor belongings now littered the tannery property of Hormel & Heyer; for at night, after supper, Father worked at his accounts, often sighing as if he were very tired and worried, and the ordinarily placid Heyer wore a troubled face as well. I knew that the company had made small loans to the butchers from whom it bought hides and tallow in return for a piece of paper called a "chattel mortgage," and now the butchers, without being asked were bringing in their carts and horses and meat blocks. Out of a clear sky, it seemed people in Toledo weren't buying meat anymore.

They weren't buying meat, Father explained, because they were not working. At such times people still needed to eat. It was true, but they couldn't eat if they couldn't work, and they couldn't find work or stay in business, no matter how anxious and willing they might be to do these things, when a panic came along. One came along every ten years or so and brought "hard times" to little businessmen, like the butchers whose customers were out of work. No, said Father, a panic was not exactly an act of God, like a flood or an earthquake, though its effect was very much the same. People lost their jobs and homes and property. And, unlike a flood where the police and soldiers stood by to prevent robbers from looting, when a panic struck, mysterious individuals called "panic birds" descended on the stricken populace and gobbled up everything in sight while men were too stunned to protect themselves.

Thinking about those hungry horses and their once jolly owners, many of whom I knew well and who had changed in a few short months almost as much as their horses, made me feel very sad.

Like all children of the poor, I knew that to be without work and money was almost as bad as being dead. When a man lost his job and couldn't find another, his children not only suffered, they were disgraced. Boys whose fathers were out of work didn't want to eat their lunches with others at school when their bread had only drippings spread on it instead of butter and meat. Little things like that separated them from the children whose fathers worked "steady." No penny for Sunday School, cardboard stuffed in broken shoes, no candy apple on a stick for a Saturday treat; these were the nice distinctions between the children of the poor and the poverty-stricken, the gainfully employed and the idle.

I was much too young in 1873 to understand the complicated causes behind this phenomenon called panic which had suddenly disrupted the lives of so many and which people discussed in subdued, hopeless voices or else shouted about on street corners and in the railroad yards, raising clenched fists and calling on God to "smite the rascals." Nevertheless, I was old enough to be immediately affected by its results, for it was my introduction—as it was for thousands of other teenage boys and girls that year—to the world of hard work and constant struggle for a livelihood. My father's tannery soon went the way of the butchers' horses and meat blocks. I quit school and went to work for fifty cents a day, glad to be able to contribute my share toward helping him feed seven hungry mouths—a considerable job for one man even under favorable circumstances.

But it was to be a long time before circumstances were again favorable to my father and millions like him. The chill winds that blew out of Wall Street with the collapse of Jay Cooke's railroad promotions brought the prolonged kind of "hard times" the American people were not to see again until I reached my seventieth birthday when another generation of overoptimists and speculators sowed the whirlwind, bringing to the common man of their time a decade of confusion and insecurity. There were differences in origins between these two disasters, it is true, but they shared one thing—in 1929 as in 1873, catastrophe was not confined to the financial jugglers alone. Men who never heard of Wall Street except when a hurricane swept out of it, or who never gambled a speculative dollar in their lives, lost their shirts.

One such man was John George Hormel, my father, who used the name George. Born in 1830 in Germany of Huguenot parents who had fled religious persecution in France, he had been brought to the United States as a child of three. Industrious, frugal, and ambitious, he had modestly prospered in his new country at his trade of wool puller and tanner. In 1865, he had left the relative security of the superintendency of a tannery in Buffalo, New York, to try his fortunes in "the fastest growing city in the West," Toledo, Ohio.

Toledo, which at the time of our family's arrival was a sprawling boom town of twenty thousand people, was justifiably feeling its oats, for in some commercial activities it had outdistanced its rival, Chicago. At Toledo came together a network of railroads and waterways. Its magnificent natural harbor, Maumee Bay on Lake Erie with its thirty miles of waterfront, made the city one of the chief ports on the Great Lakes. It was also situated on one of the principal East-West overland routes. I remember seeing long lines of creaking ox carts going through town as a constant stream of pilgrims seeking fortune in the West passed through it, some lured by gold strikes in the Rockies, others by the opening of the prairies by the railroads, all of them seeking new worlds to conquer—heirs to the American dream.

I had the good fortune to grow up in a place and at a time when the dream was very real. By some miracle, Abe Lincoln "had saved the Union," and people were looking forward to a better future than any past they had known. Although I was only five at the time, I have a recollection of the war's end and of the long troop trains passing through town, returning the soldiers to their homes.

They shouted and waved at the weeping, watching crowds and sang "John Brown's Body" and "Tenting on the Old Campground." Carried away by the excitement, I waved back and shouted too, and learned to play the songs I heard them sing on a little Jew's harp Father bought for me. I was considered too young to be taken along but my grandmother took my oldest sister, Elizabeth, who was only seven, to "see" Mr. Lincoln, who was also going home to Springfield—in a crepe-covered funeral car. And I remember the grief in our family; it was almost as though one of us had died.

With the war's ending, the nation began its westward march. The campaign slogan of 1860, "Vote yourself a mule and forty acres," had found its realization in the Homestead Act of 1862. But even people not lured by the promise of free land pulled up stakes in an effort to better their condition. These Argonauts, our family among them, poured into Toledo. An old city directory, published in 1866 which belonged to Father, boasted:

> Without rendering ourselves liable to the charge of exaggeration, we may state that the growth of Toledo has been second to no city in the West, while in commerce it has far outstripped its sister cities save one, Chicago.

But in the time-honored tradition of American city rivalry, the directory refused to admit that Chicago's supremacy was in any way due to the efforts of Chicagoans, for it continued:

This, however, is not remarkable when we consider the various channels through which are poured into *her* lap the products of the West.

It was in this "fastest growing city of the West" that Father saw the possibility of realizing his lifelong dream of going into business for himself. For years he had saved every penny not demanded by the needs of his fast-growing family toward that end. This careful saving demanded considerable self-denial on his part, for he was a naturally generous man who loved giving presents. Sometimes he bought them anyway.

I remember an elegant coal oil lamp which graced our parlor for many years. When Father brought it home shortly before we left Buffalo, the neighbors flocked in to look at the first kerosene burning lamp many of them had ever seen. They stood around admiringly while one of us touched the match to the wick and flooded the room with light—the kind of light no whale oil or candle could furnish. That lamp must have cost Father a great deal of money. Its big, chased brass bowl held a quart or more of kerosene, was mounted on an onyx pedestal and crystal pendants hung from its hand-painted glass shade. Mother was understandably torn between pride in such a possession and horror at the thought of what it had cost. She was a frugal soul who, from the moment Father began talking about going into business someday for himself, had secretly started a small hoard of her own saved penny by penny from her house allowance. This was to be her personal contribution when the great day came.

While still in Buffalo, Father became friendly with a Mr. Heyer, also a tanner. Like Father, he too had a growing family, but there the resemblance ceased. Heyer was a happy-go-lucky, easygoing man—"the salt of the earth," my father and his other friends said, but not one to salt away much else. Although he had saved no money, he was so taken with Father's idea of becoming a businessman that he urged to be included in the new venture, promising that a relative in Detroit would willingly lend him his share of capital. On this slender foundation Father agreed, so the Heyers accompanied us to Toledo. The growing city, with its network of rail and waterborne commerce tapping rich stock-producing areas, was an ideal location for a tannery. Soon after their arrival, the partners found a suitable site on the banks of the Miami and Erie Canal in what was known as Central Toledo.

Heyer had exhausted what small funds he possessed in getting his family moved into their new home and, while he was in no hurry about it himself, at my father's urging he set off to Detroit to get the money he had promised to put into their joint venture. He returned empty-handed. His relatives, he said, had refused to honor their former agreement.

This was the situation when the two men began the back-breaking work of digging holes in the heavy ground for the big, oak-lined tanning vats: two families, a dozen mouths to be fed, no money coming in, and only my father's small savings to finance a venture requiring more of everything than he had to put into it. He must have had the courage of a lion.

"We'll manage somehow," he assured my mother when she reminded him that he was not obligated to carry the Heyers or to continue the partnership. "Heyer means well. It is not his fault that the money is not forthcoming as promised. We can't fail him because others have failed him," he said, and Mother agreed.

So the partners continued to dig the heavy ground. They were both strong, robust men, but they were not accustomed to the hour after hour, pick-and-shovel labor necessary to remove the quantities of earth which had to be displaced to make room for the six ten-foot by fourteen-foot by six-foot vats. Until the job was finished, each night found them exhausted; their hands, arms, and backs swollen and sore.

Years later the scene came vividly back to me as I watched a power shovel remove more dirt in a few hours than my father and Heyer had managed to do in weeks. I saw a hillside leveled and the dirt removed with less expenditure of human energy than the two men spent in one hour using hand tools. Power-driven bulldozer, shovel, and truck had yet to free men from such toil, only to steal away their livelihood in the process.

But theirs was the courage of the pioneer, so despite sore backs and cracked hands they finished the job with the aid of a ship's carpenter who helped them build the tannery.

By the time their little plant was finished, however, there was not enough money left with which to purchase raw materials for its operation. Father, somehow, managed to keep up a brave front and no one but Mother knew how discouraged and heartsick he felt at this poor beginning. Then it was, if I remember rightly, that she turned over to him her tiny store of dollars and urged him to use them on a trip back to Buffalo. One of her brothers going to the war had been killed in a train wreck.[1] Father had helped his father-in-law collect damages from the railroad. Mother thought perhaps her father would loan him a few hundred dollars of this money.

My grandfather, like Heyer's relatives, refused, and my father must have hit bottom in the realization that he, too, would return

---

1 The Civil War.

empty-handed. At any rate, another member of the family questioned him. "I've never seen you look so discouraged, what is wrong?" And Father unburdened himself. "If all you need is money," he was told, "you may have some of mine; I'll be glad to let you have it. Repay me when you can." This was indeed a reprieve and from an unexpected source, for Father had neither known that the man had any money nor certainly not that he would lend it to him if he had.

Father's explanation was simple. "Who answers prayer? The first person who can."

On his return, a new business blossomed forth in Toledo—"Hormel & Heyer, Wool Pullers and Manufacturers of Colored Linings and Roans." So read the firm's business cards. Their facilities and equipment were crude, but both men were skilled at their trade; they were all-around craftsmen and their chance for success in that pre-machine age was as good as the next man's. They knew that from such small beginnings as their own, the great American enterprises already astounding the world had grown. The great Jay Cooke, financial wizard of Wall Street whose ability to sell government bonds had helped Abe Lincoln save the Union and who was now financing a railroad empire in the West, began life as a poor clerk in a Sandusky, Ohio general store. Jay Gould, also making a name for himself in railroad promotions, had been, like themselves, a tanner. A bright, young man in Cleveland named Rockefeller had graduated from a small commission business to the ownership of an oil refinery. Anything might happen in this land of opportunity if you worked hard and saved your money.

But Father was not the only one in our family imbued with the idea of what might be accomplished through hard work. While he and his partner were busy from sunrise to sunset creating a business out of a few small buildings and tanning vats, my mother was equally busy creating a home—perhaps a far harder task in those days considering the limited means at a woman's disposal and the home's never-ending demands on her time and energy.

Mother, born Susanna Decker, was, like Father, a native of Germany, with the difference that she was of German while he was French descent. She had come to Buffalo as a girl of sixteen. Married while still in her teens, she applied herself to the business of rearing a family and helping Father with all the skill and energy at her command—and she had plenty of both! She managed her myriad household activities on schedule, and just as soon as we were old enough to undertake the smallest responsibility, she delegated a household chore to each child. Mine was cleaning and polishing the family shoes each Saturday.

I was not more than seven when this became my task. When I finished the job, I was required to arrange the shoes in an orderly row for Mother's inspection. Never casual about these inspections, she carefully examined each pair. Frequently anxious to be off playing, I would skimp on elbow grease and time, with the result that, while the row viewed from the front would dazzle the eye, the rear view was not so impressive. I never fooled her. "Nein!" she would say. "No, George, this will not do. *Forna ist huey und hinter ist fuey!*" And no matter how I tried, if "in front they were fine but in back they were phooey," I did them over—sometimes several times to the accompaniment of loud weeping. On such occasions, if Father happened to be there, he might show his sympathy by patting me on the head, but he never interfered. Eventually, I learned, as she intended that I should, that it was quicker and easier to do the chore properly the first time. This lesson, learned the hard way, many times since has proved a gold mine to me, for it established the habit early in life of doing a task as best I could when it was first given me to do. It has been one of the rules by which I have measured the worth of the men who have worked with me, as well as my own effort.

My mother was not harsh, but she had little patience with coddling. She had a growing family and she was determined that they should be trained in such a way that they would be both a credit to her and to society.

When I was small, I would often ask her, "Does this please you?" or "Is this right?" and she would invariably answer, "First, ask yourself, 'Is this the best I can do? Is it neat? Orderly? Have I accomplished what I set out to do?' If, after you have asked yourself these questions, you still do not know the answer, what good is my opinion, George?"

Her method was Spartan, but it got results. By the time any one of her children—five boys and five girls—reached the age of ten, he or she was competent to carry out any assigned task without supervision and needed to make no apologies for the way it had been discharged.

Our first home in Toledo was the second story of a small frame building near the tannery. The family furniture, brought from Buffalo, had been much damaged in the rough passage down Lake Erie. The stove was cracked and broken; other pieces of Mother's prized furniture, water-stained and warped. But in spite of these mishaps, she soon created a friendly, livable background for her family out of what she had to do with.

Judged by modern standards (1946), what she had to do with seems meager indeed. Our beds boasted no springs or mattresses. In the place of springs there were cross slats, topped by a well-stuffed straw tick. We had kerosene lamps, the oil being furnished by one of young Mr. Rockefeller's agents, a house-to-house peddler called "Coal Oil Johnny." Bathtubs, sinks, and running water were—at least in our part of the world—unknown luxuries. At first, all the family clothing was made by hand, but when sewing machines came into use, Father insisted that Mother should have one. Our machine cost eighty-five dollars—an investment equivalent to four hundred dollars today—and occupied the place of honor in the living room. It was treated as though it were a household shrine—which in a sense it was, since with its aid Mother could keep us better dressed than the children whose mothers were still using hand methods, and with far less time and labor.

I have often wondered if anybody realized just what the coming of that first machine in the home meant, for with it the day of the mechanized American home had begun. It was the first Emancipation Proclamation for such women as my mother. She was not only without such services at her command as even people in our modest circumstances would use without question today, she had no carpet sweeper, easy-to-clean floor coverings, icebox, wire screens, enameled kitchenware, or anything else to simplify the homemaker's lot and conserve her energy.

But one thing she did have—and I sometimes think many a modern woman would change places with my mother on this if on no other count—inside the four walls of her home, her word was law. Each member of the family gave her their unquestioning obedience and such help as they were able to render. It was the price she exacted, and we were glad to pay in return for the protection and comfort of the home her effort made possible.

The Toledo of the 1860's, like the homes of the period, was a very different place from the one its lucky citizens know today. Then, there were no clean, paved streets, well-kept parks, art museums, and fine stores. It did, however, boast a public school system. Many an American city far bigger than Toledo offered no such advantages to *all* its junior citizens. In other places, we were reminded, they either went to private schools or were "charity pupils" in semi-public schools, unless their parents were taxpayers. Yea, it may seem strange to people born only a few decades later, but in America less than seventy years ago, education was largely a monopoly enjoyed by the privileged few. Moreover, sanitary codes, building restrictions, fire and police protection—a dozen public services taken for granted now, like an education at public expense—were either primitive or nonexistent.

Licenses and public inspections of any kind were unknown. A man might build a house for his own use or the use of others, and if it fell down and killed his family or tenants, it was his or their hard luck and not a matter concerning the public interest. Civic responsibility and group cooperation were social theories just coming into being, but the institutions and instruments through which these ideas were to become effective had yet to be created. Those were the days of "rugged individualism" without apology or pretense. A man could do what he liked with his own—and he did! These are points to be remembered in this story, which is only incidentally *my* story. It is a story of something far bigger and more important than any one man's life—a turning point, if you will, in a nation's history. I just happened along in time to see it turn the corner.

Seventy-five years ago the average residential district in Toledo, or any one of a hundred cities of the period, consisted of rows of narrow, dark-looking, two-story houses with unkempt front yards fronting on unpaved streets; lawn mowers had not yet been invented. In each backyard was a well, equipped with a hand pump. Nearby stood that butt of so much choice early American humor, the family privy. Fronting on a back alley was the stable for a horse or cow, usually both. Pigpens, chicken coops and runways were also standard backyard equipment. In addition to all other livestock, a couple of dispirited ducks or geese generally wandered around the premises, listlessly scratching in summer dust heaps or wallowing in winter muck. Manure from the stables and refuse from the house were piled in these back alleys. There was no garbage problem—the pigs and chickens saw to that. And since there were no sewers, greasy dishwater was thrown into the yard as well.

In the winter when we children played hide-and-go-seek in the alleys, we had to guard against stumbling over discarded tallow candle molds and women's dress hoops imbedded in the frozen earth and sticking out just enough to trip a child's flying feet. I feel sure that if the sites of these old alleys were mined, they would provide an inexhaustible treasure for the present-day crop of American antique collectors: door knockers, candle molds, warming pans—what wouldn't turn up? For the alleys were the graveyards for everything one wished to get rid of.

But they were far from being treasure-troves in my time. In summer, these yards and back-alley dump heaps were inhabited by swarms of flies: horse flies, house flies, skipper flies. Children playing in the alleys were infected and reinfected with typhoid, smallpox, diphtheria, and other dread diseases. Looking backward, I am convinced that nothing but the innate toughness of the human race ever saved it from extinction in those days. Malarial mosquitoes bred unhindered in green, stagnant pools, and every summer whole families shook with the ague.[2] Needless to say, infant mortality was terrific. It was the survival of the fittest. I was reminded of all this some years ago when traveling in Egypt as I watched the wonderful physical specimens who were at work dipping water out of the Nile for irrigation. I asked the guide what explanation he had for this and he replied, "Those who are not born physically strong do not survive."

Patent medicines, usually well-fortified with opiates, were dealt out to one and all when an epidemic swept through town. Laudanum "drops" and other opium-tinctured drugs, whose effects were worse than the diseases they were "guaranteed" to cure, were foisted on the public with no hindrance from authorities. Quacks peddled these nostrums from house to house. Any child could buy them by walking into a drug store.

"Let the buyer beware!" was the axiom of business generally, since each man operated his business as he saw fit. If he chose to adulterate food, color jams with injurious aniline dyes, sell diseased and doctored meat for good meat and shoddy for virgin wool, sweat his employees, or engage in any other antisocial practice, there was nothing but his conscience to restrain him, for the law did not. He could be penalized only by the public's refusal to buy his goods or services. This did happen and many a rogue was put out of business—good will then, as now, being a potent factor in success. But you had to be a better judge of goods and character then to get value for your money, and not all the public was by any means possessed of either standards of quality or the knowledge with which to protect itself. New concepts and new means for the widespread dispersal of

2 Shivering caused by malaria.

information were in the making; however, by the turn of the century, the "public be damned" philosophy of an earlier day was fast ceasing to pay dividends to most of its practitioners.

Since the home, like business, was self-contained and self-administered, its standards, too, judged by the present, were relative. The quantity of water available determined personal and home cleanliness. The notion of how often one could safely take a bath was not inseparable from the hard job of carrying enough water into the house in buckets and heating it on the stove, which also meant chopping and lugging in wood. Mother had passionate convictions on the subject of hot water and soap, but many people considered it the height of foolhardiness to take baths in wintertime. The germ's affinity for dirt would not penetrate the American consciousness until central water systems and sewers made altering its concepts of personal and public health and behavior a less onerous proceeding.

But if the Toledo of my boyhood offered its inhabitants few safeguards and conveniences, farm dwellers had even less. On our Sunday trips into the country, we sometimes visited with not-so-prosperous farmers who were still using tallow dips long after kerosene had supplanted candles in town. Many older farm women still carded and spun wool to clothe their families. "Boughten goods" were high in terms of the low barter value of farm commodities. Money, while used in commercial transactions, was not the circulating medium it is today; farmers, unless they raised a "cash crop" such as grain, seldom handled any. What cash a farmer did come by often went to pay interest on mortgages lent at rates as high as ten percent.

In town, the churches and schools provided a wide variety of entertainment and social get-togethers. Amusements in country districts were limited to cornhuskings and occasional fairs, with perhaps a passing minstrel or medicine show holding forth on market day at the county seat. Poor roads, horse and buggy transportation, and limited opportunities for social intercourse restricted life on the farm to work and not much else. Almost every enterprising farm youngster I knew as a child planned to leave the farm to seek his fortune elsewhere, just as soon as he was old enough and able. The drift to the cities, which became an exodus by the time I reached manhood, was already underway. "Free land" might still be bait to their elders, but it was fast ceasing to be such to the ambitious farm young of the nation.

People generally spent very little money on amusements or anything else they could do without, particularly if they had ambitions to improve their economic status. Our family was a case in point.

Capital could only be accumulated through penny-pinching thrift. Father needed it. Mother's job was to see that he got it through rigid control of household expenditures. Food and clothing were plentiful but of the plainest sort. Nothing was wasted; scraps of food and odds and ends of material were saved and converted into something useful. Wood ashes from the stove were collected, leached for lye, and the lye water mixed with the fats saved from cooking. The result was the family soap supply for general housework. To provide a large family such as ours with clean clothes takes a lot of soap; therefore, we made our own. In our household, as in others of the period, a patch was not necessarily a badge of poverty. Father might buy me a pair of red-topped, copper-toed shoes—he did and was I proud of them—but toys and playthings were rarely purchased. If a child wanted something to play with, he made it himself, sometimes with his parents' help.

I remember our first wagon. Its wheels were cut from a round piece of cordwood salvaged from the family woodpile, its axles shaped from a hickory limb. A soap box begged from the grocer was bolted to this primitive chassis; a rope tied to the front axle near the wheels completed the job. My brothers and I took turns riding and pulling each other around in this rig. When it came your turn to pull, you sweated and puffed, but every child thought his turn to ride was well worth the effort of pulling the others.

Following the lamplighter on his rounds was another prized amusement which cost nothing. A troop of us would collect and wait for him on a corner near our home. When he appeared, a dozen grubby hands would reach for the honor of placing his light ladder against the lamppost. "Let me!" "No, me!" we would shout. Sometimes, if he were feeling indulgent and in no hurry, a favored child would be allowed to climb the ladder, turn the cock, and apply the torch to the gas jet. We were always thrilled by the miracle which followed this operation as the bright beacon flamed into life. Few of us were ever abroad late at night, but we knew what light meant to wayfarers. Its protection guarded them against the perils of the dark. Once seen, mud holes and robbers alike could be avoided.

And we made music. The war had popularized the fife and drum. Almost every group of neighborhood youngsters organized a fife and drum corps. This was not hard to do. A round cheese box, such as could be obtained at any grocery store for the asking, made a fine drum frame when we scraped it smooth with bits of glass, then had it shellacked at a paint shop. We prepared the drum heads ourselves at the tannery. During the long summer evenings, all the children in our neighborhood congregated on a vacant lot near our home, attracted by the sound of my brother Henry's fife accompanied by four snare drums. Here we marched and sang the songs men had so lately made immortal on their country's battlefields. And somehow we knew what those songs meant. We knew that many of the men who had sung them before us had also died, had died to make us "free"—free to play on a vacant lot together whether we were white or black, Jew or Gentile, and to go to school and to call ourselves "The Sons of Liberty." These were the freedoms we understood.

As children still do, we created other playthings, such as kites and bows and arrows. Sometimes Father helped us make them, other times he suggested and directed the operations, but always the major effort was ours. These activities developed the ingenuity, imagination, and manual skills of all of us. Out of our efforts came a real appreciation of what goes into making anything. As Father often said, we were not apt to destroy casually what had cost us so much energy to create. He believed that every child was a potential artist and craftsman; all it needed was the opportunity for creative expression. But he also understood something else. "You will be either a maker or a destroyer," he once said to us, "for your energy must have an outlet."

I have often thought since how shrewdly wise that good and simple man really was. He understood the basic problem of human behavior—one was either a maker or a destroyer; which of the two was wholly a question of guidance and opportunity, for "energy must have an outlet."

Another keynote of the times was the attitude of parents toward rewarding children for what was essentially self-service. Money was not given to a child as a reward for good behavior or work at home. A weekly allowance in return for a few casually performed chores was the kind of unwise extravagance only afforded by the already well-to-do who, perhaps, might safely pamper their young. My parents, however, disbelieved in this on principle. They considered a child's

efforts to be its personal contribution toward its own safety and comfort, not a debt contracted by them. Only work outside the home
was entitled to a cash consideration. This point of view had one
drawback—it made children all too eager to become wage earners.

I remember hanging out the window in the early morning envi-
ously watching the older boys go by on their way to work. Their caps
set at a jaunty angle, lunch pails swinging, they were to my eyes
the sight of masculine self-sufficiency. The fact that these imma-
ture youngsters should still have been in school, that their parents
and the community owed them educational opportunities beyond
the bare ability to read, write, and calculate, never occurred to me,
as it seldom occurred to their elders. Although paid a boy's wage,
as I soon found out when I joined their ranks, these youngsters
were required to do a man's work, thereby decreasing their fathers'
ability to earn decent wages by the competition they offered in the
labor market. But only "radicals" entertained any such wild ideas
as compulsory schooling in the 1860's and 1870's; "solid" citizens
saw no harm, only benefit, in a large and continuous army of young,
semi-literate workers. But, just around the corner, time had some
surprises which were going to upset a great many of the solid citizens' ideas—in their own interest. They were going to learn a new
word: technology.

One idea of the times—and still a good one, if it any longer had
meaning—was that every boy should spend some time learning
his father's business or occupation. After school, on Saturdays and
during vacations, boys clerked in their fathers' stores, read law
in their offices, or made themselves generally useful in whatever
activity their elders might be employed. By the time a boy reached
the age where he was ready to choose his life's work, he had some

idea of what he could and wanted to do. It is well to point out, however, that in those days this training was possible because *three
out of five* boys' fathers were self-employed. By 1930, sixty years
later, this avenue of opportunity had all but closed; only *three out of
twenty* men owned their means of livelihood—the seventeen others
had become wholly dependent on the three.

Naturally, the Heyer boys and the boys in our family, as soon as
we were old enough, worked in the tannery. There, under our fathers'
supervision, we were put to work pulling wool from sheep pelts, or
spreading the wet wool on the roof to dry, then collecting the dry
wool and carefully storing it in the wool loft. In a surprisingly short
time, the youngest among us could do many of the light jobs in the
processing of raw skins into leather. By my thirteenth year, I was
able to perform any skilled task in either the wool pulling or tanning
departments of the business, and I could grade wool and leather
almost as well as my father. A few years later, just this one small
accomplishment learned in the tannery gave me an opportunity I
should not otherwise have had.

In addition to what we learned, working in the tannery had other
compensations, for if we quickly finished the task assigned to us,
we were then permitted to swim in the vat where the skins were
first soaked. Although a soaking vat is not exactly an "ole swimmin'
hole," and is not to be recommended to fussy customers; still, in the
days when no thought of germs existed to mar one's pleasures in the
simple life, a soaking vat on a hot day was a fine place for a swim.

It was the evening *Toledo Blade* and the *Democrat*, a morning paper, to which I became indebted for my first opportunity to
work for money wages. I would have gladly gone before, but I was
restrained until my eighth birthday. Shortly thereafter, I turned up

at the *Democrat's* pressroom at four o'clock of a cold morning. By the light of smoking kerosene lamps, the printers were putting the finishing touches to their night's work. Printers' ink, tobacco, and the assorted smells of burning coal, kerosene and the printers' whiskey mingled with the odors of paper and wet leather to produce a perfume familiar to the frequenters of pressrooms of an earlier day.

When I arrived, a group of patient newsboys were already waiting in line for the *Democrat's* run to begin. The paper was printed on an old style Merkle press, powered by steam. The cylinder carrying the paper revolved slowly, printing only one side at a time. A slat frame received the finished paper and placed it on a bench beside the press. When the right number of papers accumulated, the first boy in line picked them up, folded them, and left for his route. The next boy in line repeated the process. Latecomers in the line had to wait a long time before their turn arrived, for it was "first come, first served."

But the *Blade*, not the *Democrat*, was Toledo's chief newspaper. Boastful, sure of itself, it pictured Toledo as an earthly paradise. According to the *Blade*, the Creator, without a doubt, had singled out Toledo for His special favor. The *Blade* repeated this so often that everyone—including the *Blade*—began to believe it. Since you couldn't do much with perfection—and who would want to?—this uncritical attitude was far from being an unalloyed community good. As a source of news, all papers of that time left something to be desired. Front pages were devoted to small, one-column advertisements, with some bit of news of worldwide importance sandwiched in between patent medicine ads, trade announcements, oil well and land promotions. And the gentle reader who got burnt in 1929 and who thinks that time has not clipped the wings of the "blue sky" fraternity, should read those "promotions." There were no cuts or pictures to enliven the text, but in all fairness to the *Blade*'s reporters, the reader did not suffer on this account. The paper's reader appeal was in its highly colored stories of excitement on the Western Plains, Indian uprisings, local crime and last but not least, the editorial comments of its part owner, David Ross Locke, better known as "Petroleum Vesuvius Nasby."

Though the old *Blade* I knew might suffer by comparison with the truly great newspaper it became, its old-time editor suffers by comparison with no one! He was a versatile, nineteenth century combination of the late Will Rogers, Dorothy Thompson, Westbrook Pegler and Walter Lippmann, with *Information Please* and Emily Post thrown in as added attractions.

Locke, humorist and "tramp" printer, began his career in New York State, working his way west. He founded and edited various papers in Ohio before becoming part owner of the *Blade*. To aid the Union, whose staunch supporter he was, at the beginning of the Civil War he invented his famous character, "Petroleum V. Nasby," illiterate Kentucky postmaster who "loved whiskey" and "hated niggers." Locke's highly exaggerated portrayal of the Southern "Democrat" and what he stood for in those crucial times played a very important role in swinging opinion in the border states to the side of the Union. Lincoln was his enthusiastic admirer and was reported to read the "Nasby" letters as eagerly as he read accounts of battles. After the war, Locke used "Nasby" to propagandize for other causes he believed in. Mostly, he believed in one—democracy. And, what is more, he *really* believed in it.

My father, like Lincoln, was Locke's ardent admirer—and also his neighbor. Himself a passionate believer in democracy, each evening after supper, Father read aloud to the family Locke's progressive views on questions of the day. Locke thoroughly hated the hypocrites who gave lip service only to the democratic way of life. He taunted their cowardice and dared them to try it—just in case it should be a "good thing." He supported equality for women—in education, politics and business—and stoutly defended their right to other advantages enjoyed by men. Since they shared all the disadvantages, he pointed out, why not the other? And although it was reported that "ye editor" was given to personal bouts with the demon rum, he took up the cudgels for temperance. A powerful exponent of the idea that no man is ever better than he feels himself to be, Locke never tired of contrasting the social ideals of a free Western world with the caste-ridden Europe my parents had left behind.

The Bible and Locke's editorials were the two greatest influences in our family's thinking, as they no doubt were in many another Ohio home. Father read and discussed them both. It was his firm conviction that only Christian teaching could produce democracy; only Christian living made it realizable. You could not have one without the other; they were inseparable. Christ's teachings gave the principles; democracy was the result of those principles in motion. Since the principles had to do with man's relationship to himself, to God, and to other men, their honest application could only produce one political order in human affairs—democracy. Sincere belief in the one led inevitably to the practice of the other.

Many years have gone by, and mighty empires with them, since I heard my father expound his belief that no free society could be organized on any other set of principles, nor one long endure which failed to acknowledge or refused to be faithful to its origins. And nothing in time's calendar has yet disproved him.

And I have never forgotten how earnestly he tried to show us that Christ's testament was our first "Bill of Rights" on which all our other so-called rights were founded.

"Can't you see," he would ask, "when every day of your lives is a demonstration of the reason for doing so, why loving your neighbor is not sentiment, only sense? Which one of us could live safely and securely by his own unaided effort? None of us, of course. We might exist, perhaps, as animals by our own effort, but we could not live as human beings."

He would point out that we aided the greater brotherhood which in turn aided us, just as our family supported and was supported by its members. We gave what we could individually and received what we needed. In the larger as in the small family, the same thing happened. He and we contributed leather and wool, receiving in return the varied fruits of many other men's labors.

"Just suppose," he would say, "we failed to do this. I fail you, you fail me, and everybody fails us. What would happen? If that time should ever come, no one will need to prove to you why a 'house divided cannot stand.' Well, that is what Christ was talking about. It is that simple. Does it make sense?"

It was—and did—to him. He had the kind of mind that some men have who can look at a machine and never see the metal, only the principle by which it operates. He was never confused by theories of how men ought to act. If they acted in a certain way, the results they obtained proved their understanding or lack of understanding of the laws by which they lived. They profited by the first and paid for their ignorance by the second. This was the way they learned. If, in the end, they learned, who remembered or cared about their many failures? Not God. That was the meaning of grace. The only man who failed to receive it in the end was the man who stopped trying to win it.

Father loved to read, and although in those days there were no city-maintained or endowed libraries, we did have access to a few books. We could have bought books, no doubt, in Toledo, but we had so little money to spend. The church to which we belonged, and others we sometimes attended, usually had a small collection of books, however, for lending. It was from these sources that we obtained *Uncle Tom's Cabin* and other popular books of the day.

Father subscribed to *The Youth's Companion* for us. This we read and lent to neighboring children until it fell apart. Since our reading matter stressed ideas not too dissimilar from what we heard our parents discuss and saw them practice, the conflict so apparent today between what a child is taught and what he sees and hears was not present. With the same values prevailing at home as were taught to us in school and church, we accepted these values as being universal; for we met them everywhere in our childhood universe and they were not questioned.

Looking backward, though, I am conscious of the educational and intellectual limitations of that childhood. I have no feeling of having failed to receive, at a time when I could make them my own, the essential ideas by which men live. Where I have failed has been in practicing as consistently as I might have done the great heritage of liberal and Christian tenets given me to use. They are among the few things I started out with that time has not outdated. From them I have received strength and inspiration to face seemingly hopeless situations. When I have faltered, they have been the beacons lighting the way to stumbling human feet, helping immeasurably to overcome the blindness inherent in us all.

Such formal schooling as I and most of my generation received was simple. We were taught to read, write, spell, do mental and written arithmetic—"our sums," we called them—and the rudiments of history and geography. Since to attend *school* at all was a privilege, you quickly applied yourself to learning these things or you were as quickly taken out of school and put to work. In my time, there was little nonsense about sugar-coating the educational pill; each child did the work assigned to it as best it could. Teachers were not afraid to discipline the lazy and indifferent, and parents took over where the teachers left off.

In my time, they did not have the steam heated rooms of today. They had large sheet iron stoves that would take in half-lengths of cordwood. Stoves were located in opposite corners of the room. If you happened to be near a stove you might keep warm, and it might be too hot on a cold day when an attempt was made to heat the cold corners. Firewood was piled high on the school grounds and we boys had to take turns in carrying this wood upstairs to the second story; for youngsters it meant carrying a stick at a time.

The result of this Spartan training, like my mother's, was that a child fortunate enough to attend school for as long as six years—my limit—could really write a legible hand, read intelligibly, do sums quickly and accurately, and otherwise use to advantage what it had learned. It also knew a little bit about the history of its country and had a faint idea of its geography.

While I never cease to marvel at the fruits of the truly educated modern mind, I think several generations of Americans did pretty well by themselves, considering their limited opportunities and the short time at their disposal in which to acquire the basic tools of an education. They had few illusions about how much they knew, but they knew how to use such tools as they had to get for themselves better ones, if they were so inclined.

As a child I liked to draw; caricatures and cartoons fascinated me. In my free time, I was always sketching people or drawing and designing buildings and other objects. With any opportunity for the study of art and architecture, I might have succeeded tolerably well. At least, my elders thought I showed some aptitude. When I was twelve and attending the Broadway Public School, its superintendent selected me to sketch the school building and to do a drawing for a book which was to contain the compositions of the school's best scholars. This book was to be sent to the Vienna World's Fair of 1873 as an example of American schoolwork. Proud of the honor bestowed on me, I sat at a desk across the street from the school and carefully sketched the new two-story brick building with its ornamentation. For the cover, I drew the age-old insignia of the scholar —a square ink bottle and a quill pen.

But my school days were nearly over, for the year was 1872. And even if there had been no panic the following year, graduation from grammar school would have been the most I could have aspired to. There were younger brothers and sisters to be given at least a grade schooling, and there was no nearby free high school. At that time, there were not more than a few hundred tax supported high schools in the entire nation. Colleges and college preparatory schools were for the children of families which had already acquired enough money to afford the luxury of buying a higher education—not for families such as ours, struggling inch by inch toward the hard goal of economic self-sufficiency. To tell the truth, it never entered my head that boys like me would ever attend the University of the City of Toledo, established that year.

Great changes were in the immediate offing, however. In 1871, the Congress and twenty-eight states set aside seventy million dollars to establish popular education. Machines were coming into use. Industry, commerce, and trade were beginning to demand better educated workers. The country was prosperous, and the long agitation for equal opportunity for all was at last bearing fruit. Then came the panic, putting a decided stop to at least one generation's hopes for better schooling. Only two boys out of the dozen or more in the sixth grade when I left school finished the eighth.

I went to work for a neighbor who was a lather. In the tannery where the wet sheepskins were stretched and tacked on frames to dry, I had learned to handle nails quickly so that after a few weeks' apprenticeship as a lather, I could equal an oldtimer's output. The pay was two cents a square yard. I began by being able to lay seventy-five square yards a day, working up to a top of one hundred and twenty-five in twelve hours. I was not employed every day, but when my boss had work for me I earned good money for a young lad. This bonanza only lasted a short time, for soon all new building ceased and I considered myself lucky to get a job as a man of all work in a meat market.

"All work" exactly describes my duties. My day began at six o'clock. In the morning, I delivered meat and solicited orders. Afternoons and until nine at night, I helped trim bones, make sausage, dress poultry, and did whatever else my tough-talking boss could find for me to do—he always found plenty! I worked like this six days a week for ten dollars a month and board. I really was what the communists talk about, a "wage slave," and I would have quit my brutal and tyrannical master the day I began working for him had it not been for my desire to help out at home.

When I finally got a chance to join a crew of "dockwallopers," as they were called, I jumped at it. My gang took contracts for unloading lumber, salt, and other shipload cargoes into warehouses. In addition to working with the crew, I was its timekeeper and secretary. I did the figuring, kept track of hours, and divided the proceeds of each job among the men. I was probably the only one in the crew who could write or who could calculate in fractions. But the work was too heavy for a boy of fourteen and I left it for a job in Mitchell & Roland's lumber yard at fifty cents a day, taking lumber away from a surfacing machine.

Then someone told me that I might be able to get on as helper on a tenon machine, at sixty cents a day, in the Wabash Railroad's car shops. I got the job, which seemed almost like a vacation by contrast with the heavy work I had been doing. I applied myself to learning the measurements of every mortise and tenon used in the construction of a boxcar. On the strength of this showing, I was given a slightly better job making oak cleats, which were used at the joints of the rails to hold them together. These frail, oaken straps, perhaps three quarters of an inch thick and sixteen inches long with holes bored at each end to fit similar holes in the rails, were all that stood between travelers and eternity. Let the reader compare the heavy iron clamps in use today with these inadequate devices and he will no longer be in any doubt why a train journey seventy years ago was a hazardous enterprise. Twenty to twenty-five miles an hour was top speed, but that was far too fast, particularly at such times as the railroads were in financial difficulties, with little money to spend for track repairs.

It finally came my turn to be laid off. After that, no matter how hard I tried, I was frequently out of a job for one reason or another. The creeping paralysis which had spread to every part of the business structure following the panic had made a steady job all but impossible to find. I desperately wanted such a job. The uncertainty of never knowing whether I would have a few dollars to hand my mother for my board at the week's end was fast making me into an overanxious, unsure boy. I was no sunny optimist by nature. Now circumstances strengthened my native tendency to be apprehensive and to have a poor opinion of myself and my capacities. Nothing I ever did suited me. The result of my efforts was never quite good enough. I yearned to do something perfectly. I didn't care what, just so I could point to some one thing and say to myself, "No one could do that better, George," and I drove myself in an effort to realize the unrealizable. Somewhere I had heard the epigram attributed to Michaelangelo, "In trifles lie success, which is no trifle." It deeply impressed me. If success could be obtained through the mastery of little things, then someday I would surely achieve it. In a way, this thought consoled me for my poor showing.

Shortly after the Wabash dispensed with my services, Mother received a letter from her youngest brother, Jacob Decker, saying that he had achieved a dream of his own; he was now a businessman, the proprietor of a packinghouse market in Chicago.

My Uncle Jay, as we called him, was a wholly romantic figure in our family. He had run away to sea at the age of twelve, after his mother had refused to allow him to join the Union Army as a drummer boy. Mostly, his sailoring had been confined to the Great Lakes, and whenever his ship came into a nearby port, Uncle Jay came to see us, as full of adventure tales as Sinbad, his pockets bulging with candy and small presents.

He wore a shaggy buffalo coat and a big bearskin cap in winter, looking like a big bear himself except for his ruddy, apple cheeks and bright, blue eyes. In summer, he wore a sailor's suit, and a jaunty sailor's cap cocked on the side of his head. He was as strong as an ox and loved a good fight. But he was something more than the Great Lakes' sailor of his time. He had ambitions and the energy with which to realize them.

"How would you like to go to Chicago and work for Uncle Jay?" Father questioned.

"I think I'd like it," I said.

"Then I'll write to him; the change will be good for you," said Father.

And when my uncle replied, "Come along," the die was cast.

I was so excited I could hardly sleep or eat. Chicago! That was the place where things happened—the "gem of the prairies," the "garden city" that had been all but destroyed by a great fire, only to amaze the world by rising from its ashes bigger and more wonderful than before. Who hadn't heard of it? Who didn't want to go there? Like millions before and since, I knew that Chicago spelled a future certainly more wonderful than anything to be found nearer home.

CHAPTER TWO

Gem of the Prairies

W hen the train finally pulled out from the depot, all the advice and suggestions given me at home on what to say and do on the journey vanished with the familiar faces left behind on the station platform. Warily, I looked around to see what disposition fellow travelers were making of their luggage; mine was still on the seat beside me. It consisted of a large bundle wrapped in oilskin held in place by a shawl strap; in it was everything I owned but the clothes on my back. Its companion piece was a huge, string-tied, cardboard box, containing enough sandwiches and cookies to victual a large family on a through trip to the Pacific Coast! Seeing my traveling companions stow their luggage under their seats, I did likewise. Throughout the trip, whenever I left my seat, I always looked under it on returning to make sure that my possessions were still there. They and the dollar in my pocket represented security.

I was a tall, blond boy, big for my age, toughened by hard work, and looking older than my years. But I was all too conscious of my youth and inexperience as the excitement of the adventure began to give way to anxiety and a new sense of the personal responsibility I had never known as a member of a family group. Every youth on first leaving home feels, no doubt, as I did—awkward, shy, and agonizingly self-conscious of his sudden aloneness and separateness from everybody else. And, if he is going—as I was—to a strange and fabulous city, wondering what is in store for him there and just how he will meet the new and unfamiliar, his sensations are both frightening and exhilarating—the way a bird must feel when it makes its first flight from the nest.

So I sat stiffly in my Sunday suit while the train rushed through the countryside at twenty-five miles an hour. But soon I forgot all about myself in watching farmers at their spring plowing as the checkerboard landscape flashed by with its new-turned fields and winter wheat, and orchards flecked with the first, adventurous blooms of apple and cherry. Then I began to feel superior to the knots of gaping idlers on station platforms of little towns along the route waiting to see the trains go through. They were stay-at-homes in places where nothing ever happened; I was a traveler, adventure bound to that eighth wonder of the world, Chicago!

At last, many long hours later, the train began to crawl through the outskirts of the city of my destination. By now I was weary of sightseeing and only anxious to reach the end of my maiden flight. But the first glimpse of the city of which I had heard so much was far from heartening. Miles and miles of ugly, smoke-grimed, cheerless buildings stretched into the distance as far as I could see. Along the lakefront, great dump heaps of ashes and city refuse, slag and rusted iron, blotched the landscape. Big draft horses, pulling loaded drays half mired in mud, struggled along bleak, treeless streets lined with weather-beaten, unpainted shanties whose dirt-scummed, curtainless windows, screened with rags and torn window shades, looked like eyeless sockets in a skeleton's face. I wondered what jokester had called this place the "garden city" and "gem of the prairies."

I was entering Chicago's famous "South Side."

My uncle met me at the old Twenty-third Street station near the canal docks, a short distance from his home on Twenty-second and South Halsted Streets, where I was also to live. His place of business was nearby.

There were many foreign-born people in Toledo, mostly Germans, but nothing I had seen at home matched the districts where I now found myself six days a week. It was not that these people looked strange to me because they were oddly dressed—many of them wore the sheepskin hats and coats they arrived in from Europe. They were somehow brutal. Even the Irish and Germans seemed different from those I had known in Toledo. Everybody was quarrelsome. Fighting and drunkenness were so common as to pass unnoticed. I used to wonder what would happen if no club-swinging policemen should appear to put an end to their knife-wielding fights. Later, I witnessed events which answered that question.

Their children got the worst of it. It was a common sight to see a half-dressed, shivering, barefoot child walking along icy snow-covered streets on its way to the saloon for a can of beer, or towing a drunken and protesting parent home. They were always screaming or cowering in doorways, waiting for someone to let them into their wretched homes. Many of them seemed to have no homes but the streets. They hung around saloons, cadging bits of "free lunch," and many a child's best friend was a warm-hearted bartender who fed it pickled pigs' feet, or anything else he had to quiet its hunger. Because

I was not far removed from childhood myself, these scenes became fixed in my memory. I was used to being poor, for I had never been anything else, but this was poverty plus a degradation of the human spirit for which I had no explanation. I only knew that somehow I had been lucky.

There were no laws preventing the sale of liquor to minors, and gangs of drunken boys, no older than myself, roared through the districts on payday. Men abused their wives when they pleased, and they generally pleased after they had drunk enough of the fighting whiskey sold at ten cents a glass at the corner saloon.

It was a world that, once seen, is not easily forgotten. Some years after I left Chicago for good, my brother Henry began his life's work in this old stomping ground of mine. While yet a student at McCormick Theological Seminary, he launched a mission Sunday School in "Little Hell," as the district was called. He was among the first of those young clergymen who, along with Canon Barnett and Jane Addams, pioneered a new missionary movement by settling in the slums of our great cities. The mission he launched became Olivet Institute and his first pastorate, a settlement project sponsored by the Presbyterian Church which, like Hull House and others, transformed the lives of thousands.

I might say that anyone who has witnessed the conditions that these settlement workers dared to tackle can only admire their courage. It took something more than goodwill to tackle slum Chicago, as any old-time policeman who ever walked a beat there will tell you.

On my free day, Sunday, I sometimes visited, after church, the beautiful North Shore residential section or "Millionaires' Row" along Cottage Grove and Prairie Avenues, and used to wonder what it would be like to drive a matched team of satin-coated horses along these beautiful, tree-shaded thoroughfares and to turn in at the gates of the brownstone palaces which lined them. Through the massive, wrought iron gates guarding the entrance to the gardens behind the mansions, I could see green lawns and multi-colored flowerbeds and people playing croquet.

Ladies wearing stiff bustles and rustling silks were accompanied by gentlemen who twirled gold-headed canes and wore shiny silk hats and satin-lapelled "Prince Albert's" as they strolled along the broad, wooden sidewalks in this part of town, while decorous, well-scrubbed little boys rolled hoops or walked with prim little girls whose skirts were draped in imitation of their mothers' bustles. Viewing this world—as far removed from the South Side I saw week-days as though one or the other were located on another planet—I really knew, for the first time, what was meant by "the wrong side of the tracks."

One of the showplaces on Prairie Avenue—"just completed at a cost of two million dollars," the papers said—was Marshall Field's new residence. It had something, according to rumor, no other house in town could boast—electric lights!

I had never seen an electric light, nor did I ever see Mr. Field's "carbon arcs which dazzle the eye." Not until Edison invented his incandescent lamp was I privileged to view the "soft glow" of this modern miracle. How quickly the marvels of one generation become the commonplaces of the next! Nothing in all the fulsome descriptions of Mr. Field's palace seemed so wonderful to me as that statement—"it is lighted with electricity."

I sometimes wonder now if the generation which accepts the familiar without question is any less blind to its possibilities than the generation to which it is so new that it has no way of gauging its worth. Within the span of less than fifty years, the energy which produced these dazzling carbon arcs—of which Mr. Field was, doubtless, very proud—has transformed life on this earth for men. But it has yet to light their minds as it has illuminated their houses; for they continue to think about and plan their societies as if muscle power were still their chief prime mover, long after the genii of the dynamo has placed a billion inanimate, never-tiring slaves at their disposal.

I had come to Chicago, however, not as a sightseer, but as one of a vast army of humble people from all over the globe, a bit player in Chicago's fantastic drama, "Hog Butcher to the World." The stage was all over town. The players, according to the importance of their roles, lived huddled together in their thousands on the South and West Sides or in the grandeur of brownstone on Aldine Square. I saw the stage and many of the players from the front seat of my uncle's two-wheel delivery cart.

His establishment was what was known as a "retail packinghouse market." Such markets did not butcher, but bought whole dressed hogs from butchers who did. Retail packers, such as my uncle, processed the hogs into salt pork, hams and bacon, selling the other portions, such as ribs and tenderloins, to retail markets. The cured meats were sold to lumber camps, wholesale grocers, ships, and to the railroads for the feeding of their construction gangs.

For a short time after my arrival, I worked as cashier. Then my uncle introduced an innovation; he hired a young woman in my place, and I took to the delivery wagon and the cutting block. When I worked indoors, it was my task to help trim and cut hogs. Under my uncle's expert direction, I soon learned how to trim hams, bacon, and shoulders, and how to sort and prepare the meat for sale.

He was a hard taskmaster, an exacting employer. Himself a graduate of the school of hard knocks, he had no patience with coddling the young. My hours were long and the work exhausting. At a busy time, I often worked fourteen hours at a stretch. I was young and tough but at the day's end I tumbled into bed like a felled ox. When morning came, someone often had literally to kick me out to waken me. I often wonder how I stood that killing pace as well as I did.

But I learned things working for my uncle I might otherwise never have learned so thoroughly. Like my mother, he had a passion for cleanliness and order, qualities not common in the food processing business of his time. Much of it was due to his home training and a great deal of it had been pounded into him by ships' captains who were particular about their galleys. He was a big, scrubbed-looking man who usually wore a sea captain's hat and a spotless butcher's frock while working. He had a knack for keeping clean, and his insistence on cleanliness earned for him a reputation along Jackson Street and the canal docks.

"Boy, your uncle's quite a character. Yessir, Jay's quite a character," his onetime shipmates and business competitors would often inform me. They considered him eccentric because everything about his business had to be as clean as he was. Chopping blocks, knives, utensils, and floors were soused with hot soapsuds and sal soda and scrubbed until they glistened. To keep the premises clean was one of my jobs, and a scrap of trimming or crotch fat on the floor was an open invitation to a row. My uncle's objection to dirt was not solely on aesthetic grounds. "Keep the place and everything in it clean," he would say, "and you won't lose money by spoilage. Clean food doesn't spoil in a hurry; dirty food spoils while you're looking at it."

His business was almost wholly confined to provisioning Lake

Michigan ships and Wisconsin and Michigan lumber camps. During the winter, when the lakes were frozen, many captains, mates, and cooks lived ashore in Chicago. These freshwater sailors were rough, vigorous men fond of a good story, a drink or a fight. They liked to spin yarns with my uncle, who liked to listen. They were men of prodigious energy who, if they were bored with sitting around or had spent their money drinking and gambling, went to work while ashore in the packing plants and provision houses. Winter was the meat trade's busy time and such men were in demand. It was not uncommon to see one of these big fellows carry a five hundred pound dressed hog across the street and drop it in a dray to win a bet of a nickel glass of beer! Come summertime, they deserted Packingtown to take to freshwater seas in ships. Then my uncle's acquaintance bore fruit, for he got their business.

In summertime, I also took to the road. It was my job to maneuver a horse hitched to a two-wheel cart, loaded with great baskets of corned beef and salt pork—usually referred to as "salt willy" and "sow belly"—through narrow aisles between acres of lumber stacked along the docks and wharves to the ships' gangways. Often, trying to find a ship's berth was harder than trying to find a needle in a haystack, for twelve miles of wharfage along the canal docks of the Chicago River's south branch and the lake were devoted to lumber alone! Sail and steam transported millions of board feet of Wisconsin and Michigan pine to these docks to be carried out of Chicago by rail to the clapboard boomtowns of the West. The ring of the woodsman's axe and the carpenter's hammer blended here.

Among the forests of masts and spars rising above the waterfronts were hundreds of foreign ships, loaded to their waterlines with the products of the Old World or cargoes from the New—lumber to house, and grain and meat to feed the earth's hungry millions. Sailors from ports scattered around the globe swaggered along the streets leading to and from the docks, singing chanteys in a dozen languages, crowding waterfront saloons and dives, singing, fighting, or just letting off steam.

That all this activity—all these scenes I witnessed—was only a few decades old was forcibly brought home to me by an old lake captain, still hale and hearty. One day he pointed out a man standing with a group of others on a canal dock. "Know who that is?" he asked. I shook my head. "You ought to," he said. "That's Gurdon Hubbard. Ever hear of him? No? Well, he's Chicago's first packer of beef and pork."

"Why, he couldn't be," I exclaimed, "he isn't as old as you are."

"Yes, he is," the captain said. "Might be older, even if he doesn't look more'n sixty. He first came here when there was only two houses; a white man named Kinzie lived in one and a Frenchman named Ouilmett in the other. That was back in '18 or '19, ferget which. He was one of John Jacob Astor's boys in the old American Fur Company, collectin' skins in these parts. About your age then, I reckon. Take a good look at him," the captain urged, "he's history. He was Chicago's first storekeeper, first packer, first insurance agent, and one of the first canal commissioners."

"Well, he doesn't look old enough to me," I stubbornly insisted, unconvinced that these great docks and factories could have come into being in any one man's lifetime.

"Why, I helped Hubbard build the first and largest brick building in the state of Illinois in 1833," the captain said, "and don't you say I didn't. It stood on the corner of South and LaSalle Streets. Hubbard had the oak timbers cut on the Calumet in the winter

and rafted 'em to Chicago the following spring. He brought workmen from the Wabash to make the brick. I brought the hardware
and finishing lumber from Cleveland by schooner. That house was
the biggest thing ever seen in these parts, must have been six by
one hundred fifty at least, a big, two-story brick with a basement.
Everybody on the prairies called it "Hubbard's folly." People just
shook their heads at the extravagance. Said the town would never
grow up to it."

"What did Mr. Hubbard say to that?" I asked.

"Oh, he just laughed and said, 'There was only two families here
in '18; now there's a population of two hundred, not countin' Indians.
In a few years there'll be a thousand. I'm a conservative investin' for
the future.' I wish I'd believed him," the captain sighed. "I could have
bought a fifty-acre piece by the Palmer House for three dollars an
acre back in '30."

"If you've been coming here all these years, I'd think you would
have known what was going to happen," I said. "Couldn't you see
the changes?"

"Sure, I saw the changes. Ever hear about hindsight?" he answered.
"You'll be in the thick of things sometime, too. You won't know either.
Changes'll be taking place all around you and you won't have eyes to
see 'em. Trouble is, things change faster than folks' ways of thinkin'.
Only one man in a million isn't livin' yesterday today.

"Take transportation. Why I remember the first steamboat to
make port in Chicago in '32, bringin' Colonel Winfield Scott and
his troops to the Black Hawk War. That was back in Andrew Jackson's time. Them Indians was massacrein' settlers right and left
in these parts. Jackson wasn't the man to stand such nonsense, so
he sent Scott to drive 'em back to the Mississippi. Before that time

there was a few sailing vessels on the lake, but mostly we used Canadian bateaux—'Mackinaw boats' we called 'em." He waved his hand. "Instead of the thirteen thousand ships which come here every year, and all these docks, not so long ago it was just cattails and prairie. Sometimes I don't believe it myself, and I saw it happen!

"It only seems yesterday, though it's almost thirty years since the first railroad in town, the old Chicago & Galena Union, had her first run." He chuckled. "Fellows who built that railroad sure had their work cut out for 'em. First place, they had no money. Second place, most folks thought it would ruin the country. Yessir, said railroads was 'agin democracy;' they was privileged and aristocratic. If people had money to spend for roads, let 'em build plank roads everybody could use. You don't believe it, huh. You don't think people ever was that stupid. Son, you don't know yet how stupid *they* can be. Sure they change their minds, but only *after* some time and good money is spent provin' they don't know what's good for 'em. In the meantime, they cause an awful lot of fuss.

"Take the fellows who built that railroad. To throw dust in the old fogey's eyes, they got a charter to build a turnpike and a railroad. Later, folks said they was 'timid' and had the turnpike put in, in case the railroad didn't pan out. They didn't act timid to me. They gambled their shirts and all the money they could beg and borrow to buy and lay ten miles of wood and scrap iron rails as far as the Des Plaines River. They bought some old rollin' stock from a bankrupt little railroad somewheres in the East and had it brought in by steamer from Buffalo—two engines, ten cars, and a tender. They opened the railroad in '48. Took 'em some time after that to get it as far as Elgin, but they did. Now, what they started is called the Chicago & Northwestern—ever hear of it?

"People sure are funny. Ten years after that railroad was finished, if some kicker just suggested that a new railroad ought to bypass *their* wide space to those same small towners who cried back in '47 that rapid transportation would ruin 'em, he'd run the risk of providin' the fun at a lynching bee at the hands of a committee of outraged citizens. Yessir, they'd lynch him on the spot!"

"I suppose you haven't any old-fashioned notions?" I questioned.

"Sure I have," he answered. "I don't like all this talk about wimin votin'. Next thing you know they'll be wantin' to wear pants!" he snorted. "Why, it'd be the ruin of the country!"

"Votes for women" was a mighty touchy subject back in the 1870's. As for women actually wearing pants, the only one I had ever heard of who wore them and hadn't gone to jail for it was Dr. Mary Walker, a woman surgeon in the Civil War who had won a medal for bravery and, as I remember it, had been permitted to wear trousers by special act of Congress. She was considered something of a freak and was an embarrassment to her sex, for she was a great aid to hecklers at suffrage meetings who loved to point out that the next thing women would be doing would be "to dress like Mary Walker."

If the men of those days could have had just one little glimpse into the future—say, a preview of "the shape of things to come" along Hollywood Boulevard—they would have died of apoplexy on the spot, just the way that we who live today are shocked by the conditions they unquestionably accepted that we wouldn't tolerate.

From my front seat on the delivery cart, I had ample opportunity to see many of the things offensive to modern concepts, and to smell them also. The Chicago River was foul. That part of it along the South Water Street markets and out by the yards was the dumping place for sewage and offal from the packing and provision houses.

The east branch of the south branch near the yards was called "Bubbly Creek" because escaping gases from the decaying animal matter dumped into it bubbled to the surface. The river's naturally slow-moving current was further checked by debris-formed bars in its channel, and its dirty waters backed up and overran the low ground near its banks, forming pestilential sloughs and swamps.

Chicago's principal streets had been raised above the surrounding land by fill-ins to prevent them from being flooded by the river and lake at high water and to provide runoffs in wet weather. The wooden sidewalks bordering them were built on an incline. In the space underneath, millions of rats whistled and shrieked, and people wanted by the police found refuge—but not from the rats, which were reputed to be as big as terriers and twice as fierce.

Chicago was called various names, depending on the bias of the name caller. But it was agreed by all parties that it was the eighth wonder of the world, either for commerce, growth, or wickedness. The Indians had called their village on the lake *Cheecaqua*, sometimes translated as meaning "wild onion," which according to the oldtimers, once grew profusely on its shores. Two other meanings ascribed to the word were "strong" or "skunk." The wits of my time held out for "skunk" as being the most likely, and credited the original namers with a sense of humor and prophetic powers in their choice of a name. They cited the Chicago River and Packingtown in support of their contention.

On my daily rounds through the city, when not lugging heavy baskets of salt pork and corned beef between the narrow aisles of lumber up the slippery gangways into the galleys, I often went to Packingtown for tenderloins, spareribs, and other things when our own supply was not sufficient to fill orders. The packinghouses were near the Union Stockyards—the one place that visitors to Chicago always asked to see first, for its fame had spread around the world.

In view of conditions prevailing elsewhere in a time not conspicuous for its humane attitude, they were indeed a remarkable sight. Day and night, highways leading into it from the west and south were jammed with an endless stream of tired, plodding animals, escorted by swearing, sweating drovers. Occasionally, restive Texas longhorns created diversion by charging off into side roads leading toward town, followed by barking dogs, small boys, and cursing drovers. Once inside the yards, however, there was rest for men and beasts. It had clean accommodations for one hundred and twenty thousand animals; seventy-eight thousand hogs and twenty-two thousand sheep could be housed in eight hundred covered pens and twenty-two thousand cattle in open pens floored with three-inch plank. Immense haystacks and huge granaries supplied them with the best of food. When I first saw them, the yards were only partially completed. Its sponsors' plans called for facilities to eventually handle twice that number of animals on the three hundred and forty-five acre site.

The yards already had ten miles of wood-paved streets and alleys lighted with gas, thirty-five miles of sewers and three miles of water troughs so arranged that the water could be turned on or off at any point. This water was obtained from two artesian wells over a thousand feet deep which spouted water into tanks forty-five feet high. Fourteen fireplugs were available in case of fire. Visitors often commented that the hooved creatures were better cared for in the yards than were Chicago's human inhabitants elsewhere in the city.

This city of beasts was a self-contained unit in other ways. It had its own police and fire departments, a bank, stores, telegraph and post office, a newspaper, livestock exchange, churches and schools, a town hall, and a fine hotel with bathrooms for the use of drovers and cattlemen. The yards' maintenance crew of several hundred men lived in cottages adjacent to its premises. Seventeen miles of track united it with every railroad coming into Chicago. The yards were quite a place.

But it was a far cry from the sanitation and order in the yards to conditions in the packinghouses. The central authority and organized planning so evident in the one was absent in the others. Packers' methods were wasteful and their handling of animals inhumane. Dirt, grease, blood and offal covered floors, walls, and equipment. Unskilled, ignorant, seasonal workers were sweated and oppressed, and were as dirty as the premises. Processed meat, ready for the market, was without protection and generally black with flies.

I appreciated my uncle's bias against waste and carelessness every time I went to Packingtown. Packingtown was a first class demonstration of what not to do and why. And I resolved that as long as I stayed in the food business, I would never be too tired or too busy to see to it that any operation under my control was properly handled.

Words and their meanings change with the times, in the popular vocabulary, at least. I remember when the word "sanitary" had mainly to do with the U.S. Army Medical Corps; it was called the "Sanitary Corps" and ladies organized "Sanitary Fairs" to provide funds for its supplies, or formed "Sanitary Committees" to scrape lint and roll bandages. But I never remember hearing any talk of germs in relation to all this until sometime in the 1880's. People like my uncle just noticed that there was a connection between dirt and unpleasant consequences.

There were several newcomers to Packingtown, however, who were appalled, as he was, at its wastefulness, and who had different ideas about handling the public's food—men who were to clean up its dirty habits and bring order out of its chaos. Like all great pioneers, they were men who could think today in tomorrow's terms.

I first saw two of these men on the loading dock at the Armour plant where a young salesman, perhaps all of seventeen, used to help me lift the heavy barrels into the wagon. The young man's name was Ed Cudahy. He was there to learn the business, he said. At twenty-eight, this affable, energetic son of a poor Irish immigrant was ready to realize his ambition. He, in partnership with an older brother, founded in Omaha the Cudahy Packing Company, which was to become a powerful rival of the already established firms dominating his chosen field. Men like the Cudahys knew what they wanted and, with no capital except energy and imagination, began moving toward their objective at an age when most boys are content to drift with the tide of circumstance.

Alongside young Cudahy on the Armour dock, I often saw a vigorous, bearded man in early middle life whose keen eyes took in every activity within their range of vision. He would sometimes be there when I arrived on a cold winter's morning. Before he had reached the age of thirty-five, Phillip D. Armour was already "Prince of Pork" and a millionaire, having won his spurs as a Milwaukee packer for a daring coup in pork during the Civil War. Possessed of an unusual capacity to estimate men and events, coupled with driving energy, imagination and daring, he was a man to watch. In coming to work for Armour, young Cudahy had wisely picked the man and the place in which to learn the secret of getting things done.

But the man around Packingtown who interested me most was

a big six-footer named Swift who used to ride an absurdly small horse around the yards, his feet almost touching the ground. A former cattle buyer, lately become packer, he had already mapped for himself a course which was to revolutionize the meat processing business and the meat-eating habits of the world.

Other packers built their businesses around the hog and old established ways of processing and marketing. But Swift, who had started out as a small town meat seller peddling his home-butchered beef to village housewives from a cart, had other ideas—ideas so revolutionary that his onetime partner who had backed his operations as a cattle buyer in the East felt compelled to dissolve their partnership. Briefly, his great idea was that fresh beef should always be available to people who wanted it, no matter how far they lived from the source of supply. That sounds pretty commonplace today, but it didn't before Swift proved that it could be done. No one today who sees the long trains of refrigerator cars containing meats and fruits and vegetables freshly picked from the fields, threading their way across the country, ever questions the practicability of shipping these foods long distances in the specially constructed cars, but the very idea was rank folly before 1876. Men before Swift had tried it and failed, but he was not the man to set his sights by other men's failures. He had managed to run up his original capital of twenty-five dollars, given to him by his father, to the tidy sum of three hundred thousand dollars. He came to Chicago prepared to risk it all on the failure or success of his plan. This took nerve of no mean order, for his capital was wholly inadequate to the magnitude of what he proposed to do. With it, he had not only to create facilities, he had to batter down the entrenched prejudices and established business practices of centuries.

Before the coming of Swift, meat animals were mainly slaughtered during cold weather months. They could then be eaten fresh or preserved in various ways; other seasons of the year, fresh flesh food had to be obtained at the source and eaten immediately. Any distance from the source, cured meat was the only kind available during warm weather. People who were far from slaughtering areas where fresh meat might be obtained grew very tired of eating heavily salted and preserved meats in summer. They were well aware that fresh meat had food values indispensable to health and appetite, but since it was unobtainable during hot weather they assumed the inevitability of doing without it. Preserved meat, of course, was more expensive, for its preparation was labor-consuming. A few, fortunate people who lived where it was possible to cut ice from frozen water often built icehouses, covered the stored ice with heavy layers of sawdust, and as long as the ice lasted enjoyed fresh foods in summer denied to others.

In winter, Lake Michigan was an inexhaustible reservoir of ice. Its harvesting was a commercial activity of great importance. Chicago pork packers had long utilized this source of supply to prolong their seasonal operations. All during the winter months the lake was solidly frozen; men worked from dawn to dark, cutting and transporting ice to the cooling sheds and great icehouses.

Since, at Chicago, ice, beef and transportation came together, the city was the logical place for Swift to translate his great idea into action. Cheap, fresh, grain-fed beef hung in ice conditioned cars on its way to the tables of a meat hungry nation, maybe shipped in the ice packed holds of steamers to feed Europe's meatless millions— this was Swift's dream. His practical Yankee mind saw the market's limitless possibilities. But it also saw something else. A live steer shipped to Boston lost weight in transit; it had to be fed en route, and it was not as good an animal on arrival as it had been when shipped. Furthermore, only sixty percent of the average live animal became dressed beef and freight rates were figured on what was shipped. If he, Swift, could eliminate this wasteful practice by sending to market only what was edible, he could sell better beef for less money than any packer in the world! Grain and beef were cheap in the West, high in Atlantic seaboard states and in Europe. He knew all about cattle, knew how to pick them. That was his reason for riding through the cattle pens on his little horse, so he could see and feel their fat sides. The better cattle you bought, the better beef you had to sell. And he believed that another argument in favor of his plan was that carefully selected and dressed beef would improve in flavor and tenderness during its sojourn to market in an iced car. As he saw it, nothing stood in the way of his great idea—except hostility and opposition.

I remember when the news flew around Packingtown that Gustavus Swift had finally launched his refrigerator car, had helped hang the beef himself, had sealed it to prevent tampering, and had sent it on its way east. A salesman had been dispatched ahead to prepare the trade. No one envied him his job. "What?! Eat uncured meat ten days old? Why man, you're crazy!" Everyone in the meat trade knew just what those New York dealers would say. And they did.

Meanwhile, Swift sent his bedeviled salesman another car of beef before the first had arrived or been disposed of.

Barnes, the salesman, later told the story of going down to the freight yards in New York, wearing a face a mile long. He broke the seals, opened the car, and looked at the beef, as fresh as the day it left Chicago. "Come on, you skeptics," he shouted to the doubting

Thomases who had accompanied him. They looked and saw the beef, but failed to see its implications. That day marked the beginning of a new world industry and a new era in man's mastery of his food supply.

And although I didn't know it, it was also a red letter day in the life of an obscure butcher's boy named George Hormel.

But Swift's troubles were far from over. Though his beef was prime and fresh, he pocketed a loss of several hundred dollars a car on those two shipments—no mean sum considering his capital. Nevertheless, he continued to risk his small fortune by building new cars and sending them over the nation's metal highways, often taking a substantial loss on initial shipments because of trade boycotts, and at other times because the meat soured. Those early refrigerator cars were far from perfect; faulty insulation, indifferent re-icing, and the railroad's habit of leaving them on a siding during a warm spell cost Swift many a dollar. But he never complained over losses or doubted the worth of his great idea.

Within five years, the railroads who had tried to penalize his new venture by exacting exorbitant freight rates—in addition to a few other handicaps they imposed—and his rivals who had cried, "Give him enough rope; he'll hang himself," were falling over each other to capitalize on "Swift's folly."

But in that five year interim, Swift & Company had gained over the competition an edge hard to beat, and its founder's beliefs on waste, complete utilization of product, cleanliness, and more meat for less money were revolutionizing the packing industry and making his competitors, as well as himself, rich beyond the dreams of avarice.

Once having sold the great idea to his countrymen as well as to his packer rivals, he and they began the conquest of Europe. It was

Swift who first introduced fresh beef from America to England. In these days of Lend-Lease, when all the world is clamoring for American meat, it is curiously ironic to remember how hard Europeans resisted its introduction, the British meat trade in particular.

During the 1870's, the price of British-grown beef had reached what was called "famine prices." A roasting joint cost elevenpence (twenty-two cents) a pound, while a similar cut of imported American beef cost eightpence-halfpenny (seventeen cents). Rumor had it, however, that American beef was "poisoned," and English families thought themselves very daring on first buying it. Often, when servants discovered their masters had purchased American beef, they refused to eat it!

And to discourage consumption of the imported product, English butchers sold lower priced American beef at the price asked for the best British, and often sold inferior imported beef, or beef damaged in transit, for the "best American."

To put a stop to these practices, American exporters decided to sell American beef directly to the public, who, upon fair trial, found it equal to their own. In this elimination of trade abuses, Swift was undoubtedly the pioneer. He made dozens of trips to England, and while in London used to get up at three o'clock in the morning to walk around the great Smithfield Market and see for himself what was going on. He never hesitated to take issue with any English meat seller he found misrepresenting American products.

By 1880, fifty-four million pounds of American beef, valued at nearly five million dollars, had arrived in England—more beef than beef-loving Britishers had ever had to eat before. A British workman's family, sitting down to its Christmas dinner, could now enjoy the bounty of the Great Western Plains. And with that fact a new relationship was established, for the world had grown a little smaller as measured by time and distance.

Continental prejudice fast crumpled in the wake of the British. Specially fitted ships left the Port of Chicago for Germany, Belgium, France, Holland, and Denmark, as well as Britain. Peasants who, heretofore, had seldom tasted meat would also now find it a little easier to buy a soup bone or a special cut for feast days.

Swift, Armour, Morris, and Cudahy, in their search for profits, also began to devise ways and means of utilizing what had formerly been wasted. Blood and bone meal fertilizers were, perhaps, the greatest factor in the continuing productivity of the South's depleted cotton and tobacco fields. Huge quantities of these items now left Chicago to be mixed with ground phosphate rock which underlay the Southern coastlands, or were sent abroad to replenish exhausted European soils. The price of a yard of Manchester cotton cloth was possibly a little cheaper because of what went on in Chicago.

To me, when I finally understood the meaning of what I heard men discussing, when I realized the complex interchanges of value arising out of just one industry, it was a revelation. Animals grown on the fat prairie lands of the Midwest, consuming its corn and material abundance, became food for men and substance for more food and clothing grown in areas that were oceans away. It gave me my first idea of the interdependence of human societies and a vast respect for the men who could bring such things about.

During the years it became fashionable for soft-fibered critics of the American scene to find nothing but fault with such men as Gustavus Swift and other pioneers of his generation, I often wondered how many of these critics would take the risks, dare the constant threat of failure, and continue to pound away until success crowned *their* efforts in overcoming customs and prejudices hoary with age and tradition. By the record, very few such critics ever jumped in and rolled up their sleeves to do a better job at anything than the men they criticized. On the contrary, they generally demonstrated that an unlimited capacity to find fault is not synonymous with the ability to build a business, institute social reforms, or run the government. When deeds, not words, become the order of the day, many a fisherman of their ilk has gone forth to catch whales, only to return with minnows.

There were other adventures in understanding the American scene to be learned in Chicago in the first years I spent there. The problems and perplexities, the courage and resourcefulness, the small beginnings and magnificent achievements of the American people, were here to be seen in all their many parts. The city itself was the triumphant symbol of their courage in adversity, a singularly fitting place in which to celebrate the nation's first century.

As I moved about Chicago, it was hard to believe that it had been all but destroyed by fire twice within five years. There were still evidences of the Great Fire of 1871 to be seen in outlying districts, but its ravages were nowhere apparent in the solid blocks of fine stone buildings along the principal business and residential streets. Newcomers just had to take people's word for it that the fire had razed an area of over two thousand acres, destroying the homes of seventy-five thousand people, six hundred mercantile establishments, and one hundred great industrial enterprises—a total value of two hundred million dollars.

Considering the disaster's magnitude and what it had cost them, there were surprisingly few references to the fire in people's daily talk. Chicagoans were not inclined to dwell on the past; they were too busy meeting present conditions. If you asked someone for details who had been present during the catastrophe and who had lost everything but the clothes on his back, he gave them to you without dramatizing his personal loss and without self-pity. He told you that he had fought the fire "until the waterworks went up; after that there was nothing more I could do. My face and hands were singed, so I went to the lake and stayed in the water until morning."

When morning came at last, the thousands of burned, hungry, homeless, and ruined Chicagoans who had helplessly watched their city burn throughout the night, crawled out of the lake to begin rebuilding before the ashes of their former homes were cold.

Men like Gurdon Hubbard, Marshall Field, and Potter Palmer, who in the course of a day's span had lost fortunes and businesses built with a lifetime's effort, rigged up temporary quarters in barns, or any place they could find. Some of them hung out signs such as, "Everything gone but energy." Within twelve months after the fire, Chicagoans had spent forty million dollars in new buildings.

Then came the panic of 1873. And the following year another great fire swept over a large part of the recently rebuilt business section. But despite panic and continued catastrophe, the men of Chicago doggedly continued to rebuild their city. The world, which had generously rushed to the stricken city's aid in 1871 with over six million dollars worth of money and supplies, now applauded afresh the courage of a people who could start twice from scratch within so short a time. The stories of how magnificently men and women had acted during these crises, and after, made one proud to be their neighbor and fellow citizen.

The kindness of people to whom Chicago was only a name made a deep impression, not only on Chicagoans, but on the whole country.

British businessmen might feud with their American competitors, but Londoners sent over three hundred thousand dollars to relieve the city's suffering. Even the Chinese of far-off Canton sent a money gift of five hundred and fifty dollars, and this at a time when their countrymen in America were being subject to outrageous abuse. For a little while, people everywhere had acted as though they were, in truth, their brothers' helpers. Chicagoans never ceased talking about how kind they had been, and rushed to pay their debt when similar disasters overtook other communities. Hearing about it used to make me wonder what the world would be like when men didn't wait upon a fire, a flood, or an earthquake to rally to each other's needs.

CHAPTER THREE
A Second Century Begins

B efore I left home to go to Chicago, the principal topic of the day was the approaching Centennial and the Great Exposition to be held in Philadelphia to celebrate the event. Despite the continuing depression of the panic of 1872 still hanging like a black cloud over the land, people were mighty proud of their country and its achievements. The United States seemed a greater nation, just as Chicago felt itself to be a greater city, for all the changes of fortune she had come through.

As the opening date of May, 1876, for the Exposition grew near, newspapers and magazines, churches and schools, business and government, combined their efforts to tell the nation its own story. Up until now, Americans had been so absorbed in the tasks of building and preserving a nation, they were scarcely aware of the miracle they had wrought. Pausing to look back at the road so recently traveled, they were awed by what they heard and saw.

School children and churchgoers, crowds in parks and meeting places, heard again and again their nation's almost unbelievable story. That story may seem far-off and remote now, but it didn't then. As I listened, marveling with others, it seemed that only God's Providence had enabled an untried nation of less than three million people suddenly freed from foreign control but with empty hands and pockets, to survive. Empty pockets and a debt of one hundred and thirty-five million dollars, the price of freedom, to discharge somehow. We, who listened in 1876, wondered how those people in 1776, who had been subjected to all that the term "colonial exploitation" implies—without tools, techniques, or funds, with few friends among the nations and no credit, with literally nothing to give the words meaning—had yet managed to give to their great "Declaration of Independence" a reality and a vitality no power on earth could dissipate. Our throats grew tight when we thought on these things. God surely had planned a work for this nation to do.

Americans again heard the story of how early colonial governors had boasted that their American charges were without "schools, colleges, or printing presses" and how Berkeley of Virginia had prayed "that there be none for at least one hundred years." If Berkeley's prayers had not been fully answered, he and others like him, until the day they left the land for good, had ably seen to it that their charges remained in an industrial "dark age," if not wholly engulfed in a mental one.

Now, we were told, in that hundred years since Washington's footsore men had drifted back to their homes, as their commander said, "without a settlement of their accounts and without a farthing in their pockets," the nation they had created, at so great a cost to themselves, led the world. Its forty million people and thirty-eight states linked two oceans. Its trade and industry surpassed the mother country's. Its enterprise and daring surpassed that of all other peoples.

Much of the story was familiar to Americans of the old stock; their fathers and grandfathers had brought this thing to pass. But to other millions of first generation Americans, and to the foreign-born who had immigrated here only a few short years ago, it was a story whose significance they had never fully grasped until now. For them, these recitals had a special meaning.

Half Chicago's population was foreign-born. When these people read the American story in their foreign language papers and heard their orators, teachers, and clergymen recount how a hundred years before, a people composed of different races and almost hostile communities had joined together in an "experiment which was to remake a world," they knew firsthand what that earlier problem had been. For most of them, life was still like that in America. They too were divided by race and language and ancient loyalties which made them as alien to each other in the New World as they had been in the Old—conditions which seemed as perfect an obstacle as ever devised to political union and understanding.

I had heard the story of those earlier times at home and in school long before I came to Chicago, but the story had a particular meaning to me since leaving home which perhaps it would not have had if I had remained in Toledo. Racial and social snobbery are two of those unfortunate aspects of unregenerate human nature that we all suffer from when we venture into a new country or engage in an occupation considered inferior and only fit for "foreigners." In my time, anyone employed in the meat packing business in Chicago automatically became a "Bohunk." The term had originally applied to non-English speaking foreign workers in the yards. Its use was not restricted to them, however; I was often called "Bohunk." I objected, not only because I was not a foreigner, but because it was not intended as a compliment. To be a "Bohunk" was to be something outside the American scene proper, a second class citizen at best.

While I was young in years in those days, nevertheless, the circumstances of my life had forced upon me a maturity of outlook, and I already had developed a suspicion that one of the most successful ways to prevent a man from even wanting to participate in his country's life was to convince him that he could have no real part in it because of the accident of color, race, and place of birth, or that the country of his adoption was the special creation of a culture differing from his own. Consequently, to me, as to many another, it was heartening to hear again that the task of liberation had been the work of men of many cultures.

There had been "Bohunks" among them. Had not Germans, Poles, and Frenchmen—DeKalb, Von Steuben, Pulaski, Kosciusko, and Lafayette, among others—fought as brothers in arms beside men named Allen, Marion, and Washington in defense of *their* native land? They had left their Old World homes to fight for the liberation of the New because they believed in all men's rights to enjoy the fruits of their labor and to move about freely under just laws of their own devising. And their beliefs had cost them life and fortune. I thought how lucky it was for me that such men had not concerned themselves with the colonists' family trees. It was sufficient that they belonged to the human family—that alone mattered. I began to understand better my father's insistence that this one thing above all others should never be lost sight of. And I also better understood how he, as a member of a persecuted religious minority, valued the safeguards of liberty in action which had been denied to his parents in the land of their birth. I was in process of understanding what I had so often heard at home: what it meant to be an American.

As the Fourth of July drew near and Chicago prepared to celebrate, its streets and buildings broke out in a rash of red, white, and blue. Men stopped strangers in the street, inviting them to drink to the country's health. They slapped each other on the back. "Yes, *Sir*, she's a great country," they said "worth fighting and working for."

Truly, there seemed to be a magic solvent in the words "liberty and justice for all," more powerful than any prejudice a man might have against his neighbor. And, listening to the people on the streets, in my uncle's market, in the yards, it seemed that men still believed in this magic, despite misunderstanding, grinding poverty, and grueling work. "Bohunks" in the yards—men who lived meaner lives here than in the distant lands from which they came—said, "For me, no; for my son, maybe; but for my grandson, surely, life will be different." Such men might doubt for themselves but they believed in the future.

The gold of the American dream had not tarnished yet. So under flags overhead, behind massed banners and bands, Chicago's thousands paraded on July 4, 1876. Along streets packed with spectators—I among them—who yelled themselves hoarse, marched Germans and Swedes, Bohemians and Poles, Italians and Irish; white men and black freedmen, foreign and native-born. Sometimes they walked among Chicago's blue-clad regiments who had fought so recently to preserve the Union; twenty thousand foreign born, ten percent of Chicago's total population, had voluntarily joined the Union Army. Others marched in the ranks of their national societies or in their occupational groups. But no matter who they were or with what groups, I fancied, as I watched them march by, that they all felt themselves, as I did, to be as proudly American as though their fathers had landed on Plymouth Rock instead of Ellis Island. On and on they came to the strains of "The Centennial March," "The

Star-Spangled Banner," "Dixie," and "Hail, Columbia."

At sixteen and a half, one is apt to be more carried away with the excitement of crowds, the noise of cannon crackers, and the blare of bands than with the historical significance of even such a great scene as this. And so it was with me. I had to wait for time to make plain the meaning of much that I saw. Now I would know why the crowd roared and people cried when, among the floats and prancing horses of officialdom, a few carriages appeared and in them old men—ancients who had once been drummer boys with John Paul Jones and Oliver Perry. As these living symbols of a nation's victories passed, veterans of 1812, Chapultepec, and the Indian wars—hard-boiled people, like my uncle—wiped their eyes. But to me, then, those old men seemed far-off, as remote as their deeds. Theirs had been the task of enforcing a nation's will and consolidating its territories, a task that seemed ended for all time. For who could menace a nation secure behind vast ocean barriers? Young Americans, like me, could contemplate the luxury of eternal peace. I had been brought up to believe this; everybody thought so.

And so, although there was much that I could neither appreciate nor understand, for me, as for countless others all over America who participated in our country's hundredth birthday party, it was an event never to be duplicated. We should not live to see its second century end. That day would belong to our grandsons or their sons, perhaps. What the new century would bring, we had no idea. But we knew it would be different, for the signs were all about us.

I remember hearing that during the century just passed, one hundred and twenty thousand patents had been issued to American inventors. Within that period, the steam vessel, the sewing machine, the telegraph and telephone—all perfected by Americans—had appeared. In one decade alone, 1860–1870, the Patent Office issued more than seventy-nine thousand patents to invention-minded Americans—patents for improved or new plows and farm machinery, weighing scales, safety locks, steam fire engines and fire alarms, vulcanized rubber, boot and shoe machinery, grain mills, hundreds of tools, machines, and processes now to be seen in one vast mass exhibit.

Although I was not among the ten million people who went to see for themselves the wonders on display at the Centennial Exposition in Philadelphia, I was present in spirit, for the newspapers kept the stay-at-homes fully informed and some of these things could be seen in Chicago at the Exposition Building in Lake Park. But nothing to be seen anywhere else equaled the offerings in store for the lucky at Philadelphia, said the papers. Everything about it was on a scale befitting the greatest republic in the world. It was bigger and better than any similar show ever attempted anywhere at any time. It covered two hundred acres. Vienna's fair of 1873 covered fifty-six acres, while England's Great Exhibition with its famed Crystal Palace only covered a paltry twenty-six acres. The products of thirty-three nations, besides our own, were to be seen on display in its halls. Among them were etchings "graciously sent" by Queen Victoria and "done by her own hand." The exposition's acres of machinery were powered by a giant steam engine of new and radical design, the work of George Corliss, America's foremost steam engineer. And finally, the greatest world fair ever seen had cost ten million dollars!

No peacetime event in America had ever received so much attention from the press and public.

I would have given a great deal to be present on the morning of May 10, 1876, when the American flag was first unfurled over the great tower of the main building. The papers said that a "great concourse of people" stood before the President of the United States, members of his cabinet, the Congress, and ambassadors of foreign powers. And when Dom Pedro, Emperor of Brazil, his Empress "leaning on his arm," appeared, "the multitude broke into cheers as their majesties took seats beneath the flag of our great sister nation."

Every country's talent brought something to that great day. "The Centennial March" was the work of Richard Wagner, "eminent German composer." It was played by Theodore Thomas' orchestra, and "the multitude joined in singing Handel's magnificent 'Hallelujah Chorus.'" Accompanied by a great organ and the orchestra, "the multitude" also sang with a trained chorus of a thousand voices John Greenleaf Whittier's "moving 'Centennial Hymn.'" The papers reported that as the closing stanza of the hymn was sung—

> Oh, make Thou us through centuries long
> In peace secure, in justice strong;
> Around our gift of freedom draw
> The safeguards of our righteous law,
> And, cast in some diviner mold,
> Let the new cycle shame the old!

—"many eminent ladies and gentlemen were seen to dab their eyes with handkerchiefs."

When the opening ceremonies ended, the crowds surged into Machinery Hall, Agricultural Hall, Horticultural Hall, and the main building, which covered twenty-one and a half acres. Inside these walls the future awaited them. Among other unusual machines on exhibit, there was one which excited a lot of comment. A Belgian named Gramme had perfected it. Its world premiere, so to speak, had taken place at the Industrial Fair in Vienna in 1873 where it had first been placed on public exhibition. It was called a "dynamo." In some strange way, it literally "pulled" electricity out of the air. Mr. Whittier had spoken truer than he knew; an "old cycle" had indeed passed into history with the country's first century.

Judging by the reports of things to be seen at the Exposition, inventive genius had not confined itself to an industrial new order affecting factories and fields. Farmers might gape at steam plows and manufacturers at Corliss' mighty engine, but their wives must have been equally popeyed. From the list of things on exhibit, the predecessors of the "dime store" gadgeteers were already amply looking after the ladies. I wondered what my sisters and Mother would say if I should walk in the door at home with armfuls of apple parers, almond peelers, bean shellers, raisin seeders, peach stoners, flour sifters, bread cutters, knife sharpeners, improved coffee mills, lemon squeezers, and dishwashers.

Farmwives who had never owned a washboard must have marveled at such things as sausage grinders and stuffers, milking machines, chums, cheese presses, and cream freezers, to say nothing of the display of such future aids to leisure as washing machines, wringers, and a "wonderful array of brooms and mops."

The motive power for all those wonders was still, of course, muscle power, but it now seemed likely that with their help any woman worth her salt could gallop through her day's work in at least twelve hours. Furthermore, there were now "baby walkers" to keep the toddler out from underfoot while its mama worked her "new and improved, patented chum!"

Just one trip out to Chicago's Exposition Building with its array of machines, to say nothing of going to Philadelphia, seemed to prove that, from a mechanical point of view, life was certainly on the verge of the millennium.

There were some sour notes in the midst of all this national rejoicing, however—some of them close to home. Many small farmers and wage earners were anything but satisfied that the "wonderful increase of people, power, and riches" indicated by the Exposition had, in any way, benefited them; in fact, they felt far more the victims than the beneficiaries of progress.

Several of my uncle's friends had left sailoring on the lakes to take up prairie homesteads in the West under the Homestead Act of 1862. They had used their small savings to tide them over until the land could be made productive. Now, broke and discouraged by plagues of grasshoppers which had eaten their crops and by the ruinous prices offered for farm products, these men drifted to Chicago in search of jobs. They had either sold their land for a pittance to land-hungry Old World immigrants or had abandoned it outright. And they were exceedingly bitter.

I heard them talk over their troubles with my uncle. "It was just no use," they said. "We could have held out against the grasshoppers, maybe, but we couldn't hold out against fifteen to twenty cents a bushel for corn—when we had a crop to sell. It was cheaper to burn it for fuel in the winter than to buy coal."

"I had to haul my grain forty miles to the nearest shipping point," said one man, "and over bad roads, too."

"Sounds to me like you didn't use good judgment in locating so far out," said my uncle.

"I hadn't any choice" he replied. "What land the government didn't give the railroads along the right of way, the land speculators grabbed through connivin' with bogus homesteaders. Thousands of acres of good land just sits there idle, but you can't touch it. Those thieves don't want to sell at a reasonable price. It cost them almost nothing in the first place and it costs them almost nothing in taxes to keep it."

I heard the story of how the bogus homesteaders, working in cahoots with the speculators, had evaded the law. Under the Homestead Act, a settler had to build a house of a certain size, containing at least one glass window. After he had built his house and after enough time had elapsed to show his good faith, the settler might gain title by paying a small sum to the government who, in turn, issued him a deed. The crooks complied with the law by nailing a few boards on four posts stuck in the ground, inserted their glass window in the contraption, and filed a statement with the nearest land office that they had complied with the terms of the Act. When they received title, they sold the land to the speculators, removed the boards and window to a new location where they repeated the operation. According to accounts, it seemed likely that local land agents had a hand in this dishonest looting of the public domain, for they could easily have found out the true state of affairs had they cared to do so.

These disillusioned men's stories were full of references to the need for action "against monopoly." I had very little idea of what they were talking about except that everybody seemed to be against the railroads—an odd thing when everybody also admitted the wonderful benefits of rapid transportation.

"Railroads have gotten too big for their britches," one of my uncle's friends said. "They're corrupting the government, plundering the people, and impoverishing the farmer," he declared.

Later, when I went on the road as a buyer of hides and wool, I heard the same story throughout the farming districts of the Midwest.

Many farmers with whom I did business belonged to a farm organization called the Patrons of Husbandry. It was a secret order with passwords, grips, and rites of initiation which had swept the country like a prairie fire. It claimed a membership of several millions and had nineteen thousand chapters. The Patrons, among their several aims, were out to "subdue" the railroads. They demanded that state legislatures pass laws fixing "reasonable, maximum rates for freight and passengers" and declared "that the state cannot create a corporation which it thereafter cannot control."

In this day and age when farsighted businessmen accept the principle that a private enterprise exercising a public function is subject to regulation in the public interest, it seems incredible that men could ever have been so shortsighted as the railroads' managers used to be. They defied the traveling public and the small shipper, and for a short time successfully contended that what they did was no one's affair but their own.

When the Patrons declared that the railroads were "instruments of arbitrary extortion more detrimental and as much opposed to free institutions and free commerce as the feudal despotisms of the Middle Ages," they spoke the truth. The railroads had the small shipper, like the farmer, over a barrel—and knew it. On the other hand, the large shipper, who could use either of two competing railroads, could always just about set his own freight rate—so anxious were the railroads to get business at each other's expense. And it was risky for the small shipper to protest; though, in the end, he paid the bill for this wasteful and unnecessary favoritism. The railroads could—and often did—put him out of business; sometimes at the behest of a bigger rival and sometimes just to show him who was boss.

When, in the course of events, I became a "little shipper," I found out for myself what it means to be at the mercy of a "private enterprise exercising a public function which is not subject to regulation."

But there was something more to the story of the small farmers' woes than the railroads. My uncle summed it up. "From now on, it's going to take something more than free land, a homemade plow and scythe, a strong back, willingness, and a passel of young 'uns to make a successful farmer. Next time you go out by the McCormick plant, take a good look around and you'll see why."

My uncle was an ambitious man with plans but, as yet, no money. He had a very personal interest in the Midwestern farmer and anything that pertained to his welfare, for the farmer was the primary source of his product. If all went well, my uncle hoped to extend the field of his operations and his success would partially depend on the farmer.

The McCormick farm machinery factory and the machines on exhibit in the Exposition Building in Lake Park were a demonstration of my uncle's comment. Would-be farmers, like his friends, now had to invest money in mechanical equipment to compete with their fortunate fellows who owned chilled steel riding plows, harvesters and reapers, wire binders, corn planters, and wheat drills. Inventors and manufacturers were turning out new machines and devices by the dozens. I was told that farmers who were able to take advantage of these things could save at least one-half the former cost of working land and crops by hand methods.

By means of drills, two bushels of seed would go as far as three bushels broadcast. Since it was sown in rows, drill-sown seed could be cultivated with horse-drawn hoes instead of hand hoes. The reaper ordinarily in use, which cut and raked the grain, saved half the labor in harvesting as against the method of cutting and raking by hand. But a new reaper, which cut, raked, and bound the grain in one operation, at a saving of three-fourths the labor, was ready to come on the market. Machines for cutting root crops into feed were said to save one-half the labor of feeding stock in winter.

Many times, as much grain could be threshed in one day by a horse-powered threshing machine as against the old method of treading it out with horses or oxen. Three horses and two men averaged twenty-five bushels a day by this method. A ten horse-powered threshing machine with a crew of eighteen men could thresh one thousand bushels a day. But a new steam-powered thresher, with a daily capacity of three thousand bushels of threshed, winnowed, and sacked grain, was already in use on the big farms of the Far West. The same threshing crew of eighteen men needed to operate a big horse-powered thresher could treble their output with steam.

I took out my pencil and figured that where it had taken fifteen days of one man's hard labor to produce from standing grain one hundred bushels of marketable product in a pre-machine era—and that was said to be a good average—it now took one man's effort one day to produce fifty bushels with horse-powered machines to aid him. If he could harness his effort to steam, he could treble the amount. Clearly, it seemed that the price of our daily bread and the rewards of effort could no longer be determined by muscle power— man's or beast's. Henceforth, the price of a man's labor or the price of bread would be linked to the tireless energy of steam.

After a trip to the McCormick plant, I better understood why my uncle's friends kept talking about the need for "cheap money." They wanted the government to print greenbacks backed by government credit and not metal. They said tying the dollar to gold made it "dear" and that "hard money" men wanted this done because they had a monopoly on gold. With this issue I had no concern since I never had money enough, or the hope of getting any, to make the question of what was behind the few bills in my pocket worth thinking about. But at least I knew what the men were talking about and why.

One look at those fine, shining machines on the McCormick sales floor told even a penniless boy why the actual possession of money had become imperative. There was no barter arrangement by which an Iowa farmer could advantageously come into the possession of a four hundred dollar McCormick reaper. He had to have cash. To get cash, he had to grow cash crops. The farmers from whom Father had bought hides and wool had managed with very little money, but they were subsistence farmers who exchanged their surplus produce for "boughten goods" at the village store. The prairie farmer was another kind of farmer. He raised wheat and corn for cash. To get cash, he had to have accessible markets. And since he was competing in a world market in world-produced commodities, he could only farm at a profit with labor-saving tools and cheap transportation.

But the farmer was not the only one who had cause for complaint. The panic of 1873 had reduced wages as well as farm prices and they were still in the doldrums. Meanwhile, there had been no moratorium on the creation of new labor-saving devices and processes. Despite hard times and the difficulty of obtaining capital, American business was going ahead, but with no corresponding wage increases or shortening of hours. Although their ranks were decreasing, jobless, hungry men and women still tramped the streets of every American city.

In winter, working people lived in a perpetual night. At work before it was fairly light, their workrooms were dark and gloomy. The working day ended at six o'clock—dusk at any season but midsummer.

My day was typical of millions. Up at five-thirty, I ate a breakfast of coffee, bread and butter, meat and potatoes at six, and was at work by six-thirty. By noon I was starved, for I had already put in five and a half hours without a break. "Lunch hour" was long enough to eat cold beans and pork, bread and butter, pie and cold coffee. If we were in a slack season, the day ended at six o'clock. Often, I had to work later. As soon as supper was over, I was so tired I went to bed.

Not a gay life. A friend asked me recently what we used to laugh about in the old days. Did I remember any jokes of the period? "No," I said, "life was no joking matter for the cheap hired help, such as I was." Yet, judging by the standards of the times, I was not badly treated.

I earned ten dollars a month with board and room. The average laborer and his wife earned seven-fifty and six dollars per week respectively. She prepared their family meals after her return from work at six o'clock. Their working children earned around three dollars per week and generally became wage earners at the age of twelve. Most states had laws forbidding employers to hire children under ten and limiting a child's working week to "not more than sixty hours." I believe that, in Illinois, the employer's failure to obey the law brought with it a penalty of five dollars for the first offense, with a twenty dollar maximum fine for continued violation. If the law was ever enforced, employers seemed able to bear the consequences, for children as young as six years were to be seen in Chicago's manufacturing districts, working in box factories, stripping tobacco, making feathered novelties and similarly manufactured goods. These conditions continued until the late 1890's.

Throughout the poorer working-class districts, the most profitable small enterprise seemed to be the undertaking business. One was impressed with the frequency of such establishments, their show windows decorated with a small coffin lined with sleazy white satin. During the hot weather months, the death rate of children under five was appalling. I believe it was the famous evangelist, Dwight Moody, a worker in Chicago's slums, who quoted figures of two hundred and fifty to three hundred deaths each year for each one thousand living children of five and under.

As I look back over the scenes I witnessed as a youth but for the understanding of which I had to wait on maturity, I can see now that the stage was set and the players present over half a century ago whose problems and perplexities were to plague themselves and their successors for a long time to come. I was too close to those bygone years as I lived them to understand the full significance of what passed before my eyes; only time could give me perspective. But because my life has spanned so many changes in ways of thinking and living, I can perhaps be pardoned for believing that no present or future problems in human affairs are any more difficult of solution than they have been in the past. That many of the old problems I knew as a boy are still with us is wholly because we still suffer for our unwillingness to apply the means we have. Some of them are probably in process of solution at this moment, but the speed with which they become "finished business" is wholly dependent upon our ability to see where our true self-interest lies. Perhaps man's inability to gauge his true self-interest is the only stumbling block to his progress on this earth. But I have lived to see men change their minds about self-interest on many a front; otherwise, there would be no point to this story.

A great city is one theater of man's operations where, perhaps more clearly than anywhere else, this inability to correctly appraise intelligent self-interest is evident. There have been other times and places, but Chicago as I knew it in the 1870's stands out in my mind as a glittering example of how dangerous to everyone individualistic non-cooperation can be. For all the city's magnificent solidarity in the face of disaster, at other times no one except a handful of people—mainly clergymen—seemed to concern themselves with the welfare of the city as a whole. I, perhaps, should have had even less of an inkling of what was wrong, despite the fact that I was a daily witness to the sufferings of others, had it not been for one thing: my parents had taught me the value of communal worship.

The church represented something to me of inspiration and instruction to be found in no other place. I was not particularly religious in the sense that I had a vocation or felt myself to be especially "good." But I was conscious of a unity of interest with the great Christian heritage of peace and goodwill to all men. Since I was included in the "all men," it was a very personal interest. My father was an exceedingly kind, gentle, and wise man. My relationship to my own brothers and sisters was explicit in our joint relationship to him. Since children are realists in their thinking, it only needed a small bridge from the particular relationship with which I was familiar to the larger relationship implied in the fatherhood of God and the brotherhood of man. I doubt if I ever thought this out quite so consciously, but going to church gave me much the same feeling as going home. Like home, it was a place that, when you got there, they had to take you in.

Theology was a subject in which I took small interest. Creed seemed to make a great deal of difference to some people, but I went to the German Reformed Church, or the Baptist, or joined with the Methodists and Presbyterians in Sunday services, whichever circumstances favored and with equal interest. In Chicago, I occasionally went to hear Moody and Sankey. It was from these men and their fellow ministers—and later from my brother Henry—that I gained some insight into the social problems which plague humanity because of its blindness.

One criticism of the church so often made had no validity when I went to hear Moody and Sankey. No one could charge either man with bypassing humanity's everyday problems in order to make their congregations comfortable. Dwight L. Moody handled red hot social pokers and then let his congregation hold the poker. To my way of thinking, this was just as it should have been; for no man has a right to ask God to do what he won't do, and that is to clean up the mess he has made on this earth.

So it was that I found out from intelligent, scholarly, and impassioned men something of the nature of the problem which was to confront me as an individual and as a member of the larger group. The rich were growing richer and less responsible and the poor poorer and less self-respecting. Neither condition, said Mr. Moody, was "democratic nor Christian." While I knew in a general way that the introduction of the machine was somehow partly responsible for this sad state of affairs, it seemed a paradox to me then as, I confess, it does to me now. The machine was only an extension of man's natural faculties with whose aid he could increase his capacity to produce with less arduous labor. Obviously, this meant that more men could have more things. Certainly, instruments that removed the specter of famine and want, such as my mother's sewing machine which enabled us to wear more and better clothes than we had ever had before, were things worth owning. Naturally, there was no harm in owning a benefit. But in some inexplicable fashion, with greater means at hand to satisfy their needs, many men were living less securely than they had lived with little more than their bare hands to aid them. It didn't make sense.

I was not so naive, even at seventeen, as to believe that a man was necessarily "good" because he was well-fed or "evil" solely because he was hungry, but I did see that evil battened on human misfortune and that it was idle to talk to a man about saving his soul if you were unwilling to help him eat. Father had once pointed out to me that Christ had performed the miracle of "the loaves and fishes" so that his hungry audience would not be of two minds, whether to go and eat or stay and listen. According to Father, a hungry man was seldom a good listener or a good neighbor, and he had never heard him called a "solid citizen."

By the summer of 1877, there were too many hungry men walking the streets of Chicago who were neither "solid" nor safe. I was warned by my uncle to stay off the streets in certain parts of town. If I had business to transact along the west bank of the Chicago River and the regions south of the business district, South Clark and South State Streets, I was to be out of there by nightfall. Strictly speaking, these areas were never "safe," but they had grown worse, if such a thing is possible. Thugs and prostitutes ruled these evil-smelling districts, which fifty years later were to pass into the hands of the Capone gangs and their rivals. Here murder, rape, and holdups flourished with little check from the police, but not for lack of trying. The simple truth was that the police received almost no public support. Under the circumstances, they undoubtedly did the best they could.

To add to the problem of law enforcement, a steady increase of gamblers and crooks arrived to reinforce the already well-established local talent. Chicago's entrenched criminal population created a situation the like of which was probably not to be found anywhere else in America. At least my uncle said so, and he had traveled enough to have seen the seamy side of many an Eastern seaport city. In addition to the criminal scum, the streets were full of the idle unemployed. Hopeless and bitter, they were as antagonistic to employed workmen as they were to the employing classes. They menacingly stopped passersby, demanding money, or came into business establishments on the same errand. Wise men seldom refused these demands. My uncle relied on his fists to stop the too demanding, but most of his friends began to carry guns.

In July, the weather was stifling. A smallpox epidemic added apprehension to heat-frazzled tempers. Trouble broke out in Packingtown and on the docks. Police officers sent to quell the disorder were shot from ambush. My uncle was worried. "This is the way it is on shipboard before the captain has a mutiny on his hands," he said.

"What would you do if you were captain here?" I asked.

"I'd close the saloons, clear the streets of thugs, arrest anyone inciting to riot, open soup kitchens, and talk turkey to some of these business leaders. It's time someone took an intelligent interest in what's going on in this town."

In a day or two, mobs began to break windows and loot stores along LaSalle Street. The papers called it a "bread riot." Then more trouble broke out in the yards and spread to working-class districts.

Chicago packinghouse workmen were an ugly and dissatisfied lot, ripe for trouble and looking for it. Often, their only contact with management was through some petty tyrant who originated whatever labor policy suited his temperament or convenience. On the job, they were the victims of labor discrimination based on race prejudice. In summer, when seasonal layoffs took place, the first men to go usually belonged to an ethnic or racial group which differed from the foreman's. If he was a Swede or a German, he threw out the Poles and Russians. A Slav sub-boss delightedly bounced the Germans. Any white man laid off Negro workmen first. So it didn't really matter how hard a man worked to hold his job or how well qualified he was to retain it; in the end, he lost it for factors beyond his control. So now, in addition to bad housing, inadequate income and other grievances, real or fancied, workingmen fought each other along the dirty streets of their bleak neighborhoods. Often their children were injured in the scuffles or organized into gangs to fight each other.

The one thing that I have never forgotten is the look of those half fed, dirty children playing or fighting in the squalid streets alongside brothels and saloons. I was overworked and underprivileged too, but by comparison to these youngsters my life had been a bed of roses. I understood why Dwight L. Moody called down the wrath of Heaven on the people responsible for the conditions under which these children lived. It was plain to be seen why he had left a successful business career to fight their cause and to work among them. No real Christian such as he was could do less.

A great railroad strike in the East, however, was the match that lit the fuse to Chicago's social dynamite. The strike broke out this same month of July and quickly spread to Chicago. Thousands of sympathizers from other trades joined the striking railroaders in a great outdoor demonstration. Then trouble, real trouble, began in earnest as fighting broke out all over the city. Mobs began smashing and burning factories. One pitched battle took place between the police and mobs trying to burn the McCormick harvester plant. The police and armed guards beat the attackers back.

"Nothing but the Militia will stop it now," said my uncle.

Business houses closed their doors; customers were afraid to walk the streets or to come into the downtown sections. Streetcars were stoned and riders injured by flying glass. Sometimes timbers were laid across the tracks; the drivers then stopped the horses and mobs literally tore the cars apart.

Then news came that the federal government had ordered soldiers in from the West. They were coming from the Indian country. This further angered the strikers and renewed fighting broke out in Packingtown and the railroad yards. Before the troops could arrive to reinforce the police, a mob descended on the roundhouse of the C. B. & Q. on Sixteenth Street. The railroad was said to have strikebreakers working these. The greatly outnumbered police fired into the crowd which charged with clubs, rocks, and knives. There were casualties on both sides and hundreds of wounded men were dragged through the streets to their homes.

Much of this action took place near my uncle's establishment and our home on Twenty-second and Halsted Streets. I was standing on Halsted when the troops from the frontier forts arrived. Trainloads of soldiers rolled into the Twenty-third Street depot. Upon disembarking, they quickly formed ranks on Halsted and, with fixed bayonets, marched shoulder to shoulder the full width of the street out toward Archer Avenue and the yards.

The soldiers' coming ended the disorders, but not the city's fears. I do not remember that any constructive action was taken to remedy the causes which led to civil war beyond the presentation of a new machine gun to the city fathers by a group of "representative citizens."

One aftermath of the "trouble," however, was that, for the first time, reform elements were listened to with something beside boos. Every former attempt to close the saloons on Sunday and to regulate the sale of liquor to minors had been shouted down by outraged "liberals" who yelled louder than the saloonkeepers and their political henchmen. Now, a citizens' committee suddenly discovered what anyone could see any day by walking the streets—that gangs of drunken adolescent boys were running loose all over town. The committee held these gangs responsible for much of the wanton smashing of shop windows and streetcars. Laws with teeth in them, such as the Suppression of the Sale of Liquor to Minors, were quickly passed. This law brought such convincing results that "reform" could no longer be dismissed with a jest. A society which had refused to act on behalf of its weakest members for their sakes, acted now to save its own skin. Social-mindedness superseded "liberalism" whenever people began thinking to themselves about the possibilities of complacently continuing to rear generations of adolescent drunkards. I have often thought since that there is no magic like a little self-interest to clear the public's eyes of social cataracts.

My Chicago days, for the time being, were about over. Big and work-toughened as I was, I found the going too hard. From long hours of standing and wrestling heavy baskets, I developed running sores on both ankles. They refused to heal, so I consulted a doctor who cauterized them. This did no good and they grew worse. I made another visit to the doctor. "Listen, Son," he said, "medicine won't help you. You need rest, a long rest, for at least a year. You're still growing. If you want to be a strong, well man, now's the time to take care of yourself. Go home to your folks."

It was good advice and I decided to take it. My uncle had also decided to leave Chicago to try his fortunes in Dallas, Texas. He had found a purchaser for his business and was winding up his affairs. I packed my oilskin and headed for home.

CHAPTER FOUR

Traveler's Return

I returned to my father's house in Toledo many times during the years when the only other place I called home was wherever I happened to room at the time, but this first return was memorable. I was a different boy from the one who had left it a year and a half before. I was not only ill and tired physically—more so than I have ever been since then—but I was overwhelmed by the kind of life I had seen, a way of life that I doubted even my father knew existed. A greater gulf than the time I had been away or the difference in our ages separated me from my brothers and sisters. Busy with their various tasks, they were—as they should have been—as blissfully unaware of the bad, sad world I had just left as though it existed only in my imagination.

My elder sister, Elizabeth, had grown into a young lady during my absence. Still at home and Mother's chief lieutenant, she was full of ambitions and plans for a career other than housework. My brother Henry, two years younger than I, was already considering training for the ministry. The little boys and girls were just busy growing, all of them well, sheltered, and happy. They were good students and good members of society. Once caught up again in the family's life, Chicago's troubled slums seemed a long way off—a place seen in some half-remembered nightmare.

My mother's beautifully kept and managed house was like a quiet haven to a storm-swept wayfarer. I ate the good things that poured out of her kitchen at every meal with a relish and capacity that surprised even her. I particularly remember a golden "Johnny cake" she used to make from fresh ground yellow cornmeal, sorghum molasses, eggs, milk, and shortening—a far different kind of cornbread from any one can find today. She filled her hungry brood with young green cabbage coleslaw doused in sour cream, potatoes boiled in their jackets or baked, mashed rutabagas seasoned with butter and cream, and other fresh vegetables. And her vitamin-rich meat and vegetable soups, her stews and browned beef hash would have put life into anyone this side of a mummy. Before mealtimes, the most tantalizing odors stole out of her kitchen—the kind you could taste—like the yeasty goodness of baking bread mingling with the fragrant bouquet of newly made coffee simmering on the stove. Her husky, growing youngsters made those brown, crusty loaves disappear like magicians putting rabbits in a hat. And there were other smells which magnetized the impatient into the kitchen only to be rebuffed. "Nein! Run off; comes supper you will find out," she would say, shooing us out the door. But while the precise nature of her masterpiece might be concealed from us, we knew she had only to dip into her flour barrel and out came *apfelkuchen, kuchen erdbeer* (strawberry pie), cinnamon rolls, and whatever other good things time and the resources of the season allowed her to make.

No one who ever sat down to my mother's table could have said that "God sent meat but the Devil sent cooks." She was a messenger of light and her cooking proved it!

"The little general," as my sister Elizabeth called her, was more than a good cook. Father's income from the rendering plant he purchased after the collapse of the tannery was increasing with the help of my brothers Henry and Herman, and was sufficient to meet the cost of educating the growing family. Mother could always trim her budget to fit Father's purse. Furthermore, out of what he gave her she managed also to save a little something. Consequently, for any family enterprise she thought worthy, Mother could be depended upon to produce her miraculous nest egg. Because of her, despite hard times and failure, Father managed to maintain a pleasant, debt-free home and to enjoy his life and ours. A wonderful wife and mother, we valued her "above rubies."

If Mother was the family general, Father was its diplomat. It was noticeable to me, on this and subsequent visits home, with what rare skill he managed the difficult job of being a wise, understanding parent. He had the gift, without ever seeming to intrude and without violating our privacy, of entering into our lives. In an effortless way of his own, he made it his business to know the different temperaments and capacities of his children, and I think he knew us better than we knew ourselves. Mother gave the orders in everyday affairs, but in major matters he took over. He was gentle, humorous, persuasive, and persistent without being insistent. In time, he could always reach agreement with his most stubborn child. He never flatly commanded, "Don't do that because I say so." And when our wishes were contrary to his, we were as anxious to reach a compromise as he was; for we hated to displease him. My sister Elizabeth's career was one of his vocational successes.

Because she was the eldest daughter and Mother's chief helper, she had had to miss a great deal of schooling. There were just too many small children for one woman to manage unaided. Elizabeth did not resent her earlier lack of opportunity but decided, when the time came that she could be spared, to enter a newly opened secretarial school. She bought a typewriter—they were just coming into general use—on time payments, which I offered to help her meet. She was not overly strong, and the more Father thought about it, the more reluctant he became to have her enter a field where women were not too welcome. A twelve hour day, six days a week, was enough without encountering possible opposition.

In those days, to many men, the very idea of a woman wanting to keep books or to work in an office was ridiculous. It was something beyond belief. And the woman who could think of such a thing was looked on with suspicion. Father knew this and perhaps Elizabeth knew it also, but she had set her heart on being a secretary so she went to school. Father never took anything away from us unless he had something better to offer in its place, so for a time he kept his misgivings to himself.

Then one day he said to her, "Come take a walk with me, Sis. You and I haven't had much time for each other lately."

As they walked along, he asked her questions about the school and how she liked it. She was enthusiastic and told him that she was nearly ready to look for a job.

"Is it very important to you that you find a job?" he questioned.

"Yes, it is," she answered. "All the others are planning to do something and I don't want to be left out."

"I know how you feel," he said. "Mother still needs you, but that isn't the point. You want to do something on your own account."

"Yes," she said.

Father loved pictures and frequently visited Toledo's new fine arts museum. All his children inherited something of his feeling for line and color, but Elizabeth exhibited the most talent. There was also an excellent art school in the city where Father apparently had been making inquiries, for he began talking persuasively of the great opportunities for artists as against the prosy dullness of an office clerk's life. Elizabeth was not convinced that a clerk's life would be dull routine to one whose principal activity had been taking care of a succession of babies, but she was interested. Father didn't hurry her; he gave her time to digest this new idea.

But when he judged that the right time had come to press the issue, he said, "If your mind isn't fixed on going into business, perhaps you would consider giving your mother and me the great pleasure of sending you to art school. We should like to have an artist in the family. We are both sorry that you missed so much school. We should like to make up for it by giving you the best training under the best teachers to be had in Toledo. What do you say?"

"Why, I'd love to go, of course," said Elizabeth, "but I have spent so much time and money going to business school that I feel I ought to make use of what I've learned. I'm like Mama; I hate to waste anything. Besides, I might do well in business."

"Shh," said Father soothingly, "the time hasn't been wasted; every woman ought to know something about business practice. Some day, I'm sure, you'll find it very useful. It would make me happy if you cared to accept my offer."

So Elizabeth sold her typewriter to "Petroleum V. Nasby" and did Father a favor by going to art school. Later, she became a teacher of art. And when opportunity came her way and she went to Europe, she had the background with which to appreciate the beautiful things she saw there, just as Father had hoped for her. During her long and useful life, she has always been in perfect agreement that his estimate of what would give her greatest scope for her talents was better than her own first choice.

In Father's approach to life lay the secret of his successful living. He was not obsessed with its problems; he was challenged by its possibilities. What most men in his position would have considered an obligation, he considered a creative opportunity. Being a parent to a large family was not a crushing duty to be borne, it was a privilege to be taken advantage of, like any other good gift.

Before my first absence from home, I took his attitude for granted. For all I knew, all fathers were as interested as he was in making their children's lives happy and secure. Now I began to realize why none of my brothers and sisters were "problem children" or ever likely to be; how he directed our lives without depriving us of the feeling that we were managing ourselves. His method was simple. The most exciting place to be in our free time was wherever he was.

After supper, we gathered around him in the living room where he read a short Bible text, followed by a few brief and never dull comments on its meaning. Since the book's message was a living thing for him, he communicated to us the immeasurable possibilities he had found there for vital use. When he had finished, he would say, "Now how about a little music?"

By the time we got around to the music, our living room contained half the other youngsters in the neighborhood, who had come to join the fun.

When I was a little fellow, Father bought me a Jew's harp which I thought quite grand. Later, I graduated to a harmonica on which

I became fairly expert. But as the family grew up, he acquired more sophisticated instruments for our use. My brother Herman played the violin, Susan the guitar, and most of the others learned to play the piano. Everybody sang. And Father, his bearded face wreathed in smiles, joined in the singing or listened to the lovely old American and European folk songs he loved so well. Whenever he listened to music, he appeared to me to be enjoying the height of happiness.

Depending on the time of year, we rounded off the evening's festivities by popping corn or eating fruit and cookies. And when bedtime came and our young visitors reluctantly departed, we had never a doubt in the world that there was no place like home in which to enjoy ourselves. And this was so because Father offered to us what he wished to receive in return—a joyous, useful life.

He was a good listener and easy to talk to. And it was to him that I turned for help in understanding what I had seen in Chicago.

Like all deeply religious men, he believed in the ultimate justice and wisdom of Providence. But he clearly saw that since men were the instruments on this earth through whose free will their Maker had chosen to manifest Himself, progress inevitably waited on the speed with which they comprehended their possibilities. And since it was inevitable, he believed, that in the end, goodness born of wisdom would triumph over evil born of ignorance, he was not disheartened by the slowness of the onward march. Moreover, he was not afraid to subject his beliefs to the scrutiny of his logical French mind.

Much of what he said to me in our talks had to wait on maturity for true understanding. But he so ably expressed his views that, in my experience, time produced no contradiction to his conceptions of the right and wrong way to live. Without my father's guidance at this time in my life, I might very well have assumed that in a world as tough as I was finding this one to be, to achieve any kind of material success meant that a man had to be of two minds. While he might regret the necessity for so doing, he lived in a "dog-eat-dog" society where he either parted company with restraining scruples or he fell victim to men whose claws were not clipped by them. He could only afford the luxury of practicing the Golden Rule at such times as it was either safe to do so because it cost him nothing, or he must have so much that it didn't matter.

"I know," said Father, "how it seems, but let me ask you a few questions. If the Gospel is 'impractical idealism by its very nature unfitted to solve practical problems,' then did those men in Chicago buy peace for themselves by making the city a gift of a machine gun?"

"No," I said, "for the source of the trouble remains."

"Exactly," he agreed, "and trouble will break out again and again to plague them."

"Well, what would you do?" I asked.

He laughed. "Oh, I'd agree with my adversary quickly, while I was in the way with him. There's always a time when you can, you know."

"Aren't there ever any justifiable wars?" I asked. "The Civil War was fought in a good cause, don't you think?"

"Just like those riots in Chicago," he said, "it was the inevitable result of years of ill will on the part of men resolved to kill each other rather than reason together. The war cost six billion dollars, half a million lives, and who can estimate how much heartache and misery it caused. The real war didn't begin at Sumter or end with Gettysburg. It will never end until both sides make up their minds to do what a cannon could never make them do, and that is to love and trust each other."

"But it did free the slaves and preserve the Union," I said.

"Don't you forget," he reminded me, "that the freedom of every black man in the South could have been purchased for a fraction of the money cost of the war alone. The real barrier to a settlement was not the lack of means; it was hate and stubborn willful pride. When men hold on to these things long enough, only one means of payment satisfies them—blood. It was for this reason that a truly practical man once gave the sound bit of advice I just gave you—'Agree with thine adversary quickly.'

"Can't you see," he said, "that peace is not necessarily present because you don't hear the sound of a cannon. Peace is not the absence of war any more than love is the absence of hate. But the point I want you to remember is that an issue in dispute is never settled by who won the last battle. Today France is defeated; Alsace and Lorraine are now German. What the French took from the Germans in 1648, the Germans regained in 1871. But this is only the beginning. One day the French will fight to get them back and then the Germans will fight to regain them, and so on. But no matter who wins or loses, each time these nations go to war, humanity is crucified on the cross of its own blind selfishness. And this is all that really matters. Would you call this perpetual strife between neighbor nations a 'practical' way to live? But consider that both nations regard themselves as highly practical in their approach to what they are pleased to call a 'permanent solution to the Alsace-Lorraine question.' Just like your men in Chicago, they buy themselves a little truce with guns and call it 'peace.'"

"What would you do?" I asked.

"You asked me that before," he said, "and for a practical man such as I am, there is only one answer. What harm could come from practicing the Golden Rule for a change, now that men have tried everything else and failed?"

I was no more impressionable than the usual adolescent approaching eighteen. In many ways, I was less so. I had inherited both my looks and disposition from Mother's side of the house—a family which ran more to "generals" of my uncle's type than it did to diplomats like Father. I had the Decker capacity to drive myself—and others—toward any objective to which I was committed, and also the family's somewhat explosive temper and great physical energy. My mother's people could be generous and self-sacrificing, as she was, but they could be equally stubborn and unyielding. Father found no fault with the "hardheadedness" which was a family characteristic, but he always pointed out that the ideal combination for such a head was a "soft" heart, since justice without mercy was of no use to anyone. And because he was an example himself of what he talked about, I listened with respectful attention.

I was too well acquainted with the hard circumstances of his life to believe that, when he urged me to think less about my "right to happiness" and a great deal more about the need to earn it, he was only giving me what today would be called a "pep talk." He was sharing with me the fundamental first principle of successful living, which he put into action every day. Faith without works made no sense to him. He was a man of both who continually measured the truth of the one by the results of the other.

And since he was a good, practical psychologist where his children were concerned, I think he understood the need for me at this time to accept the sole responsibility for the results of my acts. Life was hard. Yes, men were often stupid and brutal. But notwithstanding these inescapable facts, I was still not bound by any standards of conduct other than of my own choosing. Whatever success or happiness I achieved here was the result of something earned; they were not debts to me contracted either by God or the world on the day I was born. On the contrary, I was the debtor. I had received the gift of life, an inheritance I could either use or squander. What I did with it was likely to depend on how well I understood the gift's purpose and its possibilities. With it, I could change the world to my way of thinking, if I wanted to and tried hard enough. But however I chose to spend it, I could never escape the consequences of my own choice.

And when I had had time to digest this idea, I could see that this was fair and right, inasmuch as my inheritance included the ability to make decisions—but decisions whose results, by the very nature of things, could never be confined to myself alone, anymore than I could exclude my family from my life just by choosing to do so. I could ignore, disgrace, hurt or help it, do anything to, for, or with it, but I couldn't shut it out. The relationship remained no matter how I chose to regard it. And logically, even though some members might disregard me, in the long run the family was bound to respond to me as I responded toward it.

Dimly, I began to perceive the why of so much that had perplexed me—particularly, the need for holding on to whatever moral values passed the bar of judgment and experience. Seemingly, these were often expensive luxuries for the poor. Many an ambitious man dumped them overboard to lighten cargo as he ran before the winds of necessity. And such men were respected, feared, and often called "smart." Unless they badly overreached themselves, as far as I could see, they were not penalized. Some of the worst rogues in Chicago were, as the saying goes, "sitting pretty." They had everything, including public admiration. I was also ambitious, with a fixed determination to "get somewhere" soon. But I could see that it might be well to remember that a halfway house en route could easily be mistaken for the journey's end.

Due to the steadying influence of Father's ideas and the recuperative magic of Mother's cooking coupled with the vitality of youth, I quickly regained my health. The running sores on my ankles healed. Soon I was as bored with resting as a young colt confined to the stall. I wandered down to the Wabash car shops "just to look around" and came home with a job.

I had acquired the work habit early and, like all people with superabundant energy, found any kind of activity preferable to none. At first, the routine work in the shops gave me all the outlet I needed. But the work grew progressively duller as my old-time energy returned. Life in Chicago had been twice as hard, but it was much more absorbing. Toledo had seemed lively enough before the "gem of the prairies" had whetted my appetite for stronger excitements; now it seemed like a country village where nothing ever happened. I began to feel homesick for the rough, tough vigor of the great continental crossroads. Now and then I bought a Chicago paper just to keep in touch with goings on there.

There was always plenty going on. At the time, Chicago papers were busy answering charges brought by St. Louis and other commercial rivals that "artful Chicagoans" had induced the railroads to discriminate unfairly in their favor on freight rates. The *Blade* joined in the controversy. I used to laugh at the thought of how mad "Nasby," the *Blade*'s chief hammer thrower, would be when he read the *Tribune*'s airy dismissal of his complaints against Chicago. "While seemingly fortunate in its situation," the *Tribune* would comment, "Toledo has had less vitality in its growth than any other Western city."

Sometimes, without naming names, Chicago papers would suggest that, if complaining cities would organize "a large number of first class funerals among their leading citizenry," they might "develop a capacity equal to ours." When other cities attempted to answer this jibe by pointing out that Chicago's business failures "greatly exceed our own," Chicago boasted that "this only *proves* the stagnating caution" prevailing in the particular community which had dared to criticize her business methods.

People, even in Toledo, laughed and said, "Now, isn't that Chicago for you." And there was always just enough truth in Chicago's rebuttal to make battle-scarred rough-and-tumble veterans like "Nasby" hastily retire to lick their wounds. There was no doubt in my mind, of course, that it was the one city where more opportunity waited for the man who knew how to seize it than in any other I had yet heard about. I was hardly a man but I would be soon, and I knew that in some fashion Chicago spelled the future. Although it was a hard, tough place to live and work, still I wanted to go back to it.

However, I was mindful of the doctor's advice. Already six feet tall and growing like a weed, I still needed time in which to gain the flesh necessary to cover adequately my big frame. A few more months at home and I would be both big and husky enough to stand even Chicago's punishment. So I continued to work in the Wabash shops and to go with Father and the family for long walks on Sunday afternoons along the banks of the beautiful, tree-shaded Maumee River.

Sometimes everybody piled into the family surrey and went out into the country to visit friends or to pick wildflowers and study birds. Father loved these excursions and utilized them to tell us all he knew about the habitants of the fields and forests. Other Sundays, friends came to visit us. Music and singing brightened these occasions. Sunday, to us, was never the dull and melancholy day it is now pictured to have been before the advent of the motion pictures and the automobile. It was a cheerful day, and anticipated in many households besides our own, when the father, released from his daily occupation, was free to devote himself to his family's pleasure and instruction.

Although cards and dancing were decidedly "not respectable" and not permitted in our home, we were allowed to attend the theater. And what an exciting occasion that was! We talked about the event days before and after. I well remember the first professional theatrical performance I was privileged to see, no less than Buffalo Bill and his troupe at the old Toledo Opera House. I still treasure a picture of the stage setting. Against a painted cardboard forest primeval, the great Buffalo Bill relived the drama of a West already bygone. I was thrilled by the deadly accuracy of the exhibition shooting and, above all, I was baffled as to how they could build a fire on the stage and grill a buffalo steak. I could see the gleaming, ruby coals and fancied I could smell smoke. Leaving the theater without discovering the secret of building a fire on a wooden platform without burning down the house, I was greatly awed by my first contact with the world of professional make-believe. There was certainly a difference between what went on in the Toledo Opera House and the transparent disguises employed by our home talent productions, which never fooled me. Yes, there was a decided difference. I became a convert on the spot to the professional way of doing things.

The next day, Buffalo Bill appeared on the street in our neighborhood, nor was there any break with illusion there. He was everything in person he had seemed on the stage. A truly handsome man whose black, flowing mane hung down to his shoulders, in his beaded buckskins he was to me the romantic personification of the West he had helped subdue.

But even the Toledo Opera House was beginning to pale as an attraction about the time a letter arrived from my Uncle Jay. His Texas venture was turning out badly, he said, and he had decided to return to Chicago. A few months later, he wrote again to say that, with just enough money in his pocket to rent an empty store and to buy a few planks for counters, he had established a market on Harrison Street on the West Side. Since the weather was cold, he wrote, for the time being he could do without an icebox. Planks nailed together and supported by barrels might not be fancy, but they made satisfactory counters. "While the market is no showplace," he wrote, "I have all the goods I can sell. Now I know what it means to have good credit. Every commission house on Jackson Street remembers that I paid my bills promptly and gladly sells me merchandise on trust."

"What every commission house really remembers," I told the family, "is that he is a demon for work."

If I knew anything, the commission houses did not stand to lose by putting him in business. With his energy and their merchandise, he would go after volume. And he did. With prices that matched his overhead and selling for cash, he was soon doing a tremendous business. Since everybody knew that fine fixtures cost money, he shrewdly capitalized on his barrel-and-plank counters and lack of an icebox. "When you buy from me," he told thrifty West Side housewives, "you pay for nothing but meat. Everything I have bought today, I must sell today." By warm weather, he had made money enough to buy half a dozen iceboxes and had formed a partnership with a man named Gale. Gale had capital and my uncle had what it takes to put money profitably to work.

Reading about his exploits, I made up my mind. "I think I'll go back to Chicago," I announced one night after supper.

Father laughed. "I've known you were hankering to go ever since Jay's letter came," he said. "And if it's where your heart is, Son, it's where you ought to be."

So I went back to Chicago. But since my uncle had no immediate openings for me, I went to work packing hogs and making sausages for Charles F. Unrath, who ran a packinghouse market on Jackson Street.

On Jackson Street, usually called "Commission Row," were located the old-time commission houses which were among the sights of Chicago. They were the outlets for small fry speculators and livestock bargain hunters who sent to them for resale small lots of animals bought in the yards or from drovers. The original purchasers, after having the animals slaughtered and dressed by slaughterers who kept the offal in payment, then consigned the carcasses to commission houses which sold them on a percentage basis. The commission houses also handled, on consignment, huge quantities of wild game, buffalo meat, and domestic poultry shipped in during the cold weather months from surrounding farms and hunting grounds.

The day began while the stars shone above "Commission Row," where flaring gas jets lighted the scene to almost daytime brightness. Buyers for hotels, restaurants, and retail shops thronged the markets filled with haunches of venison, wild and domestic geese, ducks, turkeys, and chickens. Here they bargained over whole hogs, sheep, quarters of beef, short loins, and counters heaped with hams, bacon, and spareribs. Long lines of heavily loaded drays rumbled through the night-darkened streets, bringing to the great market-place still more of these things for Chicago's tables. The city had the greatest meat consumption in the world. Though bread might be the staff of life elsewhere, Chicagoans considered meat to be its most convenient crutch. Seeing all this plentitude made it hard to believe that anyone among the city's thousands could ever be hungry except through choice.

I worked for Unrath's only a few months before joining forces with my uncle. Hard as he was to work for in some ways, I preferred being with him. He was gay and fun-loving and had a zest for living. For the experience I gained, it was a wise move.

In the winter of 1878, he said to me, "George, if I sent you to Indianapolis as buyer for Gale & Decker, do you think you could do the job?"

I wasn't sure, but I knew that if he had confidence enough in me to ask the question, I could probably do the work he had in mind, so I said yes.

My job in Indianapolis was to buy pork tenderloins from local packers engaged in wintertime pork processing for the European market. These packers, Kingan & Company and Coffin & Fletcher, made what were called "English cuts," which they shipped to England and the Continent. To make these foreign cuts, the tenderloin was removed. Gale & Decker specialized in handling quality tender-loins—for which they had established a reputation in New York's great produce center, Washington Market. Since the Indianapolis packers had developed no trade outlets for this item, it was cheaper to buy tenderloins from them than it was to buy them in Chicago.

In order to have my purchases arrive fresh in New York, it was also my job to pack the tenderloins carefully in galvanized containers which were then placed inside pork barrels filled with salted, crushed ice.

This was my first responsible job and I was filled with the importance of it since it was solely up to me to see that what I bought was of good quality, worth the price paid for it, and so packed that it arrived in perfect condition. This assignment also taught me something about the knack of bargaining. I soon noticed that on warm days the packers were more anxious to dispose of tenderloins than they were when the weather stayed well below freezing. Thereafter, as the thermometer rose, my bids fell proportionately. When the mercury indicated that I was operating in a seller's market, I offered more. At the season's end when I returned to Chicago, my uncle was well pleased with the results of my operations.

As always, I was glad to return to the great continental crossroads. The decade was now ending which had opened with the city's almost total destruction. It was the scene of furious activity. New mills and factories were rising on every hand. State Street had become a solid wall of imposing stone and fireproof brick. The harbor was filled with hundreds of vessels bringing ore from Upper Michigan, coal and coke from Cleveland. Big freighters from all over the world docked in increasing numbers by the great grain elevators, carrying away the precious loads of Kansas corn and Minnesota wheat. Refrigerator cars were no longer the novelty they had been only three years before. They streamed out of Packingtown day and night. Mills and factories ceaselessly pulsed with the roar of steam-driven machines. Hard times and caution might set the tempo for the rest of the world, but "artful Chicagoans" set their own. They were consolidating past advantages and planning for the future. Some of the newer industrial buildings were wired for electric lights; current was supplied by small steam-driven dynamos. And tomorrow's business leviathans were beginning to swallow minnows at an alarming rate.

This was particularly noticeable in the only industry of which I had any firsthand knowledge. The retail packinghouse establishments, such as my uncle's old business had been, were now on their way out. Every phase of meat processing was being centralized and controlled by the big packers near the yards. This trend was to continue.

My uncle had sensed its inevitability two years before and had sold his business because of his belief that shortly there would be no place in the new picture for small fry like himself. The correctness of his thinking was demonstrated from 1877 on through the 1890's, as failure after failure occurred in the ranks of the smaller firms in the Chicago district. Men like Swift, Morris, Armour, and the Cudahys began to eliminate small competitors through controlling their raw material sources and channels of distribution.

The change was also brought about in another way. The big firms began to concentrate on the utilization of byproducts, or rather the complete utilization of the entire product. They put specialists to work on research and developed machines and techniques for using what formerly had been wasted. In this factor lay their real mastery of the market. The little fellow had only meat to sell, and threw away, or received only a pittance for, everything else. And back in the 1880's, it seemed to me that the big fellows did a thoroughly competent job in extracting profit from these heretofore unsuspected sources. In the light of today's methods, however, those old-time packers would be considered amateurs. But that is another story which had to wait upon chemistry, medicine and research in a hundred branches of scientific inquiry then unknown. Even now, people think of packers principally in terms of their breakfast bacon or dinner chop, although this is only one part of the role they play in the everyday life of the twentieth century.

The conditions present in Chicago, however, were not true elsewhere. In cities like Indianapolis and Cincinnati, packers were still conducting their businesses in the old way. They were seasonal operators engaged in pork processing in the wintertime. Since local demand was only equal to a fraction of the portions not suitable for curing, there was little or no return for them.

Chicago packers had set up marketing divisions of their own to dispose of these items. They could do this because they were rapidly putting their business on a year-round basis. Winter was still their busy season, but this was as much because of custom as it was necessity. Ammonia refrigeration had passed the experimental stage and, while it had not as yet supplanted natural ice, it was coming into use among the larger packers. When fresh meat could be stored against the demands of the market, it was inevitable that the producers should become their own middlemen.

There were also signs that this would cause repercussions in other ways. As long as the meat industry remained seasonal and chaotic, labor was in no position to bargain. The unskilled or migratory workers, who formed the majority in its ranks, were wholly at the mercy of their employers. Such workers might get a little more in times of labor famine, but demand and supply, not their needs, determined their status, and they had no vested interest in their jobs worth making a sustained fight for.

Muscle power had been the principal commodity the laborer sold in exchange for his miserable living up until now. And very little attention had been paid to what such labor cost in terms of profit, in the days when men worked until they dropped during the short rush season. But with the stabilization and expansion of the industry, permanent, skilled labor became a necessity. Employers began to see that a logger turned packinghouse employee or a harvest hand cutting up carcasses in his off-season for a dollar a day might be costly help. For as control of the meat industry came into the hands of a comparatively few persons, efficiency and cost accounting came with it. In order to eliminate wasteful methods, practices and procedures became standardized. Competition among packers was keen and they began to stress brand names. Profit was figured on fractions of a cent, and leaks due to inefficient handling of their product could only be plugged when a trained man on the Armour and Swift payrolls had a year-round job.

Smart packers like these also began to see that markets could be expanded, without comparably increasing production costs, by a division of labor into highly specialized operations where men performed their tasks with great speed at a minimum loss of time and motion. This called for better training and better men to train.

But I doubt if even they were smart enough to see that organization inside the plant would inevitably lead to organization outside the plant. Employers as a class then held to the point of view—by no means universal today—that any increase in efficiency belonged to profits and not to wages. Collective bargaining was a conspiracy to be fought by all and any means. Nevertheless, the thing they feared now became a fact to be reckoned with in the packing industry, and they had made its eventual success possible.

Unorganized riots among dissatisfied packinghouse workers were no novelty prior to the centralization and modernization of the industry, but they had neither been costly nor difficult to cope with as long as the workers could be easily replaced within a few hours' time. But packers fought a different and losing battle when they contended with the skilled, permanent personnel they had created to meet the demands of their vast, expanding markets. Just as the little packer was being beaten because he was no match for their superior resources, skills, and techniques, the new type of industrial worker who could execute these techniques was now in a position to demand a better price for his practice. Trade unionism had come to stay in the packing industry.

This phase of the industrial revolution did not come about overnight, but its beginning was apparent as early as 1879. Thinking over the past, I realize today some of its meaning I so little understood at the time. Perhaps a germinal idea did take root subconsciously, but if so, it was a long time before it grew big enough for me to understand its significance.

And its meaning is simply this: all so-called plans for "social justice" based on giving to the worker only what he produces are misleading. If he is unskilled or if industrial organization and stability are lacking, he will not produce enough as a worker to support himself. He may protest, he may revolt, but he will still be poor. Nor can politicians nor social ideologies bring about the results they so glibly promise solely through any "share the wealth" schemes. What is really needed to give the worker social justice is, above all, men who can increase their skills, men who can fully utilize existing resources, and men who can continuously discern new wealth-producing possibilities. Freedom from want for the masses depends upon men able to organize production and distribution, and a never-ending stream of more men willing and able to undertake the risks and responsibilities of pioneering new fields.

Such men may or may not have "social vision," but once they have put into operation a continuous process of training so that large numbers of unskilled laborers become skilled, and once they create the means by which these can productively function, *then* the worker has the means of achieving social justice for himself. When this stage of industrial development has been reached, it makes little difference whether the employer is "a narrow reactionary" or "enlightened;" in either case, he has made possible the only conditions under which men can better their standards of living.

And if he refuses? Well, as a business acquaintance once said to me, "When you have built a business whose existence depends upon continuous, uninterrupted production, it isn't yours anymore. You have made a monster which owns you, and you'll have to serve it. You can't afford anything the business can't afford, which means that you can't afford labor trouble or anything else that interferes with its operation."

But back in Chicago, at eighteen, I was far less concerned with the changing industrial scene than I was with trying to find out how to be an effective actor on life's stage. I was well aware that no one else was going to create the role and learn the lines for me. My training at home and in the world to date had thoroughly convinced me of this fact. At some future time the presence of an audience might guarantee me a hearing, but the quality of the performance was another matter. Through the circumstances of my father's and uncle's occupations, I had acquired a number of skills. Brought up to believe that the most respectable career was the most useful, I was primarily concerned with making the most of what I had learned at a profit to myself. And, as yet, I had found no way to do this.

About this time, I wrote home voicing my dissatisfaction. I was sending the family very little money because I wasn't earning much. "It is now a month since I have been receiving seven dollars and fifty cents a week, but if I don't get ten dollars a week after this, I am going to work someplace else," I wrote. "It costs me five dollars a week to live in winter, which includes my washing, of which I have a great deal."

My sister Elizabeth used to keep my letters, and leafing through their time-yellowed pages long years since, I always recapture something of the time and mood in which they were written, and see how little we realize the significant and important changes in our lives when they first appear.

The fact that Gale & Decker did not place a value on my services which matched my conception of what they were worth seemed no act of Providence at the time—no more than any other turning points in my life which I related in my letters seemed significant—until long after when all the evidence was in. I notice now that I moved in new directions only when I became thoroughly dissatisfied with the old. As long as I was willing to temporize or to compromise with conditions, I stayed right where I was.

One bit of good fortune, which I partly recognized at the time, was being able to enjoy a warm room by joining forces with two other boys, one of whom was my uncle's bookkeeper. The winter of 1879 was exceptionally cold. In such accommodations as I could afford by myself, it was often so cold that I went immediately to bed for warmth on coming home.

"You haven't heard from me," I wrote in a letter home, "because for the past week it has been so cold that I couldn't write very well. But now three of us have clubbed together and rented a splendid parlor for twelve dollars a month. The room is furnished with a good carpet and good beds and has a fine marble fireplace. You have no idea of what it meant to come home tonight and sit down in a nice warm room, something I never really appreciated until now."

But my good fortune was not only in the room. The young men who shared it with me were educated and studious. One, Karl, a recent arrival from Germany, worked in a bookstore. The other, Gus Wollering, my uncle's bookkeeper, a young German-American from Milwaukee, was a student of Shakespeare. That winter was my introduction to the world of great poetry and to those ideas common to educated minds everywhere.

Evenings after supper we used to sit in our comfortable chairs by the fire, reading and memorizing Shakespeare's magnificent lines. The following night we would review what we had read the night before and penalize each other for errors. All this gave me a little glimpse of what was to be had through education. Until then, I had only dimly comprehended the gulf between the mind which responded to ideas and the untrained mind to which they were foreign through lack of recognition.

One conversation between my roommates made a particularly vivid and lasting impression upon me. They were talking about life in the Old and New Worlds.

"In many ways it is kinder and more enjoyable there," said the young German, "but the Little Corporal was right when he called democracy 'an open road to talent.'"

"Who said that?" I interrupted.

"Why, Napoleon, of course," he replied. "He was a very clever man with a great knowledge of men's motives, which he seldom applied in his own dealings with them."

"That was what finally got him into trouble, wasn't it, Karl?" asked the bookkeeper.

"Yes," answered Karl. "According to an account of his character by a man who knew him well, the real reason for his downfall was that he would trust no talents but his own. After he became Emperor, he surrounded himself with little men and closed the road of advancement to all others. In his last days, all the men who could have helped him were now his enemies. So, long before Waterloo, he was headed toward St. Helena.

"This is the real reason why I came to live in a democracy," Karl went on. "You boys don't know what it means to live in a place where a lot of little Napoleons are always shutting doors in your face. If I fail here, it will be partly my fault. In the old country I would never be sure what I could do, for I would never be allowed to try. My folks are poor and that says a lot in Europe."

"It isn't so easy to get ahead here, either," I reminded him.

"I don't ask that it should be easy, George," he replied. "I just ask that the world I live in should be alive. This country is alive, and that is enough for me."

Napoleon's fine phrase stuck in my memory long after I had forgotten many another. It summed up the possibilities of the future and explained the past to me. What really gave democracy its significance, I began to see, was what Karl meant when he said, "I don't ask that it be easy . . . just alive." He had not come to seek freedom from risk, but freedom for expression. As time went on, I began to see more and more in this idea—not "freedom *from*" but "freedom *for*." Whatever life meant, it was something like this: the freedom to use one's own special talent.

By the spring of the year, my uncle's bookkeeper and I had decided that our road of opportunity began somewhere else than Chicago. My pay envelope seemed frozen at seven dollars and fifty cents; he was earning a dollar more. A winter of plain living and high thinking had whetted our appetites for something more promising in the way of a future than a seventy-hour week of hard work and nothing to show for it but our keep.

Although we lived in one of the gayest cities of America, we rarely went to places of amusement. Our social life was confined to church attendance, a walk in the park on Sunday, and not much else. I was painfully shy and consequently made few acquaintances among girls of my own age. I was too conscious that there was little I could offer a girl besides my company, since I had no money to take her sleigh riding in winter or driving through the parks in summer, such as other boys seemed able to do. They talked about taking their girls boating on the lake or out to supper, and seemingly bought them cameo pins and gold chains by the dozens. In my innocence, I believed their stories.

So when my pal, Wollering, the bookkeeper, said one evening, "Look George, there's another passenger ticket rate war on between the railroads going to Kansas City; why don't we go?" I was ready to say yes.

The fare was five dollars. I had a total capital of a little under ten. But since Kansas City was a railroad and livestock center, it seemed safe to risk finding a job as soon as we got there. I was now a big fellow—six feet two, and as hard as nails. At nineteen, I had had six years' experience in three trades. I could seek work as a railroad shop helper, as a tanner, and in a variety of skills in the meat business. I was good at figures and wrote a fair hand.

"So you're off to see the world," said my uncle, when we announced our intention of leaving. "Well, I don't blame you. At your age, I wanted to see it too, and better myself if I could. Good luck to you!"

One thing, however, we had not taken into our calculations. When we boarded the train, it was packed with job seekers like ourselves. All young male Chicago, apparently, was on its way in search of better fortune in the West, looking for the Golden Fleece that's always to be found in the place to which you are going.

CHAPTER FIVE

The Road Opens

There were no "welcome" signs awaiting us in Kansas City. The Gold Rush had deposited a hundred hungry job seekers on its streets for every one who found a place. Every clapboard hotel and rooming house in town was full to bursting with the hopeful. My pal and I, after long and diligent searching, did find a frowsy room to share. When I paid my half of the first month's rent, I was broke.

I might have asked him to stake me until I found a job, but he did not offer and I was not used to asking favors. Anyhow, it wasn't done. I tramped the streets from morning until night in a fruitless search for work. For the first time, I knew the experience of having something to sell that nobody wanted to buy. Even in the panic years I had always been able to get a job of sorts. Now I could find nothing.

There was a penny restaurant at the corner of Delaware and Main Streets where I got my meals in exchange for washing dishes and hustling them out of the dining room; except at mealtimes, I was on the street.

Since there was no place for me in the packinghouses or railroad yards, I began to comb less likely sources of employment. I remember trying for a job in the shipping department of a wholesale grocery house and demonstrating, as persuasively as I knew how, my skill with a marking pot and brush.

"Sure, you do all right," the manager agreed, "but I haven't got a job for you. Maybe next month. Come back and we'll see."

But next month my rent was due, so I dismissed this slender hope for future employment and continued my tour.

Finally, I came to a hide and wool house and stopped to look at the stacks of sacked wool on the sidewalk. "That's a lot of wool," I commented to a man standing nearby.

"Know anything about wool?" he asked.

"I ought to, I was brought up in the business," I said. "I've just come from Chicago and I'm looking for work."

"Come inside," he offered. "I'd like your opinion of some wool we've got."

He watched me closely as I estimated the various grades for quality and the price they should bring. But when I suggested hopefully that perhaps he had a job for me, he shook his head in the all too familiar gesture. "Sorry, but I have all the men on the road I need right now."

For a moment I didn't answer him; the idea of applying for a buyer's job had never entered my head. Just any kind of a job was all I hoped for. But since he seemed to think I looked like a potential wool buyer, I asked, "Why not let me work in the house until there is a road vacancy?"

"No, that's niggers' work," he said.

Considering the kinds of dirty work I had done and the people I had worked with in Chicago, to make that distinction now seemed funny. But I didn't laugh. I needed a job and, if there was one, I meant to have it. So, disregarding his deep Southern accent and the sentiments that went with it, I pleaded, "I know all about packing and sorting hides and I don't mind working with anybody."

"No," he repeated, "that's niggers' work. You leave your name and address on a card in the office. When I have a white man's job to offer, I'll let you know."

Convinced that it was useless to argue further, I bade him goodbye after telling him again that I would appreciate any job he cared to give me.

I left him with my heart in my boots. Here was a job that I knew how to do in a place that needed my services, but I couldn't have it because it was only fit for "niggers." I was halfway down the block when I heard a shrill whistle. I looked back. The man I had just left was whistling and motioning me to return. When I retraced my steps, he said without preliminary, "Go to the office; see McDonald. He'll equip you for the road and give you a routing. Good luck."

Speechless with surprise and relief, and fright at what I had gotten into, I stumbled into the office to be supplied with report sheets of various kinds, a telegraph code book, and a book of drafts to use in payment for the hides, wool, and furs I was to purchase. On the assumption that I already knew what these things were for, I received a few brief directions on the firm's methods of handling the various transactions, but I remembered nothing of what I heard when I left the office beyond the indisputable fact that I had been hired as a buyer by Major J. N. Dubois, late of the Confederate forces. I shouldn't even have believed this if it were not for the code and draft books clutched in my perspiring hands.

Somehow I got to my room. The bookkeeper was there. As I poured forth the tale of the day's happenings and my panic at the unexpected outcome, he became hysterical with laughter.

"I never heard of anything so funny in my life," he howled. "Just wait till you get on the road. What do you know about all this? Oh, if I could only be there to see you!"

His laughing made me mad. "So you think it's that funny, huh? You just wait, Mr. Smart Aleck. Maybe I don't know how to use these things, but I'm sure as blazes going to try. You just save some of those laughs until I get back and maybe I'll join you."

The business would have seemed just as funny to anyone else as it did to the bookkeeper. I had never received a check in my life. I doubt if I knew that there was such a thing as a draft. Without a doubt, I was the worst equipped commercial traveler who ever took to the road.

Now, with his laughter ringing in my ears, I grimly packed the old oilskin (for I had never acquired enough money for decent luggage), bought my ticket, and headed for the first town on the route list, Pleasant Hill, Missouri.

On the train, I eyed other traveling men to see how they were dressed and what luggage they carried. Prince Albert coats, striped pants, and silk hats were the rule. In my well-brushed and well-worn Sunday suit, I was positively crude by contrast with these glittering specimens from Marshall Field and other well-known commercial houses. I resolved to do away with the oilskin and buy a cowhide valise if I had to go without eating to do it.

The real shock, however, of those first few days on the road was the presentation of my first hotel bill. I had never earned more than seven dollars and fifty cents a week, and my ideas of what things ought to cost were based upon what I had had to spend. In order to accumulate even a dollar or two for emergencies, I had to practice the strictest economy. We boys in Chicago often called "supper" four toasted buns apiece, which cost us ten cents a dozen; we toasted them in the fireplace and ate them with sorghum bought by the bottle. Other times, I ate in lunch cars where you could buy soup, corned beef and cabbage, or other meat dishes with bread and butter for ten cents. Fifteen cents bought these things and pie—quite a satisfactory meal, I thought.

So, after spending several days in Pleasant Hill sorting, weighing, and sacking wool, when I asked for my bill and found it was two dollars a day, I knew I was being robbed! I thought it so unreasonable that I went to the cashier of the bank to find out what was customary. He looked at me curiously. "Didn't they treat you right? Wasn't the food good?" he asked.

"Best I ever ate," I said, "but isn't the bill a little stiff?"

"It's below average," he assured me.

This gave me something more to worry about. For three or four stops there was nothing to buy. The butchers had either just sold hides and had none on hand, or the dealers were afraid of the wool market and had bought none for resale. Every time a prospect said, "Sorry, nothing for you," I broke out in a cold sweat just thinking about the tremendous outlay of two dollars a day, plus railroad fare that Dubois had invested in my services. What should I do? Here I was costing all this money and doing no business. I was hopelessly discouraged. As an honest man, it seemed I ought to go back to Kansas City and turn in my unused drafts.

On the way to the mining town of Rich Hill, Missouri, another traveler making the territory took the seat beside me. After a couple of fruitless attempts to open a conversation, he said, "You look worried. Better tell me about it. Perhaps I can help." When I had finished my tale of woe, he said comfortingly, "Why, that's the experience we all have on the road. It's nothing to worry about. Fact is, it's better to run into tough luck first than later; then you'll know what to expect."

Later, I suspected that he was humoring me, but he gave me enough confidence to continue the trip, which was what I most needed at the time.

When I arrived in Rich Hill, the little mining town was full of country people who had come to swell the crowds celebrating the tenth anniversary of the Union Pacific's driving of the Golden Spike,[3] which carried its coal to Western markets. Here my fortunes turned, but in a way that frightened me more than my hotel bills.

I bought a carload of hides from a dealer who did business with my company, but he had no wool to sell because he, too, was "afraid of the market." Wool was twenty cents a pound, which seemed high to many dealers, and if the price turned downward, the risk between what they paid and what quotations might be when they tried to sell was greater than their hope of profit. But the visiting farmers had given the Rich Hill man an inspiration!

"I'll take you to all the wool clips in my territory," he proposed, "if you'll give me a half cent a pound on all the wool you buy. That way I'll make a sure profit and you'll have something to show for the trip."

This sounded fair enough and I agreed. So we started out to buy fleece wool from every nearby sheepman. My purchases were to be delivered at the dealer's premises in Rich Hill within a few days.

---

3 The ceremonial final spike which joined the rails of the First Transcontinental Railroad across the United States.

I was at the dealer's wool sheds when the first of the caravan arrived. Shortly, both sides of the street were lined with farm wagons waiting their turn to unload wool. People rushed out to see the unusual sight. To say the least, my purchase was something of a sensation, and listening to their comments frightened me stiff. I began to wonder what Dubois would say when half the wool produced in the county began pouring into Kansas City.

The wool dealer, who had promised to receive and help me sack the wool as part of our bargain, had no facilities for such a flood as this. He began to look frightened, too.

"Man, oh, man, what are we going to do?" he asked.

"Well, at least I know how to handle it," I said.

I went to work rigging up the sort of wool-sacking equipment used in my father's wool pullery. Because the resulting bales were smoother and more compact than the other woolmen present had seen before, this gave some satisfaction.

Before I got through with my next station, Carthage, Missouri, Dubois' telegram arrived. I opened it fearfully, and then rubbed my eyes. "Congratulations," I read. "Wool arriving in fine condition. Keep it up."

That telegram brought me the first peace of mind I had enjoyed since my arrival in Kansas City. I ate my supper that night with a relish and a sense of rightful ownership heretofore lacking. The only thing missing I needed to make that meal perfect was my friend the bookkeeper's presence.

From then on, whenever I arrived at a town where the wool dealer, like the man in Rich Hill, was "afraid of the market," I made him the proposition the other man had made to me. Since dealers were always glad to make money without risking their own, I was always able to buy what wool the growers had to sell. When I returned to Kansas City, Dubois received me with open arms.

"Your salary will be seventy-five dollars a month and expenses from now on," he said. "Is this fair enough?"

I didn't dare tell him just how "fair" it sounded to me who had never earned, before I came to work for him, more than half that amount and spent all of it just to live.

My second trip was, in a sense, as crucial as the first one had been. Dubois hired a new man to work the territory with me. I worked the towns along the Missouri Pacific Railway on the Missouri side of the Kansas boundary as far as Joplin, then crossed over into Kansas, working my way back toward Kansas City. The other man started his trip down the Kansas side, which I made on the homeward stretch. My showing was better than his in the same territory, and he was let out.

If it had not been for my experience in Rich Hill, I should have failed too. The only thing that saved the trip and my job was that I had learned to go out and scratch for business when it wasn't ready and waiting for me. It was just as the Marshall Field salesman had told me on the train: "It's better to run into tough luck first than later; then you'll know what to expect." I had probably worked no harder than the man who lost his job. I knew what to expect and he didn't.

While there is no way of knowing, it is always interesting to speculate upon the kind of a life you might have had "if." It is more than possible that, if this trip had been a failure, I should have rejoined the ranks of the workingman permanently. Perhaps my morale would not have withstood the shock of failure; I had less self-confidence of a sort than I needed. While I was both hard-working and ambitious, I had yet to learn that the only man who never fails is the man who never quits trying, and that success is the result of the last, not the first, try. As it was, the trip was just enough of a success to encourage me to trust myself and to hope for larger future opportunities.

Now that I was over the first hump, I began to equip myself with fine luggage and good business clothes—though I never bought a silk hat or a Prince Albert. I was just beginning to enjoy the life of a commercial traveler whose business connections are glad to see him and who knows he is earning his monthly pay when, in the midst of this new security, I received a wire to discontinue buying and come at once to Kansas City.

On reaching the warehouse, I found it locked by order of the sheriff. I went around to see McDonald, the office manager, who greeted me with a grave face. "We're both through," he said.

Major Dubois, at one time considered one of the wealthiest men in Kansas City, had absconded with one hundred thousand dollars he had obtained by selling fraudulent bills of lading to the banks. They were accustomed to honoring sight drafts for him on shipments of hides and wool sent to Eastern firms. A shipment sent to New England would not arrive for several weeks after leaving Kansas City, and the sight drafts attached to the bills of lading were not payable until the goods arrived. Dubois took advantage of this time lag to sell his trusting bankers worthless paper on non-existent shipments. Unwise wheat speculation on the Board of Trade preceded the embezzlement, which now put the capstone on a once honorable career. And Dubois had thoroughly gutted the business before fleeing to parts unknown.

But although I was left with very little money and without a job, still the circumstance under which I lost it was not damaging to my own feeling of competence. I wrote home in hopes that Father might be able to help me land another traveling job with a hide and wool firm of his acquaintance. Just to let him know how confident I felt, I said, "You don't need to be afraid that I can't handle such a situation. I have bought lots of hides on as small a margin as they are bought in the East, and I select them just as carefully. I would like to travel around home, but I would be happy and satisfied to remain in this territory. I would gladly work six months for nothing just to learn and see as much again as I have since coming here."

But Providence was again taking a hand in my affairs. Father reported no luck in finding a job for me near home. Pondering if, perhaps, another change of scene might not be good for my fortunes, I went to St. Louis to see what Chicago's rival had in store for me. Finding nothing there, I returned once more to Chicago.

At that time, thousands of buffalo skins were shipped into Chicago from those parts of the West still wild. Some of them were manufactured into robes and other articles in this country, but thousands were sorted and reshipped to all parts of the world, particularly to Northern Europe and Russia. Most of these skins were collected by the Western branches of one firm, Oberne, Hosick & Co. of Chicago, the world's largest dealer in hides, wool, tallow, and furs.

I went around to their great fur loft and hide cellar on the corner of Kinzie and LaSalle Streets. I knew that if I found a job with this house, I was in the place to find out all there was to know about the raw materials they handled. There was nothing available on the road at the moment, I was told in the office, but perhaps the plant foreman could use me.

"Hmm," said the foreman to whom I applied, eyeing my white collar and good suit. "So you're a buyer and looking for a job." He grinned. "How would you like to try the hide cellar?"

I had hoped for something better and hesitated. Watching my reactions to this proposal, his grin became broader. "I'm your man," I said.

So I tackled the job Major Dubois wouldn't have me do because it was beneath a white man's dignity.

There were no elevators to carry the hides to and from the street level. The big drays to be loaded or unloaded backed up to a cellar opening next to the curb. One man lifted the hide from the floor to a bench where another man stood who passed it to a third man outside, who lifted it into the dray. When hides were received, the process was reversed.

There were both light and heavy hides. Because I was a "white collar man" and a newcomer, I always drew the piles of bull hides. It was a job for Samson and after a month in the cellar, I had had enough.

On the day I planned to leave, Mr. Oberne came down to look around. As usual, I was wrestling with bull hides so heavy, I staggered under their weight. I was dirty, hot, sick, and discouraged. He stopped me with, "Aren't you the fellow who used to travel for Dubois in Kansas City?"

"Yes, sir," I said, wondering what Dubois would say if he could see me now.

"There's a vacancy in Des Moines in case you're interested," he said. "They'll fix you up in the office. The manager's name in Des Moines is Crandall. When you get there, report to him." He walked away.

As I stood watching his retreating back, I knew how a prisoner feels when the warden says, "Reprieve." I said goodbye, and followed Oberne out of the cellar.

On my first trip out of Des Moines, I traveled through Iowa and Southern Minnesota and fell in love with both at first sight. I had no time for play, but Minnesota's cool, blue skies and meadows flecked with brilliant flowers were like water to a thirsty man. My months of overwork in the hide cellar had run me down and made me lose weight. I used to watch from the train the dark-shadowed lakes full of wall-eyed pike, bass, and perch, and wonder what it would be like to spend a day in the sun with nothing to do but fish.

Although my purchases were shipped directly to Chicago, Des Moines was headquarters, and after a three weeks' trip I returned there. I had done a fair business for a first trip and felt well pleased with myself when I walked into the office late one afternoon. Another traveler had just come in off the road, and we remained after closing hours to finish our reports. It was his custom to look for memoranda left for him on the office spindle. Thinking there might be something there for me, I followed his example. My eye caught my name on a letter addressed to the local manager, Crandall, and written by Mr. Hosick, the firm partner who handled the buying end of the business. Since it had been left on the spindle where anyone could read it, I saw no harm in doing likewise.

It said, "Why do you ask whether we are going to retain Hormel? Why not? His work has been satisfactory, his selection is good, and his weights hold up. We think he will make a good man for the territory."

Knowing the letter could only have been written in response to some reference on Crandall's part as to my undesirability, it naturally worried me. I had never worked for a man who disliked me and, since I had no idea why he was displeased, I was both puzzled and unhappy. Every time I came in from a trip, I expected it to be my last.

Although Crandall obviously didn't like me, he was not unpleasant. But his attitude was strictly businesslike. There were never any little jokes or pleasantries from him, such as he exchanged with other travelers who used to sit around the office between trips.

When I came home after finishing such business as I had in the office, I generally put on overalls and went to the warehouse where I washed windows, whitewashed walls, or kept busy at whatever odd jobs needed doing. Keeping busy was one way of licking discouragement. I was used to manual work and found it both an aid to self-forgetfulness and a means of restoring confidence. I was a good workman, and if I had to earn my living with my hands, it was one field of activity in which I was thoroughly master of the situation.

But I could never get over feeling hurt whenever I thought of Crandall's attitude toward me. He was one of the most agreeable men I had ever met. I liked him and wanted him to like me. He was trusted and liked by everyone. Businessmen from up and down the street were always dropping into the office to visit with him. Angry men and men with a grievance always left his presence with a smile.

Admiringly, I used to watch him handle a tough customer who had stormed into the office, swearing. Butchers in Des Moines did their own slaughtering, and their workmen brought in the hides they had to sell. When a butcher was not in agreement with our grading of the hides, he would come tearing into the office, swearing he had been robbed. Crandall always waited patiently until the angry man told his story. Then he checked and explained the transaction under dispute, topping it off with a bit of humor. If the butcher was entitled to an adjustment, he got it. Crandall never let him go until he was satisfied that he had been fairly treated.

Trying to analyze my reactions to it all, I observed that others worked for Crandall as willingly as I did—yet, he was not a slack boss. He could and did pull a man up sharp when he needed it. But when he found fault, it was never of a kind to shake a man's confidence in himself. He encouraged his men by showing them how to remove the obstacles between them and their greatest possible achievement. The best was not something they owed him, but something they owed to themselves—a matter of self-respect.

If I had been older or more experienced, I would probably have said to him, "Out with it, why don't you like me?" and cleared the air for both of us. But since I was neither, I just continued to feel hangdog whenever I returned to Des Moines, but always hoping that this time he would be pleased with me. Then, when I had about made up my mind to accept the situation as one of those unreasoning dislikes one man often has for another, he invited me to his home for Sunday dinner.

On the Monday following my very pleasant visit, he said, "I just want you to know that I am well pleased with your work, Hormel. It's a lot better than I expected."

"Mr. Crandall, what have you got against me?" I blurted.

"Not a thing," he answered. "Although, when you first arrived from Chicago, I was not impressed with your appearance; you were thin as a rail, and your face and eyes looked as though you had been on a bender for a week. The Chicago office sometimes sends to the branches, fellows in need of straightening out. Doesn't make it too easy for us, you know."

"It was lifting heavy bull hides out of the cellar which took the starch out of me," I said.

He laughed. "Just forget it. I was all wrong."

So the one man whose faith and confidence was indispensable to my future plans, when the day arrived for me to call on him, became my friend. Again, I wonder what my life might have been "if." If I had quit when I found out that my boss didn't like me, or if I had quit trying because it seemed so little use to continue making an effort to please him, or if I had learned nothing from this experience in my future dealings with others. For it certainly taught me how wrong an unusually fair and friendly man can be when he makes snap judgments based upon evidence that may fit one case but not another. It made me chary of passing judgments on other men's conduct until all the facts were in, and that, by an ironic twist of circumstance, almost ruined me many years later. But I must not get ahead of my story.

Looking backward, I am always struck with the way the right answer to the individual circumstance has presented itself whenever I have been patient enough to wait for its coming. At any rate, faith and patience had now presented me with a few of the right answers. For the first time in my life, I had freedom from backbreaking work. I earned enough money to spend some on myself without a feeling of guilt. I had friends of my own age and free time in which to play. And I was working at something I knew how to do to the satisfaction of the man I worked for. I was just twenty-one and the future looked good to me.

My territory covered Northern Iowa and Southern Minnesota. Two weekends each month I spent in Des Moines, the others in Clear Lake, Iowa, and in Austin, Minnesota. I was again vigorous and had more energy than I knew what to do with. I began to learn games and to engage in seasonal sports. Billiards, baseball, and roller skating were among my favorite recreations, and I was good at them. Those were the days when every town had its roller skating rink. I was an ardent skater, on the ice and in the rink, and joined in skating contests in most of the towns along the route I traveled. I bought a fine pair of roller skates such as were used by champions and always carried them with me. Soon I was acquainted with every man jack in my territory. A slight proficiency at poker widened the circle.

Although cards were strictly taboo at home, salesmen on the move had to do something with their evenings and I had resorted to poker. Shortly, I developed a certain skill and a great fondness for the game, neither of which do I recommend as an aid to fortune. In the beginning, I played penny ante occasionally. Soon I scorned to play for the modest sums which had seemed ample risk at first. Since I had what is known as "card sense," I sometimes won sizable stakes, but as time went on my winnings joined my losses, as such bonanzas have a way of doing. I resolved to quit. But I didn't. The itch to gamble became as insidious as the tippler's urge to drink. And I not only lost what I earned, but began to draw advances against future earnings. Apart from my losses, I knew that my preoccupation with cards was not a good thing. Even if I won, the game consumed time I could put to better use. Nevertheless, I continued to gamble, doubtless because the egoistic urge to get something for nothing was stronger than the accumulating evidence that it couldn't be done. I often thought of Major Dubois and the pass he had come to through similar folly.

But poker served a purpose. I began to see what a life on the road, with no anchors to windward, would do to me if I continued indefinitely this pleasant here-today-and-gone-tomorrow existence. It was novel and I was young, but when I began to examine critically my older colleagues, I could see what it had done to them. Most of them had become accustomed to a life which unfitted them for any other sort. They were like old actors.

And my particular business was undergoing the same change I had witnessed in Chicago. Eastern packers were beginning to establish Western branches at terminal points. Livestock in greater numbers was being shipped to stockyards near packing centers, and country slaughtering became less important. Since the big packers paid a better price for stock at the yards than most small processors with their wasteful methods could get out of it, the number of my customers decreased.

The leather fabrication business was also giving way to fashion changes. Textiles began to supplant leather coverings in house furnishings, such as chairs. Shoes began supplanting high boots for men's wear. Lighter weight leathers and split skins were used more often than they had been. The "elegant eighties" (1880's) had little use for the clumsier and more durable goods a former era had demanded. Although the leather business was still the leading American industry, the dollar value of its productions and the dollar value of the raw material had parted company. For, in addition to a more economical use of leather, the amount available had greatly increased with the opening of the West to settlement, and prices based on supply and demand had sent hides from a normal ten cents a pound to three cents.

Widespread as is the use of leather today, it is almost impossible in terms of modern life and fashion to understand the place it then occupied, representing an investment of millions second only to the lumber industry. It was for this reason that I had been so anxious to associate myself with the hide business, which seemed as solid as Gibraltar and as enduring. Since people always had used leather articles, it seemed logical to assume that they always would, and by preference. But with the knowledge that the packers would shortly control the hide market, and with the changing trends in the use of leather, I began to think about something other than poker—though it was still my besetting sin.

Since I had no capital and, as yet, no lead in any direction, there was little I could do at the moment except become better acquainted with the people and possibilities of Iowa and Minnesota. I was sure of one thing: I would never go back to Chicago to live. My new territory was still very much in the West. Thousands of acres of unbroken prairie remained in those portions untouched by railroads. In the Northwestern Iowa counties, and perhaps elsewhere throughout the state, fine farmland could be bought for five dollars an acre, which was not considered cheap for new land. In other words, for a capital investment of twenty-five hundred dollars, a young man could establish himself on a fine Iowa farm. If a would-be farmer had five thousand dollars, he could become master of a six hundred and forty acre domain and the means with which to farm it.

It was plain to be seen that the future on the American farm belonged to such men, as these, who were not handicapped by lack of capital as my uncle's friends had been and thereby forced to seek free land far from railroads. These farmers were not forced to sell their cereal grains at ruinous prices since they could buy sheep, cattle, and hogs to consume it at a profit.

Notwithstanding the tremendous supply, hogs were in steady and growing demand. Between eight and nine million a year were processed in the 1880's. Because they fattened rapidly on refuse grain, the leavings of cattle and on skimmed milk, hogs were an incidental source of profit in almost any farm operation. Corn at twenty cents a bushel and corn converted into hogs were two vastly different items—twenty-cent corn often became fifty-cent corn to the livestock fattener—with the hog's aid.

Since cattle had to be fattened, in any event, before they were fit to market, the cattlemen preferred to drive them long distances and then fatten them in Iowa before sending them on to Chicago by rail. An unfattened range steer which brought its owner thirty dollars or less at Chicago's Union Stockyards and which cost him eight dollars to market, after a winter on Iowa corn brought sixty-two dollars and fifty cents at the yards. The livestock fattener received five cents a pound for every extra pound the steer gained while in his charge. Since by good feeding the animal often gained two hundred and fifty pounds, and one hog grew fat on the spilled corn and other leavings of one steer, the corn grower doubled the market price of his grain and had his fields fertilized in the bargain, at no cost to him.

It seemed to me that here was a situation made to order for someone with my background. The states in my territory were, and always would be, one of the world's great sources of food animals. I knew how to buy hides, wool, and tallow, and something about processing meat, and I had watched the industry grow rich and powerful through the utilization of what my customers were throwing away.

If the hog butcher did not sell the carcass as a whole, as the farmer did, he cut it up for hams, bacon, and salt pork, but made no attempt to utilize the other portions, discarding them on the banks of a stream to be carried off by the spring freshets.

Some of this waste of a valuable product was unavoidable without special equipment and the knowledge of how to convert it to use—which did not exist for the small operators. The handicaps were understandable, but the little fellows' lack of imagination was not so easy to understand. I do not remember hearing one of them question, "What is this good for? How can I use it? Is there a better way to perform this operation, or to improve the quality of my product?"

That there was room for improvement in the quality of the old-time ham, anyone old enough to remember its appearance and its saltiness will testify. After curing in heavy brine and smoking, it was sewed up in thick muslin and given a coat of yellow wash to protect it from the skipper fly. Then it was stored until summer. When summer came and its outer jacket was removed, the surface of the ham was covered with a thick coat of mold. To remove the mold, the cook poured scalding water over it and vigorously scrubbed it with a stiff brush or soaked it overnight in cold water to the same end. Many old-time cookbooks prefaced directions for baking a ham by saying "soak overnight" in the belief that this method would remove the salt as well as soften the mold. The cookbooks were right about the mold but wrong about the salt, for you could soak a ham for a week and still not remove an appreciable amount of salt.

Since the proper pickling and safe preservation of a ham without the excessive use of salt depended upon a knowledge of other pickling agents and their correct use, as well as cold storage, the processor found it easier to let well enough alone. Cooks had always struggled with moldy hams, and people who ate hams were used to drinking enough water to float a battleship to quench their unholy thirst.

Naturally, there was no such thing as uniformity of quality in these country-cured meats, nor any basis of selection the purchaser could use such as later was furnished through brand identification. He just bought a ham or a side of bacon and hoped for the best.

In all this welter of waste and irresponsibility, there were a few packers in Iowa who were building businesses on more solid foundations—these were the T. M. Sinclair & Co., John Morrell & Co., the Ryan Packing Company, and the Liverpool & Des Moines Packing Co. But these were not the purchasers of the country merchants' farmer-dressed hog crop.

When the country merchant had collected a carload of frozen hogs from the farmer, he sold it to the highest bidder among the small river packers. This means of distribution was fairly profitable to the country merchant. He was the man who knew everybody and who sold everything from paregoric to salt codfish. And what a man he was! In a hundred little towns along my route, he was the oracle I consulted. He was the community's newspaper, its referee in differences of opinion and small matters under dispute. And what he didn't know, no modern FBI man could find out.

There was very little you could ask for that he didn't stock—or something "just as good." His inventory included almanacs, cardamom seeds, yardage and tubs to wash it in. He stocked patent medicines whose miraculous power to cure exceeded the bounds and variety of human and animal ailments. He offered contrivances, as someone said, "needing a second investor to figure out how to use them." Besides these, he sold groceries, wearing apparel, furniture, and farm equipment, and conducted an undertaking business as a sideline. He also sold country produce to firms like my own. He received mail for people living outside the limits of delivery and ran a "missing persons" and matchmaking bureau as a community service.

His store was the meeting place for the countryside and for visitors like myself. On many a winter's day, I found a warm refuge from the storm beside his big, potbellied, cast iron stove. When you couldn't find a man at home, you made a beeline for the "store," where he was generally to be found airing his views on life.

This was the place where housewives matched silks at the counter, children consumed yards of licorice whips, and romances were begun or ended while other rural Americans discussed the events of the day.

I was in a country store such as this when a boy from the railroad telegrapher's office rushed in crying the most momentous news of the decade. "The President—Garfield's been shot!"

Men stood still with the shock of it. When they found their voices, they shook with the same angry excitement that swept the country. What madman, they demanded to know, had dared to shoot *their* President?! The disappointed office seeker, Guiteau, who had sent the bullet, would have been torn to pieces by the men at the crossroads stores of America, if they had been able to lay hands on him that hot July day in 1881 when they learned of his deed. He had not shot a man; he had struck at the symbol of their power.

During the months the mortally wounded President struggled to live, their anger subsided to be replaced by a deep and genuine sorrow. People on the prairies wept as they read of the weeping crowds in Washington who walked beside the litter on which he was borne from the White House to the seacoast town of Elberon, in the hope that he might rally if he could escape the capital's deadly heat. While he lived, whenever I came into country stores and little towns, I was not greeted with the usual jokes. People questioned soberly, "Any good news about the President?"

When Garfield finally escaped his suffering in September, men in thousands of little crossroads country stores gathered to mourn the passing of a public figure as they had not mourned since Lincoln.

With hushed voices and wet eyes, they talked about the country boy from a pioneer Ohio farm who had become their martyred President. So much of his story was their story. As they were struggling, he had struggled to overcome grinding poverty. He had won his "edication" by a process they well knew—great personal sacrifice. He had fought, as they had fought, to preserve the Union. And his great power and position had been their gift.

An unusual outcome of Garfield's tragedy was the improvement of sentiment toward the English. Queen Victoria had exhibited the warmest feeling toward his family throughout his struggle to live. She was the first foreign monarch to send condolences at his death. She sent word to his widow directly instead of confining herself to the more formal channels of intercourse between heads of state. When Garfield was buried in Cleveland, a wreath from Victoria reposed on his coffin and the English court went into mourning as though for its own dead. As I recall, the court of Spain followed suit. It was curious and touching to see a farmer's or workingman's reaction to these tributes from the nations which had discovered and colonized the Republic. In paying tribute to his beloved Garfield, the common man felt that England and Spain were paying tribute to him as well, since a career such as Garfield's was only possible as a result of America's unique institutions which were created and supported by men like himself. In a sense, he was right; though Victoria, having lost her husband to whom she was deeply attached, was doubtless feeling more with his stricken widow than she was mourning the passing of an American president.

Their attitudes toward the events that followed his assassination were to me a revelation of the truth of Father's contention that "if you can touch a man's heart, you can reach his head." It was his opinion that "when a man talks about 'using' his head, he really means he is following his heart. And if it's results you're after with people, don't appeal to their heads without working on their hearts a little too, otherwise you won't get far. For when his heart speaks, even a *dummkopf* (stupid fellow) listens."

I discovered that if I wanted to take the measure of a man, or of a nation, there was no better way than to listen carefully—not so much to what he said he thought, but rather to what he expressed in words of what he felt. When a man said, "I feel I ought," he generally acted. When he said, "I think I should," he was apt to forget or he had second thoughts and so never got around to making up his mind at all. People were forever doing the things they "felt like doing," forever following their hearts.

I have always prized my long contact with the "Whistle Stop." No better listening posts can be found in which to gauge the nation's character and temper than the meeting places where rural and small town Americans congregate. When circumstances have demanded action to support beliefs, these crossroads Americans have never failed the nation or themselves. They have been capable of greatness at such times because they are capable of great feeling, of acting on what they feel to be true, of following their hearts at whatever cost.

CHAPTER SIX

A Chance at Fortune

The year 1884 opened auspiciously. For the first time in sixteen years, gold shipments were returning to the United States. Europe, at peace and prosperous, was a ready customer for the great grain and meat crops that poured across the Atlantic in exchange for her yellow metal. The American farm, as well as business, had at last emerged from under the dark cloud of "hard times" brought on by the collapse of the railroad promotions in 1873.

Changes were taking place everywhere. Brick replaced clapboard along the Main Streets of the little towns I covered. Commercial travelers from Chicago and points east brought tales of marvels happening in their bailiwicks. New York had a central electric power station. Chicago had five thousand telephones. The engineering wonder of its time, the Brooklyn Bridge, was open to traffic. New Yorkers boasted of its great piers sunk in pneumatic caissons, of the huge steel suspension cables by which it was anchored.

There were other wonders! Mr. Edison had invented a machine that "talked;" engines ran on ball bearings; you couldn't feel a dentist's drill or a surgeon's knife after a dose of a new painkiller called "cocaine;" a Marshall Field traveler had seen what he called a "fountain" pen. But these were minor miracles. People were talking about "harnessing" the great falls of Niagara and turning all the wheels for miles around with electric power!

New words were entering the American vocabulary. In *Leslie's Illustrated Weekly*, in *Harper's New Monthly Magazine*, and in other illustrated periodicals, you could see pictures and read descriptions of incredible structures built on steel frames called "skyscrapers." An American engineer, Frank Sprague, had invented a new kind of streetcar powered by electricity—a "trolley" car. Even little towns, too small and poor for any kind of public transportation, flirted with the idea of installing these seven day wonders, mostly to impress some rival hamlet "getting too big for its breeches"—meaning their own commercial comfort. Such things as steam turbines, gas engines, and manganese steel were pictured or talked about by fortunate eyewitnesses who had actually seen them. When money became so easy that even the farmers began to view the future with optimism, the time seemed ripe for me to settle down. The booming town of Fort Dodge, Iowa, was my first choice. But since I had not accumulated any capital of my own, the problem of what I was going to do and how to do it was still unsolved when I returned to Des Moines in May.

Then, without warning, the hurricane struck. General Ulysses S. Grant's New York investment house closed its doors and touched off a panic that swept through Wall Street. On the heels of Grant & Ward's failure for seventeen million dollars came word of the failure of the Marine National Bank and the suspension of both the Metropolitan and the Second National Banks of New York. From then on throughout the summer, each day brought further tidings of disaster. Many of these failures uncovered thefts and destroyed reputations notable in banking and finance. Banks, railways, and industrial enterprises had been looted by conscienceless contrivers entrusted with their management. These gentry had hooked "smart" men like old Russell Sage and James D. Fish, president of the Marine Bank, along with such innocents as General Grant, the one victim of the disaster for whom the country felt sorry. Inexperienced in finance, he had trusted his equally inexperienced son who, in turn, was the prey of his partner, Ferdinand Ward, would-be Napoleon of finance.

Angry as they were over a repetition of the disaster which had engulfed them for years after the panic of 1873, and despite their well-founded apprehension that they, too, would suffer from the results of this new looting of the country's fluid capital, the little men with whom I talked were genuinely sorry for the ruined Grant. His political enemies, who tried to take advantage of his tragic situation by insinuating that he had been party to the thefts, got nowhere.

"You can't tell me Grant's a crook," men said on trains and in the crossroads stores; "he's just too danged honest himself to spot a thief when he meets one." They were particularly grieved when the General—to make good a personal loan of one hundred and fifty thousand dollars from William H. Vanderbilt, which his son had persuaded him, reluctantly, to borrow to tide the house over a "temporary emergency"—now turned over to Vanderbilt deeds to all his properties and his personal trophies. The financier, so the story went, had refused to loan the money to the firm of Grant & Ward and had told the general that he distrusted the firm's partner, who was reported to be gambling away its money in various harebrained schemes. But the deluded Grant had persisted in trusting Ward and in disregarding Vanderbilt's advice.

Little did I know as I heard the story of Grant's stripping himself and his family of every resource they owned, that circumstance would one day place me in the General's shoes, and for much the same reason. While I would have no exquisite, costly and treasured gifts to offer my bankers—no cherished swords and jeweled caskets or other tokens of the world's esteem with which to pay my debt— nevertheless, I would be as thoroughly plucked when my turn came as the general had been.

The possible effect on our business of what was going on in Wall Street had us all worried. "I don't like the look of things," said Crandall. "The panic may end with the bankruptcy of a few more railroads and financial houses—after all, the country is sound—or money may be so hard to get that business may be crippled and prices turn downward."

The panic did both. All during the remainder of that year and the next, business found it hard to borrow money for its legitimate needs, and prices fell. As American panics go, however, its effects were relatively slight. One benefit that I can remember resulting from this gambling bankers' panic of 1884 was a countrywide insistence that a form of business organization must be instituted that was not a standing invitation to dishonesty. People felt that even such inexperienced men as Grant and his son might have saved themselves by an adequate system of bookkeeping. Not even a cash book or journal had ever been kept by the firm of Grant & Ward. A roar went up for state and federal banking laws to govern the conduct and inspect the operations of men handling other people's money. Men insisted that the time had come to clip Wall Street's wings. What went on there was not a matter to be settled by "gentlemen's agreements," since its operations affected everybody.

Fifty years went by before some of these demands were met, but people were determined that they should be met and, from then on, all the opposition could do was to fight a delaying battle. Long before Roosevelt, it was no longer a question of what, but of when. This is a point to keep in mind, for if business is not pleased with the results of government interference in its affairs, it has always had ample warning of the public's attitude and time enough to put its own house in order before such interference came about.

So I kept my road job and thanked my lucky stars that I had not gone into business on a borrowed shoestring. Though, as month followed month and year followed year, I was greatly discouraged at my prospects. I was still playing poker. I wasn't saving money. I wasn't getting ahead, and I wasn't happy. I decided to break my deadlock by going home to Toledo.

The journey home accomplished what I hoped it might, as I slipped back into the tranquil current of the family's life. My younger brothers and sisters had grown into attractive young men and women since I had last seen them. The youngest children, who had been little more than babies then, were now in their teens. All of them were as good as gold, and my membership in such a group filled me with pride and satisfaction.

On my first night at home I sat up smoking with Father after the others had gone to bed.

"I wonder if you know how lucky you are," I said. "The children are so well and happy and attractive. For all her hard work, Mother is in good health and still looks handsome, too. The house is filled with pretty things and your business is prosperous."

Father smiled. He was fifty-seven, but there was scarcely a touch of gray in his dark wavy hair. Above his beard, his cheeks were rosy and unlined. The crinkles at the corners of his twinkling eyes I always remembered seeing there, for he was doubtless born laughing. "Don't forget," he said, "I've been working at the business of rearing a family for thirty years. It's time I had something to show for it, don't you think?

"When are you going to begin working at something you can show me in the next thirty years?" he asked presently.

"I don't know, Father," I replied. "I don't even know what I want to do, let alone how to do it."

He smoked in a silence for a while, then he said gently, "Have you asked?"

"Not very hard, I'm afraid," I confessed.

"If you wanted help from me that I could give you, you'd ask for it, wouldn't you?" he questioned.

"I suppose—yes, of course I would," I said.

"You'd be so sure that you'd even go ahead with your plans while you waited to hear from me, if you were in Iowa and I were here at home, wouldn't you?" he asked. "You'd say to yourself, 'Since my plan is good and Father has the money, he will certainly send it at the first opportunity. I can count on him because he is as anxious as I am that I should have a chance at fortune.'"

"Yes, that is how I would reason," I agreed.

"That is how I have reasoned all through the years," said Father. "Many's the time when someone fell sick, or a man I'd been counting on couldn't pay, or the business hardly brought in enough to give your mother her house money. I'd start fretting, for I couldn't see for the life of me where to turn or who to go to for help. And that was my good fortune, too. Since there was nowhere else to turn, I turned first to the place where most people turn last. After a while, I learned not to worry. He never failed me."

We smoked on in companionable silence.

After thinking over for a time what he had said, I ventured, "But you are naturally a prayerful man, Father. It comes easy to you."

"All men are prayerful—after their fashion," he said. "It just depends on what you choose to pray to—what you have faith in. Some men carry a rabbit's foot for charm against misfortune—to bring them luck. I prefer to turn to the Source I believe made the rabbit."

I laughed. Every gambling man I knew, and many farmers and businessmen of my acquaintance, did something to propitiate the gods of chance. Lucky horseshoes, a pinch of salt thrown over the shoulder, a special hat, a good luck pocket piece—an act or a thing to avert evil and bring good.

"Is there anything I could do to help you get settled, George?" Father asked.

"Why, no," I said. "I haven't any plans."

"That leaves me in the same boat as your Heavenly Father," he said. "We can't help until you tell us how."

"Thanks, I'll remember this," I said. "You've helped me a lot."

A few days later I returned to Des Moines, feeling better and more hopeful than I had felt in a long time. The rest from the continual sameness of life on the road and the sense of once again belonging to a loving and interested group—of not always being the stranger at another man's table—had done wonders for me. It had opened my eyes to what was, in part, wrong with me: I had nothing to work for. Working for myself wasn't enough. I needed to be part of a family and part of a community that needed me as much as I needed them. I needed someone to say, "Lend a hand on this," and I knew that I would never amount to much unless, like Father, I meant more to others than I did to myself. This self-knowledge was the beginning of wisdom.

I began looking around in the towns I visited, more particularly in terms of the people who would be my neighbors if I should cast my lot with theirs. I began to ask myself, "What besides a living does this place offer me?"

The little town of Austin, Minnesota, came nearest my idea of where I should like to locate. It was small—around three thousand people—very active and growing. Although it was not much to look at in the 1880's when its streets, lighted by smoking, coal oil lamps, were quagmires in wet weather and ankle-deep in dust in summer, and the courthouse square was a tangle of hazel brush, I liked the people and the countryside. I had been spending a few days here each month for seven years, and during that time I had become well-acquainted with its hospitable and friendly people.

My principal customer in Austin was Anton Friedrich & Son, which operated the leading meat market. When I made my usual buying trip there shortly after my visit home, I was greeted by the news that the Friedrichs had been burned out—down to the ground. The town had no central water supply, only wells, and no modern firefighting equipment. As a result, people thought it a wonder that the fire had been confined to one establishment. During hot, dry spells often accompanied by high winds, a fire, once it gained headway, roared through the clapboard structures of the prairie towns, razing them in an hour or two at the most, sometimes with an appalling loss of life.

It generally took one bad scare, however, before people taxed themselves for the means of prevention. Since the wooden walls and floors of butcher shops contained as much grease as a candle, scared Austinites knew that luck had been with them. When I arrived, they were holding meetings to discuss the fire hazard. People agreed that it was better to bear the cost of installing a central water system than it was to continue to run the risk of being cooked alive.

On my next trip to Austin four weeks after the fire, I found the Friedrichs erecting a brick structure somewhat larger than their former building. The elder Friedrich, who was known as "Fritz" to everybody in town, was supervising its construction.

"Going to start up again, Fritz?" I asked.

"Not by a *verdammt* sight!" he replied. "I've worked hard enough. I am going to quit. My son, Albrecht, takes no interest in the business. Just when customers begin to come, if Dr. Allen stops in front of the market too and points toward Jimmy Hay's, Albrecht takes off his apron and they go off to play bill-yards. No, George, I am through. I am going to quit."

"What would you say to Albrecht and me running the business?" I asked.

"All right," he agreed. "You just tell me what you want and I'll fix it that way. There is a *schlauter* house, two smokehouses—everything ready."

"What's the rent going to be?" I asked.

"Sixty dollars a month."

I thought this a very reasonable figure since it included facilities for butchering and curing in addition to a fine new market.

While he was talking, my mind was running over the possible sources of money. Poker and the expenses of the trip home had exhausted my ready cash and I had overdrawn my salary account at least one hundred dollars. I wanted to settle down in Austin; I loved the place. Here was my chance. But how?

"Give me a thirty day option," I said. "I have to finish the trip—and arrange other things. It will take you at least a month to rebuild."

"Sure, George, take your time," he said easily. "There's no hurry."

I left Austin determined somehow to get the money for my share of the capital. To stock the market would require an outlay of around a thousand dollars. Now the penalty for having frittered away an eight-year opportunity to acquire money came home to me. Having a good time had cost me a maximum of five thousand dollars—what I might have saved out of my expense-free income. Even if I had put aside only a third of my salary, which would have been easy enough to do, by now I should have had a two thousand dollar stake. Once again, I was learning through firsthand experience what a hundred preachments and other people's examples had been unable to teach me—that you can't get something for nothing, and any man who thinks he can will, in time, have nothing to show for what cost him plenty.

The only man I knew who had money and who knew me well enough to loan it to me without security was Crandall. On my return to Des Moines, I went out to his house to talk over my prospects.

As always, he listened patiently to what I had to say and then asked, "But what are you going to do for money? The place may be all you say it is, but you can't run even a little business without some money."

I took the plunge. "I want to borrow five hundred from you," I said.

He shook his head. "You've overdrawn now. I'll grant that you are a good traveler. But a good businessman is something else again and—well, cards and business don't go together."

"Listen," I said, "I'm all through with cards. I owe the firm a hundred and four dollars. Here's the four dollars. Lend me four hundred more, and I'll give you my note for five hundred. I will either pay it back to you within six months or come back and work it out. You are my one chance to make more of myself than I have been doing for a long time."

Crandall gave me a searching look and then nodded. "I believe you mean it this time," he said. "Though I hate to lose you, I won't stand in your way. The money is yours."

So I started on my last trip for Oberne, Hosick & Co. with nothing to show for eight hard years of tumbling off trains at wayside stations at three o'clock of a cold winter's morning—besides a lot of experience and a debt of five hundred dollars.

While stopping off at Stuart, Iowa, I wrote a letter home to the family, telling them of my new venture. Partly in earnest and half joking, I said, "Now, don't say that I am going to be a common, everyday kind of a butcher. I am not. I am going to be a packer. Now laugh. But we must hold up our heads in this world."

Then I outlined my plan of operation as I conceived it. "In the course of a year I intend to have a general supply depot in Austin, where butchers from towns within two hundred miles or so can get anything they want. I will secure a manufacturer's agency for tools and forward circulars to butchers soliciting orders for tools, sausage casings, and sausages. There is a twenty to forty percent profit in these things, and no capital is invested in them. The market, which will be complete and up-to-date, will be helpful in disposing of offal and trimmings while I start the pork packing business in a small way. I will also solicit consignments of hides, of which I can get a great many. Once I get straightened around, I can get plenty of business to keep me active."

On that hot August night, optimism exuding from every pore, I continued my letter, adding, "I should like to get Father out of his hard business in a year or two." My brother Henry, who had been his right hand man, was now in college preparing for the ministry and my brother Herman, next younger, had become a jeweler. My letter concluded, "I am glad Herman is faithful to his work. Should I make a great success of business, he will profit by it."

During the remainder of that last trip, I spent every minute I wasn't working with customers planning what I should do now that I was to be a junior partner in a business enterprise. I held the picture in my mind of what I wanted to accomplish until it became as real to me as the people with whom I talked. This was possible because the enterprise, as I conceived it, really represented what I wanted to do and, with the boundless confidence of youth, I saw no hazards ahead.

On trains and in blistering hot hotel rooms at night, I jotted down figures and drew blueprints of a roseate business career on the backs of used envelopes. Naturally, I left out of my picture drought, hard-to-get markets, hard times, falling prices, my own discouragement, and all the rest of the headaches I was to know as a businessman. But, looking back on that time from the vantage point of fifty years of learning what I didn't know at twenty-seven, I am glad they were left out. My mind was free to plan without that hardening of the business arteries we oldsters think of as prudence—and our juniors call "lack of enterprise."

Friedrich & Hormel opened for business in October, 1887. Very shortly, however, it became obvious that we were of two minds. Friedrich's ideas of what he wanted the business to be were based upon his experience; he wanted to run a butcher shop. I wanted to build a business as a meat processor; to a beginning packer a retail market was an indispensable outlet, not an end in itself. Manufacturing entailed a lot of extra work—too much work, Friedrich thought, for what one got out of it.

Although his hours might be long, the life of a retail merchant in a little market town in those easygoing days was a pleasant one. He had time for leisurely chats with his customers. If he ran a market, as we did, he passed out free beef liver for bait to fishermen and discussed how the bass were biting. And when the urge seized him to find out for himself, he turned the business over to an employee and went fishing. This was just the way things should be, said Friedrich. Otherwise, what was the use of being a proprietor? If a man who was self-employed couldn't take things easy, who could? Certainly no man in his right mind became a businessman just so he could work himself to death. As for being packers, well, that was a cut above ourselves. Better let well enough alone. We had a nice little business, what more did I want?

I tried for a while to make him see what I believed to be true, that we had a chance to raise ourselves by our boot straps. By using our heads and following the example of men like Swift and Armour, we could capitalize on other men's lack of initiative and enterprise, on their waste of profit-making raw materials. We were establishing our business in a farming area that was sure to become a great livestock center. All we had to do was to see the possibilities before they became apparent to every Tom, Dick, and Harry. Then it would be too late. Some of those Toms and Dicks would have money. They wouldn't have to start from scratch as we did. But they wouldn't bother us until such a time as the farmers grew enough stock to make large-scale operations feasible. By then, if we worked hard now, we should be well enough established to hold our own. We should have friends, facilities, and know-how; and, everything else being equal, people preferred to do business with their friends. But my argument failed to convince him. Seemingly, it required too great a flight of the imagination for a man with his background. So I gave up trying to do what he could only do for himself—sell him a chance at fortune.

Despite our differences, however, the partnership continued until 1891. Friedrich ran the market and I plugged away at making sausage, hams, and bacon for the jobbing end of the business. Indeed, far more of these things were produced than could be disposed of at retail in Austin. I sent a carload of mess pork to Chicago, and solicited orders for our other products from every likely prospect.

Everything I had learned from my Uncle Jay could now be put to some good use. My mother's family had been meat purveyors for centuries. From them, he had accumulated a store of valuable business secrets—methods of pickling and curing hams and bacon that were superior to the techniques and formulas generally used—and I followed them with good results. Consequently, Friedrich & Hormel had something to sell that was good enough to bring us repeat orders after we sold a first lot. By the time we mutually agreed to dissolve our partnership, the firm's cash balance was surprisingly good for a little business whose initial capital had been less than a thousand dollars four years before.

The tools, market, and equipment represented one division, and cash the other. I inventoried the first at a figure high enough to make the cash the more attractive proposition, hoping that since Friedrich was "not interested," as his father had said, "in the business," he would take the cash, and I the business. He decided otherwise, however, and took the latter. I acquired most of the cash and such things as were of use in manufacturing—and a wonderfully mounted deer presented to me by a friend, which I thought would be highly ornamental placed in my new retail market.

Then began another period of indecision for me. I knew by now what I wanted to do and why, but I was undecided as to where. I liked Austin and felt that the town liked me. I was a partner in many of its activities. Before we acquired a central water system and professional firefighters, I was a member of the volunteer crew, rushing out with the others to muscle power the pump and drag the hose to the nearest available well or helping to pass the water in rubber buckets from man to man until it reached the fellows who poured it on the blaze. I belonged to a church and, of course, I had a girl, someone I meant to marry if she'd have me. And I had the kind of masculine companionship I craved. The young business and professional men of the town had made me one of them. I was a charter member of the "Bachelors," a group of young blades who organized sleigh rides, bicycle tours, balls, and oyster suppers. We went on camping trips together and caught creels full of black bass from the Cedar River. In the dull, summer season, when farmers were too busy in their fields to come to town, and in the long summer evenings after work, we played baseball.

The teams were composed of young fellows in business along Main Street. One side of the street played the other. I was captain on my side and Dr. Johnson captained the opposing team. Not even a present-day World Series can produce more excitement and wilder betting among the fans than we produced among our ardent supporters. We also played a game we fondly believed to be polo—the papers called it "horse shinny." I also took part in the doings of our local Turn Verein at Turner Hall.[4] For the first time in my life as an adult, I really belonged somewhere. When I visited nearby towns in search of business, it gave me quite a thrill to read in the local *Enterprise* or *Herald*: "George Hormel, young businessman from Austin, was among our out-of-town visitors last week."

Two young men of the many I knew in Austin, Russ Shepherd and Doak Catherwood, were especially important to me. They were attorneys and had had the educational advantages I was so conscious of lacking. Catherwood had been the prize orator of his class at the State University. But notwithstanding the difference in our backgrounds, we three began a friendship that has lasted through the years and to which I am indebted for many things besides the sound legal advice and shrewd business counsel they so unstintingly gave me. They gave me perhaps the greatest gift one man can give to another—faith in himself. Considered among the most eligible young men in town, all doors were open to them. Since the town numbered many cultured and intelligent people among its residents, I had the opportunity to make acquaintances that a newcomer might not otherwise have enjoyed.

I still have a picture of myself and Catherwood attired in the height of fashion and about to set forth on a Saturday evening's social round. He wore a long Prince Albert with satin-faced lapels, wide-striped black and grey trousers, a low-cut vest, a dazzling hardboiled shirt, gates-ajar collar and dark bow tie. A large, cream-colored, broad-brimmed hat, sweeping handlebar mustachios, and a tightly rolled umbrella completed his ensemble. I was elegantly

4 Vigorous athletic, cultural, and social societies organized by German immigrants and exiles carrying the torch of liberty and democratic reform, in the tradition of the German Turn Verein societies.

attired in a square-crowned derby, a huge watch chain and charm, a black, braided, cutaway coat, and a white tie on a shirt as stiff and glossy as starch and a hot iron could make it. The parts of our apparel that can't be seen in the picture were probably red flannels.[5]

When I came to Austin, I knew nothing about the profit side of a retail meat business. What I learned convinced me that the profits were too meager. So that I might find out for myself where to place the selling emphasis, when I had first started in business with Friedrich, I had worked out a special kind of ledger in order to compare costs in relation to selling prices, and the results were revealing. When we slaughtered an animal, its cost was entered on a separate sheet of the ledger, and every time we sold a piece of meat from that particular carcass, we entered the selling price against the original cost. This brought clearly to light the fact that much waste was involved in the sale of beef, veal, and mutton, but pork could be utilized completely, bringing its original price per pound. This led us to specialize in pork. When a customer was in doubt, we always recommended "a nice cut of pork."

As I planned my future business, it became increasingly evident to me that a plentiful hog market would be a crucial factor in success—and packers in the "Twin Cities" of Minneapolis and Saint Paul were already complaining of a scarcity. I went up there to look things over, and went through the plant of a small packer whom I knew to be operating at a profit. What I saw convinced me that, if he could make a success of small scale packing, so could I. As to hog supply, farmers grow what they can sell, I said to myself. I can make it to their advantage to raise stock for me to buy. Suddenly all my

5 See photo insert.

doubts vanished as I felt myself to be the determining factor of my future. Within limits, it would be whatever I chose to make it. The past was fixed but the future was fluid, as subject to change as I was.

I took home with me the plan of that small plant I had visited that was efficient beyond anything I had seen. Among other improvements, it had a "strong-arm throw out," a device that picked up a hog from the scalding tub and landed it on a scraping bench. When a workman had finished with scraping and shaving the hog and the gambrel stick had been put in place, it was hung on a trolley and run into a cooler where it hung overnight, to be further processed the next morning. I bought materials to make one. I have never been so proud of a piece of equipment or an improvement since; it was the beginning of a business and a chance at fortune for me and for a great many others.

Once having reached a decision, I began translating my shoe-string capital into the physical means of a new business as skillfully as I knew how. I wanted to start off debt-free, or as nearly so as could be managed. Through a combination of luck and Crandall's kindness, I had been able to pay off my debt to him. On his recommendation, his firm had financed my purchases of hides and tallow. About the time I had collected my first carload, the price of hides advanced substantially. The profits of the transaction had cancelled my note. Since then I had collected two more carloads on a rising market; the profits from these plus my share of the old business had given me just enough money, if I spent it wisely, to establish the new enterprise. A great deal would depend on the use I made of my retail outlet.

One thing I was determined to do was to make my local outlet the most attractive place in town in which to buy meat. I had always disliked the unsanitary and unsightly establishments in which the most perishable of all food products was handled. Now that I could do anything I pleased within the limits of my purse, I set about to create a place that I, as a customer, would like to patronize.

The matter of a location was my first problem. There were no vacancies on Main Street. The only available room large enough for my purpose was on Mill Street, called "Bourbon Street." Except for two other establishments that did not cater to women, the street was solidly lined with saloons.

"You just can't do it," my friends warned me when the location came up for discussion. "How can you run a shop on a street where a woman or a child, to get there, has to step around some staggering drunk or one flat on the sidewalk?"

The possibility that this would happen about every time a woman or child did go down the street was true enough. Austin had seven churches and twice that number of saloons. In this respect, however, it was no different from the majority of American towns in the 1890's and since. The farmers, after the spring wheat planting and until the next harvest, spent their idle months on "Bourbon Street," buying "rot gut" whiskey with whatever money received from the sale of their last crop they were able to withhold from the merchants to whom it was often owed and who carried them from harvest to harvest on credit.

But since the Mill Street location was Hobson's choice (take it or leave it) for me—I could take whichever horse was nearest the door—I determined to go ahead with my plans. My Dutch was up.[6] I thought of the traveler who had said to me on my first trip on the road, "It's better to run into hard luck now than later; then you'll know what to expect."

---

6 To get angry or to lose one's temper.

It was now or never. Within two weeks I should reach my thirty-second birthday. If I was ever going to launch out for myself, it was high time. It had taken twenty years since I started to earn a living to get this far. If I failed, I was back in the ranks of the wage earner—in all likelihood, to stay.

By the first of the year, however, one question was settled: I could do business on "Bourbon Street"—for by then I had the largest trade of its kind in town. And the amazing thing about it was that I was actually receiving cash in return for the goods.

This was an achievement so remarkable as to merit a little special explanation. To get business was only half the problem confronting merchants in those days; the other half was to remain solvent. Most retailers received credit from their wholesalers equivalent to the credit they extended their customers. In one-crop farming communities, the merchants' accounts were settled after harvest. Although industrial payrolls were generally on a monthly basis, wage earners did not necessarily pay their bills on such an orderly schedule. Everyone lived on credit until "settling day," whenever that day arrived. This system soon froze the cash assets of all but a few—and was especially deadly in the case of a business like mine, since I paid the farmers cash for their products before the raw material they sold me could be processed into saleable goods.

Credits were handled by issuing passbooks, but all too many customers "forgot" to bring their passbooks. Busy or indifferent clerks, in turn, "forgot" to enter the transaction in the daybook and the result of this happy-go-lucky custom was that on "settling day," the merchant's and his customer's books were often at variance. That we were not the only merchants losing money through the failure of this poor method was borne in upon me whenever we purchased goods from other merchants. We ran an account at a nearby hardware store and each month there were items, often expensive ones, that we had purchased which did not appear upon its statements.

In trying to beat this problem while in partnership with Friedrich, and over his protests, I had hired a cashier—the first in town—and attempted to install a foolproof system of bookkeeping. This was achieved with some difficulty; there was then the problem of collecting. At the first of the month our working funds were exhausted and we were obliged to go after our accounts with hammer and tongs. One thing I did consistently: I went after a dime as hard as after a dollar. All accounts were made due the first of the month and if delinquent by the tenth, credit was withdrawn. This was a hard thing to take for the merchants and professional men among our customers who had been in the habit of paying their bills when the spirit moved them, and Friedrich protested that we would lose all our trade.

Friedrich was right. We did lose trade but I collected every bill, and because we sold only quality meats, our wealthier customers who had left in a huff soon came back again. Our working-class customers came back too, when they found how much easier it was to pay us one month's bill than the two months they owed our competitors. Our collection policy proved a blessing to other merchants. Their billheads also began to carry the caption in bold type: "All bills are due the first of the month and must be paid." This is accepted as matter of course today, but to establish a cash policy fifty odd years ago was like trying to make water flow upstream.

As the market on "Bourbon Street" was successfully under way, I became even more deeply engaged in other activities. Like a juggler throwing and catching and throwing at the same time, I was buying livestock, building and equipping a packing plant, getting married, and establishing a home. But blessed with a fund of energy equivalent to the demands upon it, the days ended before my desire to do more went with them.

An abandoned creamery, situated by a beautiful, flowing spring on a ten-acre site across the Cedar River about a mile from town, was the scene of my greatest activity. This was to be the plant. Here, my first employee, George Peterson, and I worked tirelessly installing machinery, some of which I purchased from a defunct packinghouse in La Crosse, Wisconsin. With the exception of a hundred pound sausage chopper powered by a two horsepower engine, everything else was to be powered by muscle. When he first heard the engine and chopper going, my younger brother John, who had come from Toledo to help me, was so impressed with the clatter that he burst out, "Whew! Sure sounds like industry!" We built two small smokehouses, one for hams and bacon, the other for sausages, and constructed pens, feeding troughs, and other necessary adjuncts to a packinghouse. As we worked, Peterson and I speculated upon the future. Who would be married first? There was a difference of opinion, so we began making bets. Before we were through, we ran up quite a stake—the best cookstove in Decker's store! Peterson won it; he married two months before I did.

Finally, the little plant was finished and its small icehouse packed with every ounce of river ice we could squeeze into it—every tub and kettle, trolley and tool in its place. My capital was exhausted and I had borrowed small sums to complete the facilities, but the plant was there. Only a few small brick and frame buildings of no importance to anyone but me, to George Peterson, and to my family and the girl I was shortly to marry, but to us—well, those little buildings meant everything. They were our hostages to fortune.

For me, the next year was unique. It ushered in three new partnerships with life, which were to test and endow whatever is a man. The little buildings by the Cedar River took on life and became a going business about January 1, 1892. On February 24, I married Lillian Belle Gleason and set up housekeeping in a rented house on Saint Paul Street where, before the year's end, our son was born.

My wife had been a teacher in the Austin High School. Of New England descent, she brought into our partnership a love of music and books, rare good sense, insight into human nature, and the patience and understanding necessary to surmount the problems and uncertainties of our first years together. They were not easy years for either of us. They brought sickness and death, struggle and worry—the hard things to which the flesh is heir. But for me, they were made endurable by her never-failing help in any capacity in which she could serve. Like Father, she believed that the test of love is what we are willing to do for others and, like him, she was never afraid of the test.

I could never have ventured simultaneously into business and marriage on my slender resources but for her help. On a monthly budget of thirty-five dollars, she paid the rent (twelve dollars and fifty cents) and all other household expenses, which took a bit of doing even in 1892. Not a nickel was spent for anything not absolutely necessary.

Our house was about a mile from the railroad depot. To save cab fare, I usually walked home on returning from out-of-town trips. It cost a quarter to ride home and quarters were scarce. As I walked up the road in the September dusk after a brief absence in the fall of 1892, I wondered how things were with my wife. We expected our child within a week. The bag I carried seemed heavier than usual, for I was tired, and I almost wished that I had given Johnny Mears the quarter to drive me home. As I neared the house, I felt sudden alarm, for I heard someone crying. The door opened and my wife's sister ran to meet me, tears streaming down her face.

"Don't get excited! Don't get excited!" she cried.

"What about?" I asked.

From her incoherent answer, I couldn't make out whether my wife or the baby had died, or both. I rushed past her into the house and into the room where my wife lay in bed. She said weakly, in response to my query, that she was "all right." But I noticed that there was no child beside her and no sound of one in the house. I knew enough about babies from the arrivals of brothers and sisters at home to prick up my ears for that thin, angry wailing with which newcomers greet their entry into this sad and sorry world.

I found the doctor in the kitchen, where the baby lay wrapped in a tiny bundle on top of the cold cookstove.

"Is it going to live?" I asked.

He shook his head. "I don't think so—stillborn," he said. "But we might try artificial respiration."

"For heaven's sake, get busy!" I shouted.

In response to the doctor's manipulations, the child began to move, to stretch. While the doctor worked over the baby, I hastily built a fire to heat the cold room, to warm water and blankets. Then I rushed to a neighbor's house where there was a nurse. Not long afterward my son uttered his first cry.

I went into his mother's room. She too had heard his cry and was smiling wanly with happy relief.

We named him Jay Catherwood, for his great-uncle Jacob and for my best friend, and he was as vigorous, healthy, and active as the men whose names he bore. Indeed, his mother and I had reason to suspect, when we got to know him better, that on the occasion of our first acquaintance he was simply exercising a personal prerogative—he, and not the doctor, would decide when he should breathe.

CHAPTER SEVEN

"The Good Old Days"

From here on, this story, like all such stories, is the story of a business—a story that can no longer be told in the first person singular. For a business is a joint venture, by its very nature communal; an entity that embraces all the men who spend their lives in its service, all the people who serve it and whom, in turn, it serves. But no matter how many others compose the organism in which the founder's "I" becomes the "we," a special responsibility continues to rest on him who heads its activities, for someone must act as the mind to its body.

Many times I have been grateful that we could not look ahead on that Sunday before I opened the plant, when my fiancée and I had spent the afternoon skating. At sundown we crossed the river for her first inspection of the plant. It was a thrilling moment—and, as we walked about, never a hint of what those little buildings would really represent crossed our minds; we were to find, with time, that they often represented a taskmaster so hard, so demanding, that we would ask ourselves, again and again, what can we ever gain to compensate for what this monster costs us? For myself, many were the times when I should have gladly served it in a less exacting capacity and let someone else feed its rapacious maw with money, energy, and ideas—but always money; it lived on gold!

Even with the most rigid economy at home and at the plant, I could see as that first year went by that we were becoming dangerously extended. All-out operations required capital and I had borrowed every cent the bank would lend—with the market and packing plant as security. The retail end of the business was doing well on a cash basis. By itself, it would have made us a good living, but it was not a big enough goose to lay the kind of golden egg needed to run even a small packinghouse.

I tried all possible means to add a new dollar to working funds. Circulars were sent throughout Southern Minnesota and as far west as the Dakotas to every likely source of furs, since beaver, muskrat, marten, otter, and other valuable fur-bearing animals were still being trapped in considerable numbers in this territory. Hides and wool, of course, were purchased, wherever they could be found, for resale to my former employers, Oberne, Hosick & Co. I shipped poultry and eggs to R. E. Cobb, a leading Saint Paul house which gave us a sizable contract for Thanksgiving turkeys that year. I immediately engaged three teams from the livery stable, instructing the drivers to go in different directions into the countryside and buy turkeys— with the result that thirty turkey pickers were kept busy for two weeks, plucking the birds they rounded up. All these sideline activities produced profits, but never enough. Many a time at month's end, Geo. A. Hormel & Co.[7] had almost no cash in the bank.

---

7 The company name was officially changed to Hormel Foods Corporation in 1993.

Nevertheless, we managed somehow. When the books were closed in October in accordance with packinghouse accounting practice, the record of our first fiscal year's partial operations—we had been in business only ten months—showed that we had handled six hundred and ten hogs and that our business for the period totaled two hundred and twenty thousand dollars. While this was nothing to alarm Armour or Swift, it did prove that we were in the pork packing business and might possibly be competitors someday worthy of their notice.

As the year drew on to a close, disquieting rumors of attempts to organize monopolies in hides and other basic raw materials began to emanate from Chicago and New York. Stock issues in trusts to control staple commodities had been launched. Mergers among the independent producers and distributors were highlighted on the financial pages of the *Chicago Tribune*, which I read to keep abreast of the market quotations on products I bought and sold. There was a great ado about "huge savings in operation costs" of inestimable benefit to the consumer which these combinations were to bring about. I observed, however, that there was no lowering of prices for the things we bought that had come under trust control.

However, I had little time to consider the state of the nation that fall. As often as I could get away from the plant, I took one- and two-day trips on the road, selling sausage, buying hides—making any kind of dicker in which a red cent's profit could be seen. Business was "good," but it was already plain to me that we couldn't carry on at a profit except by expanding. Caught between high prices for raw materials and labor costs, there was only one answer—and that was volume. To get volume, we must expand plant facilities. To do that, we must have more money. And to get money, we did everything.

It was one of those periods of "easy money" produced with the aid of the printing press, and the speculators' new wealth in stock issues created by the same means were no harbingers of good times to come. The kind of optimism exuding from the Chicago Board of Trade and Wall Street, so freely expressed as "faith in the American future," should have been a danger signal to everybody. But, at the time, all the phenomena of a dangerous inflationary spiral seemed to me to be indication of an expanding economy, with which our business would be forced to keep pace in order to survive. Volume had to run ahead of the avalanche of rising costs to keep the small profit margin from being snowed under.

With this idea in mind, we broke ground for a new brick building which we hoped to complete in the spring of 1895, at cost of around forty-five hundred dollars. I knew that, undercapitalized as the business was, this was a daring venture. But I felt about it much as I had about buying the Rich Hill wool clip. If I didn't buy wool, there was no point in being a wool buyer—and I wouldn't be one long. If present facilities were too small to operate on a volume basis and the business couldn't live without volume, the ship just had to carry the sail it needed to run before the wind.

No working day was long enough for one man to do all the things that had to be done. Up at dawn, I was at the plant before seven. In winter, McBride, the grocer, an early riser too, used to joke me, "I just stay in bed until I hear the sound of your sleigh bells, then I know it's time to get up." After the day's work at the plant was over, my wife and I spent our evenings on paperwork. We made price lists on a homemade hectograph. An impression of the hand-lettered original was transferred to gelatin and shaped in one of her square bread pans. We billed customers, wrote letters, addressed circulars, kept books, and figured payrolls until bedtime.

Even a more plentiful supply of money would not have enabled me to delegate to others many of the jobs I took upon myself; for if I were to stop the leaks in this stage of our expanding program, I must keep an eye on everything. Competition among buyers and sellers was keen, profit margins small, and carelessness at any one of a dozen points would be fatal.

A farmer in my district was not dependent on any one purchaser; if he didn't choose to do business with one livestock buyer, there was always another not far off. He sold to the highest bidder—and sometimes the competing bidder was not too scrupulous. He might overbid the market and cheat the farmer by means of dishonest scales—there were no inspectors of weights and measures in those days. All we could ever hope for from the farmer was a preference on an equal price basis with the others. The new business had to sell itself to the farmer as a more reliable organization with which to trade. Hence I did my own buying and as soon as we could afford it, I installed a second scale, requiring that everything we bought and sold be weighed on two scales by separate scalers. I did not feel I could safely delegate this responsibility to another, until papers in farming communities round and about Austin began to run items like the following, which appeared in the *Wells Forum* of fifty years ago: "W. H. Taylor, prominent farmer, reported selling another carload of hogs to Geo. A. Hormel & Co. and tells, 'This firm is one of the best I ever had dealings with; I find it profitable to do much business with it.'"

Securing the best available livestock and maintaining good farmer-packer relations was, however, only part of my "juggling act" in this busy period. There must be careful supervision of the curing process of the mild sugar-cured ham we had begun to feature. There was a right time to take it from the pickle. Every day it remained out of smoke after it had reached the final curing stage, it deteriorated in flavor and color. There could be no variation in temperature in the curing room while it remained in pickle. A door left open, an unusually warm day or insufficient ice in the cooler above hastened the cure but increased the risk of taint. On the other hand, if the temperature dropped, curing was delayed, and a ham prematurely removed from the pickle and sent to the smokehouse came out spoiled and worthless.

I was also devoting careful attention to eye appeal in relation to the customer's purchase. One naturally assumed that an article which looked attractive was more desirable than another whose workmanship was crude and slipshod; therefore, I trimmed the hams and bacon myself. They were made as uniform in their appearance as we tried to make them in quality, and they were also as carefully graded as though every buyer knew as much as we did about what constituted a first class product of its kind. Only the finest were marked "Dairy Brand"—our top quality. I supervised the grading. Any that, in my opinion, were not entitled to such a distinction did not receive it. The hardest people to sell on this policy were the workmen, who thought I was fussy beyond all reason. My insistence on perfection was no joke around the plant.

"You ought to see Hormel look over a ham," a former associate told a group of men one day. "Why, he looks at that ham the way most men look at a pretty girl, isn't that so, George?"

I laughed with the others, for I knew just how funny it must have seemed to them. However, while we had to sell at the market, as we had to buy at the market, we had the privilege of selecting the kind of market we were trying to reach. I believed that, by never ceasing to aim at perfection, we should one day reach a quality-conscious group able and willing to pay for the best of anything. Already the best hotels in the "Twin Cities" featured our products by name on their menus. I also wanted to see them on the menus of Chicago's best hotels.

Curiously enough, considering how the American public felt about quality, its attitude was all but ignored by the majority of commercial food processors who, to judge by their operations, believed that adulterating their product and cheapening it was a quick and easy road to riches.

This was our opportunity, our point of attack, and our means of defense. Quality was our only defense against the competition we had to meet from the big packers. To stay in business, we had to do everything a little better than they were doing it; the entire organization was keyed up to this one idea. I constantly hammered home the need for improving our working methods to the end that we could produce superior food while reducing costs; for in a highly competitive field it was impossible to accomplish the one without the other.

There was special opportunity for quality in an item to which we had been giving increasing attention during the latter years of my partnership with Friedrich—sausage. Since we had already built a reputation for our product in a small way, it was not hard for the new business to establish volume in the product for many varieties which found a ready sale among wholesalers in the "Twin Cities." Because we could always find a market for sausage, its manufacture made it possible to keep our men busy every hour of the day.

An old friend, commenting on the early days of our acquaintance, once said to me, "I never thought you'd get anywhere; your sole ambition in life seemed to be to make a better sausage."

To onlookers, it certainly must have seemed a small ambition. But first things come first. "A better sausage" was one thing we could make with the limited means at our disposal.

In the following spring I had reason to be very grateful that I had geared the infant enterprise to something we could do well. Only businesses firmly grounded upon reality survived the panic of 1893. No one escaped—no one ever does. Panic in New York and Chicago meant panic at the crossroads. Frightened bankers in Austin called in their loans just as the bankers in the big cities were doing. Who could blame the bankers? Panic had the public in its grip and ready money disappeared. We purchased small bills and coins at a premium of two percent. Certified checks took the place of bills of larger denominations.

Fortunately, our new brick building, started the previous fall, was completed just in time. Like everything else we owned, it was mortgaged, but it was built and ready for occupancy before the panic made it impossible to borrow money for any such purpose. Father had lent a thousand dollars toward its erection. We were ready to move into it when he arrived on his visit in the late spring.

I took him down to look it over. "There it is," I said proudly.

He gave one startled glance. "Boy, oh, boy!" he exclaimed. "What are you going to do with all that room?"

The two-story brick building, with its thirty-two windows gleaming in the sun, looked pretty big to me, too. But it looked a lot bigger later on when I had to find the money to repay the debt incurred in its building, plus cash with which to buy livestock and to meet the increased payroll needed to keep it running. Whenever I hear the words, "the panic of '93," they bring to mind the kind of recollections shared by a lot of people since. For me, as for the men who wince now at the mention of 1929, life was just one long series of question marks. How to buy on a falling market? How to sell the product without cheapening it or else selling below cost? How to keep from cutting wages and lengthening hours past all decency? And last, but not least, how to keep the banker off our necks?

Since these were questions for which we had no answers, we tightened our belts and stressed the one product people seemed willing to buy. When I wasn't making sausage, I was on branch line trains going from one town to another, selling what we had on hand and taking orders for the next lot. I sold other things, too, but sausage was the mainstay. My brother John, who had lately joined me, took to his bicycle and scoured the countryside for prospects nearer home. He even rode to Preston, fifty miles from Austin, to promote our quality sausage; distance never daunted John if he could make a sale.

By some miracle, in the years 1893 and '94, the firm bought and processed into hams, bacon, and sausage a total of five thousand and sixty eight hogs—four times as many in each year as in 1892. But this showing was not wholly the result of our combined efforts, long hours, and pinchfist economies at the plant, important as they were. Without help from other sources, we should have failed despite all we could do.

My wife stood guard on the home front. She was patient and unruffled at times when there was enough tension in the house to blow off the roof. My nerves were raw from the pressures placed upon me. At times when the strain seemed greater than I could bear, her support and belief were of inestimable value; she never doubted that we would come through. She mailed price lists or practiced small economies with the best grace in the world. How much men owe to such women at times of great crisis in their fortunes is hard to estimate. I left home each morning with enough renewed energy and confidence to see me through the day.

To make matters more difficult for us at this time, the big Chicago packers, trying to find a way out of their dilemma, began to invade the selling territory of the little fellow by means of refrigerator "peddler" cars, which covered regular routes out of Chicago, "Twin Cities," and other Midwest packing centers to all the little towns within a week's journey of their source of supply. The cars were switched to a siding while the salesman in charge sold the local dealers. When he boarded the train for his next stop, the coupled "peddler" car went along. Since it was to the joint interest of railroads and packers, they combined to make this distributing system work smoothly and efficiently.

From the dealers' point of view, the new method of buying was an advantage also. To gain their trade, the big packers had cut prices. They, and not the railroads, owned the cars. They had perfected and built them in the days when the railroads shortsightedly refused to have anything to do with such cars. Consequently, the packers owned both the refrigerator car patents and the cars themselves, and the railroads, which wanted to use them for shipping fruits and vegetables from California and Florida on the backhaul to Chicago, leased them under conditions laid down by the owners.

Small packers doing business west of Chicago went down like ninepins before the onslaught of hard times and such competition. The big packers had, in addition to their transportation monopoly, modernized plants, labor-saving devices, and material-saving techniques—all the means by which the price of their product could be legitimately reduced. They could almost sell meat at cost and still make money from the things others wasted. This eventuality I had seen coming for a long time, and I had tried, within the limits of our slender resources, to narrow the gap between the big and efficient and the small and inefficient. Of the hundreds in business before May of 1893, only four independent packers remained in the territory between Chicago and the Missouri River by the end of 1894.

That we were not among the casualties was undoubtedly due to our emphasis on quality and to the fact that we converted raw material, which would otherwise have been wasted, into quality sausage. Even if refrigerator cars had been available to us, we couldn't have had them to dispose of fresh meat in nearby communities as the big packers were doing, for we lacked the sales volume. More, we lacked capital. Working funds had reached the vanishing point and everything was mortgaged.

The only out for us in this dilemma was to establish additional retail outlets of our own. But where to get the capital? At this point in our affairs, the bank decided we should be thinking about reducing our loans. It was the last straw.

I went over to the bank and handed the president the keys to the market and plant. "You're a packer now," I told the astonished banker. "I'm going to get this thing off my back. You take it. Pay me enough to live on and I'll run it for you. Just give me a job. I can't stand any more harassment over money."

He took one look at me and knew I meant it. "Let's go into my office where we can have a little talk," he said soothingly.

I knew exactly how he felt. The last thing any man in his right mind wanted to be was a packer. He talked persuasively for an hour before he convinced me that I could make better use of those keys than he could. While he didn't say so, he conveyed the idea that the bank would rather lose the money than take over the business. He was a very smart man. In his shoes, I would have done the same thing. When he agreed not to press me, I picked up the keys and left.

I went to see my friend, Shepherd, who was lending money for a wealthy uncle of La Crosse, Wisconsin. We had known each other ever since I came to Austin, and I felt if any man had reason to trust me, Shepherd was the man.

I told him my story. "I've got to have two additional markets," I said, "to dispose of things I can't throw away and can't ship. I need working capital. The bank won't give it to me. I have no collateral to offer they haven't got now. I need five thousand dollars. Can you help me?"

He thought it over for a few minutes and then said, "As you know, my uncle requires security on his loans, but perhaps I can arrange a loan for you on your personal note. Will this put you on your feet?"

I told him it would and thanked him.

Shepherd's faith and the money he procured tided us over one of the most critical times in the company's history. Like Crandall's loan of five hundred dollars on my unsecured note of seven years before, his was a gesture of confidence worth whatever it cost to maintain it. I went back to work determined to make that business a success in spite of all the hurricanes out of Wall Street and all the refrigerator cars out of Chicago.

Businessmen of today complain a great deal about the restrictions and regulations that handicap them in the conduct of their enterprises. Some of their complaints against government are justified. But in other days, businessmen had troubles too. *Laissez-faire* is a doctrine that cuts both ways. Non-interference in one department can mean indifference and non-cooperation in a dozen others of life and death importance to individual enterprise. Business has every right to demand that tax collection agencies spend wisely and economically the large sums extracted from its income. On the other hand, it is well to remember that when business paid few taxes, neither did the other members of the community tax themselves for good roads, water and sewage systems, nor for other utilities and services of sometimes greater importance to business than to non-business members of the community.

Our operations depended upon livestock raised in the surrounding countryside; good roads as well as railroad service were of paramount importance. But there was no system for road maintenance and repair—let alone for building highways to tap new sources of supply. Although each district had a road commissioner, the farmers had the right to work out their road tax. In good years they paid money taxes by preference. But at times when they decided to work out their road tax, each farmer followed his own notions of how to repair a road. One farmer might be fairly competent in repairing his strip, but another might take his plow and scraper and so damage his piece that on the first rainy day an empty wagon would bog down in it. I have seen farmers unhitch their teams and leave their wagons in the mud until two weeks later when the roads were sufficiently dry to get home without killing the horses. Culverts, drainage runoffs, gravel and crushed rock surfacing were unheard-of expenditures. This condition was by no means confined to country dwellers. Streets within the town were just as bad as roads leading into it. To cross from one side of Main Street to the other in wet weather meant wearing boots or sinking in mud deeper than high shoe tops.

Public carriers, of course, did as they pleased. There was no organized business and community support to aid small business in its stand against monopoly, just as there were no laws with teeth in them to force big business to recognize the rights of the public—and even less, the rights of their small competitors. Today a different spirit prevails. Great transportation systems and other corporations exercising public functions have been educated to regard good public relations as indispensable to their success. Their employees and officials make every endeavor to aid individual and community enterprise. But they didn't do that fifty years ago.

Few railroads today would refuse to install a sidetrack bordering their right of way to enable a business to receive and send carload shipments. The Chicago & Great Western, which bordered our property, took the position that putting in a spur was to our advantage but not to theirs. Not until 1902, after years of wire pulling, did the C. M. & St. P. agree to put in rails if we bought nearly a mile of right of way. But officials were far from enthusiastic and the road superintendent in charge of the work growled, "the sidetracks we've laid into little plants like this would furnish rails enough to lay a track from here to Halifax!"

He was probably right. I merely cite the instance to give my younger colleagues some idea of the problems faced by the small businessman of the last century. He was a "rugged individualist" by virtue of necessity. If nobody "bothered" him, nobody went out of the way to help him, either. And by the time he had reached the top of his particular heap, what had once been necessity became an obsession. He had climbed where he was by constant struggle against great odds. Personal initiative had pulled him through; therefore, he refused to give up any part of what had so greatly aided him. The struggle had been so intensely personal that, in achieving success, he had long since lost sight of ends and aims larger than his own.

Decentralization of industry is a favorite "spread the work and income" panacea for the ills of the modern industrial order. But from the operator's standpoint, the "factory in the field" has pains and aches quite unknown by its enthusiastic lay advocates. Even with American Railway Express, parcel post, telephones, airmail, and paved highways, it still offers difficulties. Consider what it was like in a country town without these things.

If we needed bolts and screws of a certain size and thread to repair a broken machine, we wrote to Minneapolis or Chicago and waited until they arrived. Wrapping paper, packing boxes—a hundred other things—had to be bought in large quantities and stored. To protect ourselves, we had to make a sizable investment in items that a packer located in any large city could pick up daily as he needed them. Every increase in activity added to the expense of stock keeping and necessitated the accumulation of a stock—care and control of which was a business in itself.

We had to be self-sufficient in a dozen ways: our water supply, sewage disposal, and fire protection were personal and not municipal problems, and there were no credit bureaus, research technicians, or trade associations to which we could turn for help or information. However, this was by no means all loss. The need for self-sufficiency increased our resourcefulness. Ingenuity was valued above rubies. A man who could think of a substitute for a broken machine part, or who could make one, or who could simplify an operation or improve a technique, was the man for our money. We were our own time and motion experts, our own plant and efficiency engineers. How to do something better, quicker, and cheaper became a fixed idea with every man in our employ who had ambitions for his own future and that of the business.

The mechanics of running even this small enterprise and supervising all its operations finally grew too much for me. My day often started at four in the morning, but at that it wasn't long enough to buy livestock, trim hams, sell sausage, repair and install equipment, teach workmen, and keep books. So I left off buying livestock and keeping books—two jobs I could safely delegate to others.

As time passed, with the more I learned, the more convinced I became that before I could tell another man what to do and how to do it efficiently, I should have to find out for myself. This included learning to know the right from the wrong way to do even the disagreeable jobs around a packinghouse—and there are many of them. I cleaned hog pens, sausage casings, and dirty floors, until I found the most efficient ways of doing them. The need for continual experiment convinced me that where I belonged was in the plant. Someday, I hoped, the business could afford a white collar executive six days a week, and I meant to apply for the job; but right now a boss in overalls, watching temperatures in the curing cellars and smokehouses and stopping leaks wherever found, was of prime necessity.

The buying I turned over to the best man in our part of the country, a successful young livestock dealer named Elihu Smith, known to his many friends as "Gid." As an independent buyer for the Chicago market, Gid had built up an enviable reputation among the farmers for his fair dealing. He was just the man to represent the kind of business we were trying to build. But how good Gid was going to be, I had no idea when I hired him.

The evening of his first day on the job for us, he briskly drove into the yard at the plant.

"Well, George," he said, "you've bought a lot of hogs, Robert Guy's whole herd, sixty-three of 'em."

I was stunned! This was more than we processed in a week and, in addition to his purchase, farmers sent in a few hogs each day that we had to accept. Incidentally, it meant also that the farmer was now the owner of a sizable chunk of the Hormel bankroll. I felt very much as I had on the occasion of the Rich Hill wool purchase.

"What are we going to do with them?" I weakly asked nobody in particular.

"Oh, we'll use them," Gid said cheerfully.

The next day he bought thirty-three cattle. This was another blow since we should have to retail most of the beef ourselves; the majority of butchers among our customers killed their own. I groaned at the prospect of what this would mean. Clearly, something would have to be done. We finally decided to ship the cattle to Chicago. They were sold at a profit, and from that time on we made such shipments every now and then.

The next week, our new buyer stayed at the plant dressing his hog purchase and thereafter we confined his excursions into the countryside to three days a week, keeping him busy at the plant the other three. Not for several years after he joined forces with the company was it altogether safe for my peace of mind to let Gid get away from home too often.

In this day of high prices, it might be interesting to know what Gid paid the farmers for what he bought. Livestock prices fell after the panic to about half what they had been. In the spring of 1893, I paid up to six and a half cents a pound for hogs live weight; a year and a half later, he bought them for three cents a pound. The farmer received correspondingly low prices for all other products he had to sell.

The price of a day's work had also fallen. Skilled labor now got, on the average, one dollar and fifty cents for ten hours. This represented a drop from two dollars and forty-two cents, the national average day's wage for skilled mechanics in 1892. Common labor was lucky to find work at ninety cents a day.

There was no scaling down of interest or debts, of course; so bankruptcies and the auctioneer's hammer made quick work of those unfortunates caught between the twin scythes of hard times and fixed obligations. Until 1900, practically every piece of equipment we bought came from some defunct little packinghouse or industry liquidated by the events of 1893.

The firms that survived earned their solvency the hard way. We did twice the work processing double the amount of food, for which neither the farmers nor ourselves gained an additional penny. Peterson, my right-hand man, and I often put in a good day's work before lunch. My younger brothers worked killing hours too; it was the only way we knew to stave off disaster.

Father had lately sold his business and, with all the family who were still at home, had come to Austin and rented the house next door to ours. The boys, John and Ben, had come into the plant, Herman took over the market, and Father became the new bookkeeper. But having him for a next door neighbor meant a great deal more to me than acquiring a good bookkeeper for the business. His presence was a continual source of cheer at times when I almost succumbed to the blackest discouragement—a constant reminder of what faith and courage could accomplish in spite of all the "slings and arrows of outrageous fortune." Whenever we talked together, I remembered how much more confidence he had needed than I to leave behind him a job and friends; to venture his hard-earned savings in a strange place in the effort to establish a business, for he had a family dependent upon him. I might grumble about

Friedrich's lack of enterprise, but Heyer had failed to furnish his share of capital. By contrast, my start as a businessman had been almost sinfully easy. But he never reminded me of such things.

He was so gay and light-hearted a man that it would have been easy enough to forget that there was nothing in my picture with which he hadn't grappled all his life. But he had learned the secret early in life of using his energy to lick the obstacle instead of letting it leak away in worry. This was very hard for me to do. When obstacles blocked my energy drives, I exploded in anger or sank into despondency. Father thoroughly understood the situation—as did my wife—and by allowing me to talk things through, he helped me to deal with them constructively. His ready sympathy and capacity to evaluate a problem at its true worth were priceless aids at such times.

"Steady, my boy," he'd say, "light your pipe and tell me about it."

Before he came to Austin and during the years I spent on the road, we corresponded frequently about our activities. I discussed every development with him and always found his comments helpful.

But even though he refused to take "anxious thought for the morrow" or to speculate upon what it might bring, he was no optimist, as the term is usually applied to businessmen. He continually cautioned me, "Don't gamble on the future price of anything you have to sell. Don't get caught in the greedy man's trap. Yes, perhaps six months from now the price of hides or lard or bacon may be higher. But you can't know for certain. Even if you could, the knowledge would be bad for you. Think how many times a man can turn over his money at a little profit he's earned while he's waiting for a big speculative profit he hasn't earned to make him rich."

Or again, "Just think of what it would mean if all the wealth—not money but the hides, wool, wheat, cotton—things people need to live by—if these were shipped to one vast storehouse and couldn't be used until they brought more profit to somebody. Why should the countryside be stripped bare for such an end as this? Is this the reason for commerce and industry? No! They are the means for the distribution of the results of labor, not means for you to get rich by speculating. When men lose sight of this," he warned, "look out!"

He often illustrated his comments by accounts of men of his acquaintance who had been successful and those who had failed. I sometimes suspected that these stories were intended as delicate hints to a onetime poker player. Father had intensely disliked my gambling, and while he knew that I had not touched a card since I entered business, doubtless he hoped to make me think twice in case I should ever be tempted to "speculate in futures," either on the Board of Trade or by withholding goods—and most packers did both.

It was certainly a comfort to have Father around. His coming not only heartened me and took some responsibility from my shoulders, it also enabled me to take a combined vacation and business trip of considerable importance that I probably should not have felt to be advisable had he not been there to take care of things during my absence.

Next to getting money, distribution is the principal problem that plagues the small industrialist when his production expands beyond the demand of his local market. Although we had now three retail markets catering to a population of four thousand people, there remained the problem of what to do with what we couldn't sell to Austin housewives. Our only opportunity to market out of town such things as fresh pork loins and shoulders was to ship them to

Minneapolis during the winter months, when freezing weather made it possible to use local freight.

I had made it a practice, whenever possible, to visit other plants doing a larger business than ours, or a different one, and a trip through the Drummond Packing Company of Eau Claire, Wisconsin, had brought to my attention possibilities of the Southern market, where, I was told, profit was too small to tempt the big packers—but, nevertheless, it was profit. At home again, I began experimenting with the troublesome pork loin, one of the choicest cuts of meat in its fresh state. Was there something I could do to make it equally desirable when cured? The outcome of my experimentation was a brand new product, rather similar to what is now known as "Canadian bacon." Once the customer, who liked bacon but preferred it lean, tried "Hormel's Sugar-Cured Pig Back Bacon," the reorders began. It was only a short time after its introduction that the demand became greater than the supply, in spite of the fact that we kept advancing the price. What had been a drag on the market now became a sure source of profit. By the time competitors entered the field, the new bacon was firmly established in popular favor.

From then on, throughout my active business career, I kept constantly before me the challenge, "originate, don't imitate!" and made it one of the key commandments of the organization.

I also began to think more of how to get business in the South and less about refrigerator cars and cutthroat competition in Minneapolis. Drummond had said of the South, "There are too few centers of population, outside a half dozen cities, for the sale of fresh meat. Rail communications between them and the outlying towns are poor. There isn't enough good livestock available to make it worthwhile to establish regional packinghouses. And most Southerners prefer—at any rate they buy—dry salt-cured and smoked meat to other kinds. St. Louis and New Orleans are the gateways to this trade, which is still in the hands of the old, established distribution firms that mean to keep it. We sell to these people on a mighty small profit margin, but it enables us to stay in business."

Someday I would get those cars, but in the meantime, acting on Drummond's suggestion, I wrote to a St. Louis firm of which he had said, "the profit is mighty small;" but a profit, instead of a loss, was all we needed to increase our output of other things in which a better margin could be made.

When my Uncle Jay wrote that he was thinking of taking a vacation, could I come along? I replied that I too had thought of a trip: how about steamboating down the Mississippi? We set off to St. Louis soon after, where we called on the broker with whom we had made a recent sales connection. He took us to the Board of Trade and entertained us at a luncheon with other leading brokers—all of which opened our eyes to future business possibilities in the South.

Our steamboating then took us to Cairo, Illinois, which had been one of Father's old stomping grounds when he steamboated on the Mississippi as a boy in 1845. We had planned to return home from here, but when my uncle said, "Say, we don't get many chances to be gentlemen of leisure; let's go on to Memphis; things will keep 'til we get back," on we went. By the time we reached Memphis, we were enjoying life on the steam wheeler so much that we went on to Vicksburg. "I'd like to see New Orleans again—you'll enjoy seeing it, too, George," said my uncle. So we stayed aboard.

Wherever the boat stopped for a few hours, we got off and made the acquaintance of distributors. By the time we reached New Orleans, I had a sizable list of future customers and a fair amount of orders.

But the South was poor. With the exception of the principal river cities, the towns were down-at-the-heel places, and the buildings were weather-beaten, needing paint and repairs. Cotton prices had tumbled along with those for everything else the agriculturist had to sell. Many small planters and small merchants with whom we talked were exceedingly bitter.

"I was poorer after the last good crop I sold than I was before picking. After I had paid my debts to the provision merchant at a carrying charge of two percent a month, bought clothes for the family and fertilizer for next year's crop, I had to sell some small piece of property in Memphis to keep me going until the next harvest."

A forwarder in Vicksburg complained, "The planters think we're getting all their money. We're not. As long as they persist in raising cotton and nothing else, we just turn over the money to fellows like you—to the corn growers and hog raisers of the West. Precious little sticks to *our* fingers. If we don't start pretty soon making cotton our *surplus* crop, the next generation of Southerners will be poorer than our former slaves. We're already slaves to Wall Street! If we could get our people to forget cotton until after they thought about food, we'd have a little surplus money to build up our own manufacturers. The North would respect that kind of a South. We wouldn't be poor relations, always seeking favors; we'd be in a position to grant a few."

Uncle Jay and I talked it over on the way home. "They don't raise as much or as good livestock here," he said, "as they did thirty-odd years ago. Most of their animals went for food during the war. They've never replaced them. All they think about is cotton. Just suppose you aimed your business at one market; where would you be?"

"By now I wouldn't be in business," I said.

I understood more of the meaning of what I saw on the homeward journey than I had when we started out. The falling fences, tumble-down houses and outbuildings, the half deserted little towns—all the aspects of neglect and ruin that stretched across the rich Mississippi delta—told the story of war and mass delusion. Even my sales told a story. I had taken orders for several carloads of the cheapest and least desirable types of cured meat. Millions of pounds of these items were cleared through St. Louis and New Orleans each year. People able to consult their palates would have quickly tired of these heavily salted products, but they were often the only form of meat eaten by Negroes and poor whites—this in a land potentially flowing with milk and honey.

When I arrived home again, it seemed to me that, if I had journeyed to the moon and back, I should not have encountered stranger contrasts, so great were the differences in point of view between the men of Minnesota and of Mississippi. The South I had just seen was a topsy-turvy world of idle acres and hungry men, of labor shortages and exoduses, of planters who turned their backs on the present in a vain attempt to recreate a vanished past. To me, the crux of it lay in their attitude toward labor—that ingrained sense of the onetime slaveholder that, not only his fields, but the men who worked in them were property. In this spirit, some Southern states had established bureaus of immigration in the hope of luring the English, Germans, and Scandinavians to labor in the cane and cotton fields in competition with Negroes. It couldn't be done, as they soon found out; for not even the most poverty-stricken Europeans would voluntarily submit to a way of life that was no more than chattel slavery. Thinking of all this and the sturdy farmer of the Midwest, the miracle was that they could be united at all, that there was any common denominator between them.

I mentioned it to Father. "It only seems like that," he said. "What, to my mind, is really strange is men's habit of forgetting that they are engaged upon a common task—the way they lose sight of their great common interest."

"And what do you think that is?" I asked.

"Why, it's so plain," he said. "Nothing else makes sense. We're here to work as best we can to create the freest possible opportunity for individual growth. That's our common interest; it's what we mean when we talk about 'equal rights to self-development'—what is meant by the brotherhood of man and the fatherhood of God. It's the 'kingdom on earth as it is in heaven;' it's the idea behind "The Sermon on the Mount," "The Lord's Prayer," and the Constitution. It isn't I against you, we against others, North and South, master and slave, saint and sinner. Ever notice how fast men move backward instead of forward when they begin to think and feel that their separate interests are greater than their common interests? How, in the end, if they won't share good fortune, the circumstances they create make them share common misfortune?"

"I'm afraid it will be a long time, Father," I said, "before men generally agree to any such definition of self-interest as yours."

Father looked at me and laughed. "You're thinking about those refrigerator cars," he said. "Your time will come to use them and, when it does, don't forget that until someone else could use such a car to his advantage, it didn't exist for yours."

Despite difficulties, the end of our fiscal year in October, 1895, showed that we had doubled production over the previous year. More important than volume, however, was our growing ability to combat waste. We had improved our working skills to the point where very little was spoiled in processing, and because no sum was beneath our notice, the few pennies saved here and there were beginning to mean a hundred dollars that could be spent for improvements. The time seemed not too far off when we might dare to risk removing money from our working capital to increase facilities.

Most heartening of all were the reorders, which were coming in faster and faster, especially for our featured items, those we tried to make a little better than others of their kind on the market. This indicated that we were receiving a preference over competition in areas we could reach—a preference not based upon price.

The more I examined these small straws in the wind, the more I could see, in terms of my own experience, what Father meant: the better world or the greater success men were always hoping for was never any nearer or farther away than their own capacity to make the most of what they had to work with at the moment. They were often less handicapped by circumstances than they were by poverty of thought and their inability to grasp the fact that they were masters of their own destiny.

The Christmas holidays that year were like the old times I remembered from boyhood. As a family, we were all together for the first time in many years. My brother Henry had also joined us to become the first minister of the newly organized Presbyterian Church, feeling that Austin was a better place for his wife and baby than "Little Hell" of the Chicago slums where he had begun his ministry. And when the family got together, it always meant music. There was Sue's guitar, Herman's violin, my wife or sister Charlotte at the piano, and everybody singing! The Hormel quartet was a special feature of these gatherings, as my four brothers had beautiful, natural voices which they used well together in best "barbershop style," with Herman as tenor, Henry, baritone—as well as a yodeler of some talent—and John and Ben as first and second bass. My wife's sweet, contralto voice joined theirs when she played the accompaniments; she was an accomplished musician who brought much enjoyment to the family circle—and all joined vociferously in the refrains. Mother's presence assured the old *gemütlichkeit*—the German word that means so much sentiment, kindliness, tenderness, and freedom from care. I can think of no better way to describe what Christmas ought to mean always and what that particular Christmas meant to me.

Not least important under the circumstances was Father's generous gift of a new delivery wagon for "Tip," the calico mule. Evenings of gay and rollicking song ended always with the singing of that tender hymn, long since the family favorite, "In My Father's House are Many Mansions"—which father had first heard and brought home to us from a Y.M.C.A. convention in Chicago some years before.

In April of the following year I went South again—this time to call on the trade. On the evening of my return early in May, I dropped over to visit with Father. Mother and my wife had gone to a church "sociable" and we two sat alone on the porch in the long twilight, smoking corncob pipes and talking. Father was in a reminiscent mood. "I can't get used to the fact that so much has happened in the last fifty years," he said. "You tell about big cities that weren't even landings when I was steamboating on the Mississippi."

He ruminated as we smoked in silence. "Not counting Indians, there are more people living in Austin right now than there were in all Minnesota when I first traveled the Upper Mississippi. Saint Paul was only a landing with a few shacks and shanties, where French and Indian half-breeds lived. The Chippewas and Dakotas used to shoot arrows at the riverboats when we came close inshore. Once in a while, one would let fly with an old ball musket he'd come by; though, as I remember it, the Indians never did hit anybody. They just liked to see the pilot head out toward midstream—and how they yelled when we ducked behind the cargo. It made 'em feel important. They were like small boys letting off steam."

"What would you say is the greatest change in the last fifty years?" I asked.

"Well," he answered, "just offhand, I wouldn't know what to say, but perhaps the first thing that comes to mind is education. In my day, we were lucky if we got enough schooling to learn to read and write. Well-to-do folks just wouldn't tax themselves for public schools to be used by the children of the poor. They sent *their* children to private academies; what happened to the others didn't matter. Except in a few places, other people's children—when they went to school at all—went either as 'charity pupils' to schools partially supported by public contributions or to Sunday schools maintained by the churches. I went for a time to Sunday school."

"Did they teach you to read and write in Sunday school?" I asked.

"Yes," he said. "I didn't want to be a 'charity pupil' and my folks didn't like the idea either. Lots of people wouldn't send their children to schools where they would be looked down upon. Our German Reformed Church ran a Sunday school where children too young to work attended weekdays and where working children were given the opportunity to learn on the one day they were not employed.

"You would have thought," he went on, "that people able to send their children to private schools would have welcomed the church schools, since they were not taxed to support them; instead they agitated against them continually on the ground that teaching the poor to read and write would make them discontented and so spread the growth of 'radicalism.'"

"That sounds absurd," I said. "Anybody with a grain of sense knows that a free country depends upon a literate citizenry. Mass ignorance is what people need to fear."

"Yes, that's ordinary common sense," said Father. "But you'd be surprised how many people in 'the good old days' were afraid of exactly what you're talking about. They were afraid that when everybody learned to read and write they'd take to reading "The Constitution" and "The Bill of Rights" to find out what their rights really were. The rich wouldn't stand for anything as 'radical' as that. But in spite of all they could do to prevent it, by the time you came along there were public schools, and if you didn't get to go very long, you went long enough to learn that you did have rights and to be able to find out for yourself what they are. But there are plenty of people who still believe that mass ignorance is more desirable than dangerous."

Again, we smoked in silence.

"I'm glad I've lived to see the beginning of equal opportunity for all," he said presently. "I went to school only a few months out of each year. It wasn't enough, but you went six years steady. The younger boys and girls finished high school, Charlotte went to kindergarten college,[8] Henry through college and professional school, and my grandchildren will do such things as a matter of course. We started life as common laborers with no chance to engage in the professions—no chance to do what we might have done. But now the monopoly in education is broken. Perhaps in the next few years,

---

8 To train kindergarten teachers.

any poor man's son will have a chance to develop his talents and to rise in the world—if he cares to."

I had worked hard that day and it was bedtime for me.

"I think I'll turn in," I said. "It's getting late."

"Light another pipe," he urged. "By the time it's finished, the folks will be home."

I filled the pipe. "Tell me about the South," I suggested. "What was it like before the war?"

"Well, I saw my first slave auction in Natchez, Mississippi," he said. "Those colored folks were so scared, their faces were gray. They were somebody's house servants, according to the auctioneer; octoroons or quadroons, many of them no darker skinned than I. It made a terrific impression on me, and though I was only about fifteen at the time, I'll never forget how angry and shamed I felt when the auctioneer invited the bidders to see for themselves how young and strong the slaves were. They pinched their arms and legs, looked in their mouths, handled them as if they were cattle. First thing I did when I came North was to join Mr. Garrison's Anti-Slavery Society."

He ruminated.

"Steamboating was a lot of fun for a young man, though," he said. "We used to race other sternwheelers—sometimes from Natchez to Memphis. Nothing was ever so exciting! But the really gay time on board was at night. There was music and dancing in the grand salon. Handsome gentlemen in sprigged silk waistcoats danced quadrilles with their ladies. The black people made music in their quarters. The white men who weren't dancing played cards all night—sometimes with the professional gamblers who traveled up and down the river. Often, more money changed hands on one trip than you or I have earned in our lifetimes. When a man ran out of money, he gambled his land or his slaves or his cotton. Gentlemen carried derringers in their sashes. Any dispute over cards—or anything else, for that matter—was settled in favor of the man who reached his pistol first. The gamblers, naturally, were dead shots. At short range, the little guns tore a hole as big as your fist. Since everybody carried them, the survivor always claimed that he shot in 'self-defense;' and if any witnesses were present, things happened so fast that nobody knew just what had gone on—and dead men can't defend themselves."

"Sounds lively enough," I said.

"Oh, it was," said Father, "those were lively days. Well, such times are over. The gay, young blades I used to envy—they took life so easy—died by the thousands defending a way of life the rest of the country believed to be a monstrous wrong. The Chippewas and the Dakotas long ago shot their last arrow from the river's west bank. When I look back over my life and the changes I've seen take place, I often wonder what the future can bring any stranger than what I've lived to see."

"You'll live to see more surprising changes—you're only sixty-six," I said.

He shook his head. "No matter how long I live, there won't be any change to compare with what's already happened. In 1843, I rode with Engine No. 9 on the first steam railroad, the Mohawk & Hudson, which ran from Buffalo to Albany. Today, from coast to coast, this country's seamed with railroads and filled with people. I've read by the light of candles, whale oil, kerosene, gas and electricity. There were only half as many stars in the flag when I first saw it as there are today. The country's limits are fixed; it can't grow any bigger. And it is so powerful, thank God, that no one will ever dare attack it. And also thanks to Him, we are a peace-loving people. My boys and your boy can look forward to a better time in a united nation than my generation ever hoped for. Mr. Lincoln and General Grant saw to that."

"I'd like to be able to say, 'I saw Lincoln,'" I commented.

"He wasn't much to look at—sort of unfinished looking," said Father, "but there wasn't anything unfinished about his heart and head. Boy, oh, boy, to be as humble as he was but to know when to put your foot down, to have faith always that right makes might, and in that faith to dare to do our duty as we understand it. That's something to aim at. To hate slavery but not to hate your fellow countrymen for believing in it—to realize, as he said, that it is 'just what we would believe in their situation.' Boy, oh, boy, that takes some doing!"

"To put yourself in the other fellow's place always takes some doing," I agreed. "Well, here come the folks. It's late and I must hurry off to bed. Goodnight, Father."

As I rose to go, I felt that in some way he was reluctant to have me leave, but he said, "Of course, you need your rest. Goodnight, boy."

The next morning, Mother came over very early. She looked troubled.

"Your father had a terrible chill last night," she said. "I piled covers on him but he couldn't get warm. He shook the bed all night."

"Mother, you shouldn't have waited until morning to call me," I protested. "Why didn't you send one of the boys for the doctor right away?"

"Your father didn't want me to call anyone," she answered. "He knows how much you all need your sleep."

I didn't wait to run over to see him first, but started after the doctor. Father had been in good health and best of spirits the night before; there was nothing to worry about, I told myself. But, nevertheless, something I couldn't put into words—something I felt—disturbed me. His reluctance to have me go—had he been less well than he seemed? There had been a note of leave-taking in our visit that I couldn't put out of my mind. Had he felt this, too?

Perhaps he had. The doctor's verdict of double pneumonia preceded his passing by three days. It was, indeed, our last visit.

Nothing I had ever faced before required so much fortitude. The world had become an indescribably lonely place. While he lived, there had always been a warm, flowing sympathy—a well of inspiration ready and waiting for each one of us to partake. And none of us, I think, until the day he wasn't there, had ever realized how often we had gone to him for understanding and help. Now we should have to do as he had done—go to the Source.

CHAPTER EIGHT

New World in the Making

The closing years of the nineteenth century brought with them events of so great a magnitude that, as I look back upon them, it is small wonder we were not awake to their implications. Almost overnight, many old certainties vanished, the old ways changed, men and the hour met on a hundred fronts to inaugurate a new age. The genie was out of the bottle for good or ill.

Just two short years after Father had said, "The country's limits are fixed. It can't grow any bigger . . . my boys and your boy can look forward to a better and more peaceful time than men of my generation ever hoped for," my brother Ben was on his way to fight in the Spanish-American War. Among the members of Austin's Company G who went with him was my uncle's son, also named Jay Decker, who had come to work with us, and Harvey Chapin, another one of my boys at the plant.

When they returned, their country was a world power, committed by the march of events to a role in Far Eastern affairs few of us relished and none of us understood. The flag flew over one hundred and twenty-four thousand square miles of islands, and phrases like "imperial America," "American protectorate," and "America's role in the Orient" began to appear in the papers. Much to our amazement, not everybody in the conquered territories welcomed their "liberators." We sincerely believed that we had gone to war solely to rescue cruelly oppressed peoples. It now came as something of a shock to learn that, after chasing out the Spanish, we had to "pacify" the Filipinos with bullets. Dissatisfaction in Cuba and in Puerto Rico, Funston fighting Aguinaldo, stories of "native uprisings" among the Moros—all the problems which are part and parcel of alien peoples under alien rule—now became something for Americans to ponder over. But no matter what they thought about these matters, it became evident that place names like Guam, Mindanao, Luzon, and Sulu Sea were in the news to stay, along with the recently annexed islands of Hawaii and Samoa.[9]

To add to the perplexities of the American voter, already up to his ears in the time-tested and familiar campaign issues of "free silver" and "monopoly," his politicians now harangued him on his "duty to the Filipinos" or urged him to "settle the problem" by turning them loose.

But, on examining these propositions, a great many people hitherto unversed in the "white man's burden" and the joys of colonial overlordship found they had a bear by the tail. Cubans, Puerto Ricans, and Filipinos might not like their newly acquired Uncle Sam, but once we cut them adrift, since they were "weak," they would quickly fall prey to others who might find uses for them by no means to our advantage. Though Americans might sympathize with the deposed Queen of Hawaii, nevertheless, since the Islands were "strategic,"

9 References to U.S. military involvements in the Caribbean and the Pacific that were frequently in the news around this time.

they must be held. But to hold these various possessions meant to admit into the American economy raw material producers who competed with Utah sugar beet growers, Louisiana rice and sugar planters, Montana cattle raisers, and Minnesota dairy farmers.

Now the American farmer, confronted with cheap butter substitutes made out of copra and soap made from palm oil, began to look at the word "tariff" with eyes from which the scales were falling fast. It was a very different word than it had been when he thought of it only in terms of himself as the consumer who paid more for manufactured goods. Now that the shoe was on the other foot and he was in competition with low-cost, duty-free products, he became less sure of the blessings of "free trade"—a change of view which was natural, inevitable—and ironic!

The shifts in our political thinking were as nothing, however, to the changes which were taking place in American homes, on the farm, and in industry. Inventions and discoveries continued to come so thick and fast that plants and methods were obsolete almost before one left the blueprint and the other became established practice.

Within the space of a few short years, automobiles, electrical steel, aluminum, reinforced concrete, airplanes, submarines, x-rays, radium, elevators, transatlantic radio telegraph and telephone, jackhammer drills, disc plows, around-the-world messages in twelve minutes via the Pacific cable, monotype, motion picture, adding and automatic screw machines, diesel engines, gas welding, wireless telegraphy, electrolytic copper, and turbo generators came on the scene. These things came faster than we could adjust our thinking to them. Before we knew it, they had changed our industrial system, and our relations with each other and the world. No phase of civilized man's life was unaffected.

Had my father lived only ten years longer, he would have seen or heard about these things, for some of them were changing life at home in Austin. And this was only the beginning of the new world taking shape all about us. That we were ignorant of the possibilities for good or ill in these new means is understandable; our almost instant readiness to identify ourselves with them is less so. People began talking about the "new machine age man" to the total exclusion of the moral man, as if they could be separated safely. As time went on, events proved that they could not. And in this, perhaps, lies the story of the new century's tragic failure—a failure not of means but of men.

Much as I missed my father, I was often glad that he had been spared some of the anxieties that fell to our lot after his passing.

In August, four months after the evening of my last visit with him, we were awakened around midnight by the sound of the whistle at the city water works, signaling a general fire alarm, and someone pounding on the door and crying, "Fire! Fire!"

Yes, fire had broken out in the smokehouse which, before its extinction by the Austin Fire Department, did a lot of damage. In the cleanup next day, the grinning crew ate baked ham for lunch—which cost the insurance company about seven thousand dollars—but the business was saved. Although the loss in merchandise and facilities would seriously cripple sales and operations until we could make replacements, I felt myself to be the luckiest man in the world. Under such circumstances, people's ideas of what constitutes good fortune undergo surprising changes.

While we were eating our expensive lunch, I remembered that I was in Austin because of another fire nine years before. This was August and, on another hot August night, I had written to my mother that I was coming here, not to be a "butcher," if you please, but a "packer." The nine years between had been a liberal education in many things not set down in my original calculations of a roseate business career. I was fast learning that being a businessman was a far different affair from the inside than it had seemed from the sidelines. I wondered what the next nine years would bring to me, the business, and the country.

I hadn't long to wait for some answers to the question.

In the summer of 1896, gold was discovered in the Klondike. Gold fever swept the country. My old partner, Friedrich, who had sold his share of our original business, went off to try his luck in the new El Dorado. Half the restless farm boys in Mower County seemed bent on following his example. By May of the next year, other boys, like my brother Ben, had gone to war. Americans were again on the march. New heroes, fortunes, legends, and a new chapter in our history were in the making.

Our escape from the fiery furnace seemed a good omen and I was sufficiently encouraged by it to tempt fortune further. The icehouse we were using was inadequate—so were other facilities. Thirty to forty thousand dollars would enable us to build a cold storage plant, a poultry house, replace the burned smokehouse and abattoir. Somebody, somewhere, certainly had that much money. It only remained for me to find the right somebody. I started out with the belief that it was possible and that, somehow, I could do it. By fall, these new facilities were taking form under the carpenters' hammers. The brick walls of the cold storage plant were seventeen inches thick, its overall dimensions sixty by forty feet—all in all, an "icebox" big enough to hold five hundred carcasses.

When the new plant was completed in November, 1897, a great many people privately thought of it as "Hormel's folly." The Austin papers, while admitting that if the business could be maintained at its plant capacity "it would mean at present prices many thousand dollars annually to the farmers," doubted that it could be done "because of the scarcity of hogs." Fortunately, there were to be a number of effective ways of remedying this scarcity.

For one thing, each year sturdier strains of hybrid corn were being introduced into Southern Minnesota, which flourished in a climate heretofore considered much too cold for that warmth-loving grain. Cooperative creameries were springing up everywhere. Farmers and consumers had discovered that there was something in the soil which grew the kind of dairy feed that made Minnesota butter as fine as any in the world.

The growing emphasis on dairying directly benefited our product because, in a dairy belt, young, growing pigs are fed on the skim milk brought back to the farm each day from the local creameries. Skim milk, supplemented with corn and mill feed, produces just the right mixture of fat and lean which means the choicest bacon. Such firm-textured, sweet-tasting meat produces a superior product and is mostly obtainable in the cooperative creamery district of Southern Minnesota. Since we had long ago learned that our products would be no better than what the farmer had to sell, these changes meant that we could now have uniformity in quality not possible to processors whose hogs were bought at stockyard centers where the quality varied because the animals came from localities far and near which had different feeding methods. A slop-fed pig, or one fed on cottonseed cake, soya beans, or straight corn, again differs from a corn- and milk-fed pig. With adequate facilities, we were not only in a position to offer the farmer a quick cash market for the best he could raise, we could make it worth his while to aim at the best that could be produced. And, to this end, we could work with him to improve and stabilize breeds.

Perhaps no single factor so influenced my thinking at this time as that very great and farsighted man, James J. Hill. He became for me a symbol of the businessman I wanted to be, and his railroad the kind of a business I wanted to help bring into being.

Much has been written about him, but not half enough. He had the vision, the inspiration, and the insight to help himself by helping others. He was not—and never pretended to be—a philanthropist. He didn't like the word; it smelled of charity. His idea of social responsibility had nothing to do with ameliorating the condition of the poor through establishing soup kitchens and "milk funds" for their undernourished children or through political maneuvers designed to help the politicians more than the sufferers. He thought the poor had sense enough to endow themselves if men in his position had the wit to help them come by the means.

His beginnings were modest. He started life as a clerk in a steamboat office in Saint Paul in 1858. Always observant, after he became a forwarding agent for his steamboat line and for the new Saint Paul and Pacific Railroad, he noticed on his trips to the Red River Valley how high and rank the grass grew wherever cartwheels loosened the soil. Hill reasoned that a land that could grow grass like that had trade possibilities. On the strength of his feeling for this country's future, he founded a partnership with Norman Kitson in the Red River Transportation Company, which ran steamers from Fort Abercrombie to Fort Garry (now Winnipeg).

By the time its Dutch owners were tired of carrying the failing and ailing Saint Paul and Pacific, he was able to persuade Kitson and the Canadian financiers, Baron Strathcona and Sir George Stephens, to help him finance its purchase. The year he acquired control, 1878, Hill completed it to the Canadian boundary. By 1893, he had built it into the Great Northern System and carried it across the Cascades into Seattle. And he did this without a penny of government subsidy or land grants, which was sufficient in itself, perhaps, to mark Hill as the greatest American railroad builder of his time.

By any other man's calculations, the northernmost transcontinental railroad ran through unpromising territory. The Great Plains of the Dakotas and Montana were pasturelands at best, sparsely settled and nonproductive. But Hill, unlike the stock speculators and land gamblers in search of instant profits at their victims' expense, saw potentialities based upon scientific development of the territory—its arable land competently tilled by real farmers equipped with every resource of modern agriculture and animal husbandry. He conceived it to be his job to develop markets in Europe and the Orient for the sale of their produce. It was not enough for his agents to tell farmers and their wives of the "wonderful opportunities in the West," and then leave them to shift for themselves, as others were doing and had done. When the settlers by the thousands came into new territory at his invitation, his interest in their welfare increased rather than diminished. His agents arranged credit facilities, opened highroads, and helped the new communities in every way possible.

I was in Saint Paul on business in the early 1890's when one of Hill's great, organized excursions to the new country was about to set forth. He addressed the trainloads of prospective settlers. "Now you can see for yourselves," he said, "the kind of soil which awaits your plows. Don't take our word for anything. Investigate, ask questions, but make up your own mind as to what the future offers you. We will help you become as prosperous as you are ambitious; we promise no more than that. If you want your children to be free citizens in a free land, something more than slaves working for others, then together we will work toward that end. You farmers talk a lot about free trade and protection and what this or that politician will do for you, but remember they can do nothing you cannot do better for yourselves. All wealth comes from the land. It is here and free for the asking. Help us build the prosperous farms, thriving cities, and great industries of the great future which awaits us both."

When I walked into his Saint Paul office a few years later, that "great future" was already taking shape. It was in the fall of the year when Hill was getting reports from the five-acre patches planted under the supervision of his agricultural experts. He looked up from his reading and said, "Take a look at these, George; here is the proof. Farmers are sometimes a stubborn lot of people to convince—they distrust newfangled ideas on principle. But look!"

He produced report after report showing the results of the five-acre plots for which he paid five dollars an acre to the farmer who would cultivate the plot according to his experts' instructions. The yield, in almost every instance, was double per acre what the farmer produced on the rest of his farm.

"I think," said Hill with a chuckle, "they'll believe the 'perfesser fellers' now!"

"I wish you could see some of the interesting experiments in growing alfalfa we're conducting at my place," he continued. "It won't grow, you know, in acid soils or in soils with poor drainage, but we think we're on the track of soil treatments and systems of

drainage which will enable a lot of our people to grow it successfully in parts of the country where it has failed to grow before. We're
growing it now in my conservatory in soils taken from our right of
way in five states. When we hit on the right methods for the different
soils and climates, we'll add fifty million dollars to the value of the
farmers' livestock. Alfalfa's got the kind of protein content that will
make the finest beef and milk you ever ate. When we get the fodder
problem worked out—we're experimenting with other new grasses
and grains that don't mind cold weather—then we're going to step
up the importation of more blooded Pole Angus and Hereford bulls
to build up the herds."

For a half dozen years, Mr. Hill imported the very best breed of
bulls from continental Europe and leased them to the farmers along
his line of road, and the result was that the livestock coming from
the Hill railroads made the South Saint Paul Stockyards one of the
leading livestock centers of the nation.

"I don't understand," I said, "how you can afford such a costly
program now. Some of the railroads are crying poverty and going
bankrupt."

I have always remembered his answer: "I cannot expect my railroad to make money until I first put money in the hands of farmers
along my right of way. It occurred to me that, during our depression
years, we could not correct our national economy until we found
better ways of putting money into the hands of our people so they
could buy the products of the farm and the factory.

"Every dollar we spend," Hill continued, "helping a farmer along
our right of way, puts him in a position to buy needed farm imple-
ments and home necessities, which spells income for the railroad.
Maybe if we aren't afraid to risk a few million helping these farmers

to make this nation great and prosperous, perhaps someday the Great Northern will mean enough to the people who depend on it for them to help us save it from unfair legislation."

This reflection was occasioned by Hill's belief that Attorney General Knox's edict—that the Great Northern, the Northern Pacific, and the Chicago, Burlington & Quincy, now operating as a unit under Hill's management, constituted a violation of the Sherman Antitrust Act of 1890—was a "cheap political trick" wholly unjustified under the circumstances. He believed that Theodore Roosevelt's attack upon his railroads had less to do with the public welfare than it had to do with the President's desire to succeed himself. Hill argued that the evils to the public in a series of disjointed and conflicting lines, inadequate to the task of transportation, was the thing to be feared.

"The farmers want cheap freight rates—so do you," said Hill. "But I can't give them unless we can cut operating costs. Low costs of operation mean one continuous haul under one management from producer to consumer. That's not monopoly; it's horse sense. Someday, people in this country will wake up to the fact that what they need to encourage is greater railroad consolidation under wise management and under wise public supervision. Then, neither the politicians nor the promoters can bring sickening losses to our people."

Throughout his life as a railroader, I watched Hill develop the economic ties which bound the new empire he had helped create to the Far East and Europe, and watched him fight off attacks by hawkeyed speculators and freebooters like Harriman, who attempted, unsuccessfully in 1901, to wrest from him the results of years of hard labor. He was always full of plans that would have taken two lifetimes at least to realize in their entirety. His agents scoured the Orient to discover what products his farmers raised that the men of Asia could consume, and what products they had to give in exchange. He established Pacific Coast terminals and steamship communications between the great Oriental cities and the Northwest. He encouraged men wherever he could find them to exchange the fruits of their labor and to collaborate in the practical fraternity of men engaged upon a common task, as my father would have put it, "of replenishing and subduing the earth."

Along with Carnegie, Edison, Jane Addams, Charles W. Eliot, and a host of other distinguished Americans of his day, Hill belonged to and supported international peace associations. The old Indian fighter had lived long enough to know that it takes twice the energy to fight a man than it takes to work with him toward some constructive end. He once said, "We can have peace whenever we're willing to work toward making the productions of industry so profitable everywhere that no man can offer his countrymen any gains through war."

How right he was! Like another Man of Peace, Hill, in his particular way, was as wholly practical. One enunciated the principles behind successful group effort, the laws of peace and abundance; the other put the principles into operation as best he knew how. Before he died in 1916, Hill had the satisfaction of seeing a life "dedicated to self-advantage," as he once phrased it, bear fruit across three thousand miles of prosperous farms and communities where only the prairie dog and the gopher had reigned twenty-five years before. And so passed from the American scene a hard-headed businessman who never pretended to be a "do-gooder," but whose efforts enriched millions of lives. My contacts and association with him were quite frequent in later years, and I count them among my outstanding privileges. When the millennium comes, the J. J. Hills will be somewhere in the foreground.

It might be well to point out here, however, that the man who proposes to engage in Hill's variety of intelligent self-interest, if it calls for public collaboration, must also be prepared to put up a good, stiff argument and his own cash to win supporters. It took both to convince a class as traditionally conservative as the farmers that there was anything to "this newfangled livestock talk." The big Chicago packers who first tried to convince stock raisers that to improve their herds was anything but "nonsense" found that out.

When Swift and others began shipping beef to Europe in the late 1870's, they quickly discovered that only the choicest quality of beef could be shipped abroad at a profit and sold in competition with the best European stock. This meant introducing blooded Shorthorn, Hereford, and Pole Angus bulls into American herds, since experiments proved that purebred steers, weighing from one thousand to fourteen hundred pounds, were ready for market in eighteen months to two years, while it required twice as long for scrub stock to reach that weight. By that time, the flesh of the slower-growing animals was much too tough to stand comparison with the best British beef. But stock raisers didn't leap at the chance to cooperate with the packers, even when the packers bought and lent the bulls. Some, of course, were smart enough to see advantage in the obvious, but others said, "Just nonsense, it will blow over—a steer's a steer, isn't it?"

"Practical" breeders appraised a fine cow, not on her milk yield, but on the appearance she would make on her owner's lawn or country estate. The standard by which she won prizes at fairs was her aesthetic appeal. I'm not fooling. "Superb beauty of form," according to the judges, won the ribbons.

But long after the principle of better production from blooded lines had been thoroughly established, many farmers still persisted in buying three scrubs for the price of one good animal in the belief that they were somehow getting the better of the bargain. Scientific agriculture, animal husbandry, and business management on the farm met the same fate on its introduction. And this attitude was not confined to the farmers, either. All the commonplace ideas of today were once the exclusive property of "radicals" and "crackpots"— rugged individualists who, fortunately for the rest of us, kept right on promoting their "funny" ideas until facts wore away prejudice and inertia.

As the new century dawned, old ways of thinking were being challenged on a dozen fronts. Doors were opening and closing so fast, as one new factor after another entered upon the scene, that, as I look back upon the times, it seems remarkable that we managed to make as wise decisions as we did. No system of society demands so much from its individual members as does ours. When and where to change the "stop" to "go?" How to encourage or restrain each other and ourselves? When to abandon the tried and true in favor of the new? These problems confronted us at every turn. Business, big and little, like the farmer and the nation, was undergoing a change no less dramatic and far-reaching in its consequences to the old way of life which had conditioned our thinking until now.

The passage of the Sherman Antitrust Act in 1890, over the determined opposition of big enterprise, defined a new era in American business policy. But like the Interstate Commerce Act of 1887, it too got buried for a time. So much public feeling had arisen against trusts and trade combinations of all kinds after the panic of 1893 that by 1900 the Republican Party felt compelled to include an antitrust plank, drafted by Senator Joseph B. Foraker, in its party platform of that year. Few, if any, prosecutions were undertaken at first, but the signs of the times were unmistakable. The Interstate Commerce Commission, hitherto slow to act, came to the aid of small businesses like ours. With the advice and counsel of my friend Catherwood, we presented our case before the I. C. C. By the close of 1900, we had won the right to use refrigerator cars on the same terms as other packers.

I was forty that year. The business had now reached the stage where it could no longer be conducted as a one-man show if it were to go ahead. So I took off my overalls, hung up the cleaver, and devoted my energies to management. We had the good fortune to secure the services of a first-rate, experienced packinghouse superintendent, John Schmidt. Four full-time salesmen, among them my brother Ben, safely home from the war, opened up nearby sales territory.

Ben and Frank Sump went to Minneapolis. They sold out of a refrigerator car, using bicycles or horse and buggy to get around the city with their order books. Sam Moe, our first full-time salesman, and Bill Yelland traveled as far as Duluth singing the praises of our products. I was mighty proud of the boys. We were now a full-fledged business concern with a bookkeeper and a "lady stenographer," whose presence made the boys a bit nervous at first—she didn't like grease on the office doorknob.

We were also catching up with the twentieth century in other ways. The first mechanical elevator, powered by something besides a half dozen men of muscle and referred to as our "armstrong elevator," was installed at the plant. It too made the men nervous at first. Suppose it fell and you dropped with it?

Now that the business was past the formative stage, it presented new problems. We were reaching out for volume and getting it. If we were to achieve more than a flash-in-the-pan success, however, policies had to be established and people trained to represent them: how to get new business and safeguard credit losses in new accounts, and how to collect overdue bills and still keep customers. Even men who eventually paid their bills were somewhat touchy on the subject of "when" in those days. Since there were no credit bureaus to tell the story, we worked out a system that still seems pretty good to me. When the boys went into new territory, I told them, "Don't ask a man how much cash he has in order to determine his credit standing. Watch how he handles his customers. Ask yourself if he understands his business. Are his habits good? Is he clean? Are his tools and shop in good order? If the answer to these questions is yes, then ask to see his books. If he is a good collector himself as well as a capable businessman, he is a good credit risk."

Everything I had ever attempted had been done on a shoestring. Other men's faith in extending me credit had been based on nothing more tangible than that I worked hard and perseveringly to improve my skills. Since they had lost nothing by it, I determined that we, in turn, could afford the same risks on the same security. I urged our people to be especially considerate of the man just making a start and, above all, not to take advantage in any way of his inexperience, but to encourage him and to give him the benefit of whatever knowledge they had.

We trained each other in "experience" meetings. When the boys came in, we discussed why Sam had better luck collecting than some other salesmen. Then Sam would tell the others how he did it.

"I start off by saying, 'Good morning, Joe. How are you today?'" said Sam, "and then after he tells me, I present the bill and say nothing about orders until the bill is paid. We are creatures of habit and we can get our customers in the habit of paying their bills when once they understand they must be paid. After that, I seldom have any difficulty getting a good order. I make a habit of handing out bills when I first go into a shop. Now my customers are getting the habit of paying them right off."

Since Sam was also an outstanding salesman and account getter, the rest of the boys decided that they could do what Sam did.

In going over their orders, I noticed that one salesman would sell nearly every item on his list or another would be outstandingly successful in convincing every customer that he ought to buy certain items. Each of these fellows, like Sam, would be asked to tell how he did it. Sometimes their answers were surprising. The result of this interchange of ideas and selling technique was that, in a short time, we developed salesmen and a sales plan that spelled increased profits for the business.

When this had been accomplished, I felt that we had reached the place where it was important to create a permanent business structure, so we became a corporation.

It was my hope that through the sale of preferred shares we should at least acquire an adequate working capital. It was no longer a question of asking people to invest in the "blue sky," for we were making money. However, there was always a place for every dollar and we were always handicapped for lack of them. The securing of money was our greatest problem.

But I was soon disillusioned on the score of what constituted a legitimate business risk. Men, wise in the ways of corporate finance, proceeded to enlighten me. It was not enough, it seemed, that we should offer guaranteed earnings against borrowings secured by assets. "We can sell your preferred shares," they said, "if you will give a common share with each share of senior stock as a bonus. Otherwise, people won't buy."

"Then we'll never sell a share," I vowed. "Every preferred share we sell is a prior obligation against earnings and assets until the day we buy it back at a premium. We recognize the right of a money-lender to such preference, but we don't agree that, in addition, the lender is entitled through common stock ownership to a perpetual lien against the energy and enterprise of the men who make this business possible. Any common stock bonuses we pass out will be to our own people. They're the ones who've earned it. And as long as I have anything to say about it, they're the ones who'll get it!"

Needless to say, this unorthodox attitude didn't sell the one thousand two hundred and fifty preferred shares overnight. Fellow townsmen did buy them—slowly. But by then I didn't care. I was not a stockjobber. By pinchpenny economies, luck, and unlimited hard work, my brothers, my wife, myself and my associates had created a wealth-producing mechanism. It was small but growing. If we had to, we could continue to build as we had begun. Even a small backlog of ready money would make the task ahead easier, but men and not money were the creators of wealth, and with the right kind of men all things were possible. We would sit tight until the day when owners of money came asking us to employ their dollars and would probably be content to take a fair return for their use. Until that day arrived, we would confine our promotional activities to men and ideas and trust to these to accumulate capital.

Time proved the wisdom of this particular decision. On this and on subsequent occasions when I have experienced setbacks and disappointments because of money, I have lived to be thankful they occurred. Because it was never available to make the way easy, I ceased to think of money as a prime mover. It became, in my think-ing, the end result of something I or some other man did. I have

George Albert Hormel (1860–1946), *circa* **1872**
As a youth.

John George Hormel (1830–1896), *circa* 1890
George A.'s father.

Susanna "Susan" Wilhelmina Decker Hormel (1836–1910), *circa* **1908**
George A.'s mother.

The five Hormel brothers, 1896
(*left to right*) Henry, John, Herman, Benjamin, and George A.

The five Hormel sisters, *circa* **1890**
(left to right) Charlotte, Susan, Elizabeth, Emma, and Emilie.

George A. Hormel, late 1880's

Samuel D. ("Doak") Catherwood and George A. Hormel, 1887
George A. took great delight in describing this photo when discussing his early days in Austin
(see page 150). George A. thought so highly of his friend that he used "Catherwood" for his
son's middle name. Photo courtesy of Hormel Foods Archives.

George A. Hormel, 1903

Lillian Belle Gleason Hormel, (1867–1946), *circa* **1905**
George A.'s wife, who was known as Belle to her family and friends.

Ludwig "Louis" Decker, George A. Hormel, Jay C. Hormel (George's son),
and Jacob E. "Uncle Jay" Decker, *circa* 1897

George A. Hormel, *circa* 1910

The five Hormel brothers, 1923
(left to right) Herman, John, Henry, Benjamin, and George A.

**George A. Hormel, Samuel D. ("Doak") Catherwood, and
Russell E. Shepherd,** *circa* **1940**
Longtime friends.

Lillian Belle Hormel and George A. Hormel, 1942
At their 50th wedding anniversary celebration.

Jay Catherwood Hormel (1892–1954), 1907
In his Shattuck Military Academy uniform.

Jay C. Hormel, early 1900's

Jay C. Hormel, *circa* **1917**
In his World War I uniform.

Jay C. Hormel, 1945
Photo taken by Pach Bros. Studio, New York, NY.

The George A. and Lillian Belle Hormel home, Austin, Minnesota, *circa* **1910**
Restored and open to the public, it is known today as the Hormel Historic Home.

The Hormel family home, Toledo, Ohio, *circa* 1880
Photo courtesy of Stephen E. Rowe, from the Elizabeth Hormel photo album.

The George A. and Lillian Belle Hormel home, Bel Air, California, *circa* 1930

Geo. A. Hormel & Co. Provision Market, *circa* **1891**
The company retail store, with delivery carts.

Geo. A. Hormel & Co. plant, 1894
The two-story brick building in the back was the first addition to the
former creamery turned meat packing plant, with staff and delivery carts.

Geo. A. Hormel & Co. plant, 1901

Geo. A. Hormel & Co. plant, *circa* 1940
Photo courtesy of Hormel Foods Archives.

Geo. A. Hormel & Co. staff, *circa* **1898**
George A. is standing at the far right.

Sausage room, *circa* **1903**
Photo courtesy of Stephen E. Rowe.

Cutting room, *circa* **1896**
George A. is at the far right, supervising.

Hog cutting room, *circa* **1902**
Photo courtesy of Stephen E. Rowe.

George A. Hormel, 1930
Photo taken by C. Elmer Grove, California.

been confused about a lot of other issues in life, but rarely about the function of money or what it can or cannot do. It is a good servant but a miserable master. And the real evil in thinking about it to the exclusion of everything else is that it eventually compels the man who does so to think in no other terms. Imagination unlimited has its wings clipped to the size of a five dollar bill. The power of Niagara is harnessed or utilized according to some man's conception of its money worth instead of what it can do.

So the common stock of the company, issued in one certificate in my name, remained in that state until 1928, the year we offered our common stock to the public through the Chicago Stock Exchange. When the common stock then sold as high as sixty dollars a share, I felt greatly rewarded for the fight and energy it required to retain all the shares of the company in my name.

However, a special employees' stock was devised which participated in the company's earnings the same as common stock. These shares were non-negotiable. When the owners of such shares left the business for any reason, they surrendered their stock and received the book value for it in cash. When a dividend was declared on the common stock, employees' shares received a like dividend and any earnings above the dividend were credited to the owner's personal account. I took the position that the human brain was the most richly valuable asset in the business I could utilize. One of my school teachers used to say that if a man would tie his arm to his body and not exercise it, the arm would become useless. Just so with the human brain. If it is not exercised, it will yield no benefit. The idea of employees' shares was an incentive for all of our employees to think of ways and means to improve our product and produce it at the lowest minimum cost. Every time an employee submitted a useful idea, he was rewarded with employee share certificates. This incentive kept him alert and his brain active. In a way, these men were made partners in the business. The money paid out in employee share earnings each year paid big dividends and did more to prosper the business than any other one thing.

I knew that when the business grew large and profitable enough to pay high salaries for brains we could hire them, but I was more concerned with developing the talents of the men we already had. I wanted the country boys who came to work for us to be so good and efficient that when an opportunity arose, they, and not outside talent, would fill the better job. An increase in capacity of every man on the payroll meant an increase in the company's assets impossible to estimate in dollars. And every increase in the company's capacity to reward better men meant better men to hire. Bright boys in our town would have no reason to go off to big cities in search of a future when economic success was possible right at home.

From my own working experience, I also knew that other factors besides money would play a part in how successfully we could develop our human talent—and not the least of these was pride of performance. Men did their best work under conditions which identified them with excellence in some degree. The job had to offer constant incentive for further development; for the man who took pride in his own skills was always seeking to extend the range of his competence, and the community as well as the employer played a vital role in how well he thought his job deserved the best he could put into it.

Perhaps no single circumstance from this point on played so large a part in the development of the business as putting into practice these few simple truths. The time and the place were ripe. Indeed, we should have failed without concepts of self-advantage based upon the spirit of the new century. I counted it my good fortune to have been conditioned against a form of labor exploitation which would have gained me nothing at the time and in the place I happened to be, as it was equally my good fortune to have come to a place where a sturdy, independent and intelligent people made a union of ideas and action possible.

Together, we created a wealth-producing medium which has been mutually advantageous over the years. Its history has become the history of a great many of my fellow townsfolk, just as their story is part of mine and the organization's.

During the years I worked for other men, I found myself instinctively classifying them as men who build you up or tear you down—leaders and drivers. Analyzing my reactions to a man like Crandall, I noticed that others worked for him as willingly as I did. He was not a slack boss but he knew how to pull a man up sharp when he needed it without losing his good will. The distinction between Crandall and other bosses I had worked for and heartily disliked was that, even when he found fault with you, he never said anything to shake your confidence and belief in your own talents. He encouraged men by showing them how to remove the obstacles which stood between them and their greatest possible accomplishment. The best you could do was not something you owed him, but something you owed to yourself. It enabled you to view yourself with the proper kind of self-respect. Contrasting his attitude with what I had seen take place around Chicago's Packingtown and South Water Street further pointed up the fact that, when men were driven by necessity to accept any kind of treatment, when because of it they no longer felt "just as good as the other fellow," they were not. Under such conditions, men somehow lost the power to function as reasoning human beings.

Perhaps because I was young myself when I first experienced the economic facts of life, I particularly noticed the effects on their social attitudes of the conditions under which men worked and lived. Coming to Chicago from a friendly and protecting home was like entering into another world. My father was poor. Most of the parents of the children I knew were poor. Only a couple of boys out of a dozen who went to school with me graduated from grammar school. They went to work as I did and for the same reason. But none of them went to jail or became public liabilities. So the difference between what I saw on the streets of Chicago and at home had something to do with other factors besides lack of money and education. It seemed to me that the difference lay in the fact that great numbers of working people in the great city had lost all hope of bettering themselves. Nothing in their daily lives gave them any belief in their own importance or any assurance that they could materially affect the future. There was no basis on which to build a proper kind of self-respect. These beliefs were a man's stakes in life—the measure of his humanness. Without them, he became ugly and explosive—a menace to himself and everything called civilization. Of no value to himself, he became a bad citizen, a quarrelsome neighbor, and a worse parent. The Chicago papers were always full of stories of neglected children who confessed, when ferreted out of their dens by truant officers, that they had not been near their homes in months.

It seemed obvious to me that when people were drawn to great cities and kept in them under conditions of hunger and degradation because commerce, instead of being a method for the distribution of the results of labor, had lost sight of its function, they lost sight of themselves. When things became more important than a man himself, then his viewpoint became warped in regard to himself and the other fellow. He suffered some hurt to his humanness which rendered him incapable of any longer acting "like a man." The process of dehumanization was cumulative and spared no one. Brutality and indifference in one department of a man's life spread to every other. Master and toiler were equally affected. The driver became as brutalized as the driven, whom he came to fear. I had seen such men, when the labor pot boiled over in Chicago, afraid to walk the streets without bodyguards—and for good reasons. And the other exempted nothing, not even his own children, from his destructive and calloused feelings.

Tramping the streets of Kansas City had been a further illustration that whoever controls a man's job controls his life. As an overworked boy in Chicago, barely earning enough to live, I was just another "bum" at the bottom of the social heap. Without a job and money in Kansas City, I wasn't anybody. And anyone who has ever walked the streets from morning till night, looking for a place to sell something nobody wants, knows what that does to a man's assurance. People did not go out of their way to be unkind, but it was plain to be seen that one's status was determined, in their eyes, by the job factor. And I realized how quickly a jobless workingman becomes a man without social importance, since that is how people see him and how, through their eyes, he comes to view himself. Or he sees himself as a mean fellow doing menial work somehow beneath all human dignity and he loses the feeling of being other men's equal— and soon he isn't, because he acts the way he feels.

By the time I reached the stage of an employer of other men's talents, I had acquired a fairly broad experience of the worker and his job, of what it means to be the underdog. I knew at firsthand why it was a "mortal sin" for one man to oppress another, to make him lose sight of his worth and importance. It was socially indefensible and morally wrong because it was wasteful—wasteful of the only conscious productive force in the world: the human mind and heart. And since that mind and heart would inevitably express its thoughts and feelings constructively or otherwise, it was everyone's business and to everyone's advantage to see that nothing blocked the creative channels through which a man could make the fullest use of "what God gave him to use."

As I watched men at work in the plant, I realized why that shrewd humanist, "Petroleum Nasby" in Toledo, has stressed in so many ways the importance of believing, "you're just as good as the other fellow." For it seemed to make no difference to a man what he did if two factors were present: encouragement and hope.

If he received the proper encouragement at the right time, even a very ordinary fellow came up "with bright ideas every now and then," just as "Nasby" said he would. And whenever a man with few skills could be convinced that by using his brain as well as his brawn he could go on to any future he chose to aim at—where the business was concerned, the sky was the limit—he began to stir himself—or his wife did. Women have an intuitional grapevine which always tells them about the better job their men might have by going after it. He might not be brilliant—for men who have not thought of themselves as having a future beyond the life of a manual laborer do not suddenly acquire the power to think creatively—but when he did get the idea that, although he worked in the hide cellar, he didn't have to stay there once he made up his mind to graduate to the better job he could have when he gave some evidence of his ability to fill it, he began to look around in the hide cellar. It was surprising how many things he could find that needed improving right where he was—things he had never bothered to notice before.

Personal recognition from his superiors and the fact that we considered him intelligent enough to have profit-producing ideas were as important in quickening his perceptions as the more tangible rewards he earned. In brief, whenever I could convince a man—and this I conceived to be my most important job—that the only limiting factor in life was himself, and that the job he was now doing was both useful and important enough to engage his whole effort since it was the means by which he lived, he proceeded to make greater use of such talents as he possessed. And he often possessed more talents than he dreamed he owned.

I believed the first step toward accomplishing these ends was to get a man to question the "why" of what he was doing, to get him to ask himself, "Why am I performing this operation in a particular way? Is there a better, easier way to do it?" Once this wedge could be driven in the old habit pattern, the process was cumulative. It was Sam Moe's method in reverse. He got his customers to pay their bills by "getting them in the habit;" we established the habit of questioning habit.

Another factor which influenced the worker almost as much as the possibilities of advancement was the opinion of others toward his job. This meant how his family, his co-workers, his superiors, and his community regarded his means of livelihood. When what a man does for a living determines his social standing and not how well he does it or how important it is to the people who benefit from his labors, then he isn't "as good as the other fellow"—and he knows it! Such a man is not fooled by patronizing talk about "the dignity of honest labor" by people who never perform any. And "labor's rights" and "democracy" also leave a bad taste in his mouth when every day of his life he is treated meanly by someone because he does the world's dirty work. No one fools him on this score, and it is the cause of much deep-seated dissatisfaction, the real reason for much so-called "labor unrest." For the fact that neither in the business nor in the town did this kind of job snobbishness gain a foothold, I take some of the credit, but most of it belongs to the people of Austin.

Our business, in the old days of hand labor, demanded long hours, hard work, and painstaking attention to detail. Since we were handling the most perishable of all food products, it was decidedly no place for a blind man. Dirty tools, scraps on the floor, waste and uncleanliness could only be eliminated by a real love of order and pride in workmanship. A workman who had never thought of his work as an exercise in craftsmanship had to be trained to identify himself with these aims in a very personal way. He had to be proud of his part in the hundreds of operations which led to perfection as nearly as we could achieve it. For we were aiming at nothing less. On this issue, I refused to be tolerant and it earned for me a well-deserved reputation for a quick, explosive temper and a caustic tongue. I don't think I ever flew off the handle at an honest mistake in judgment, but a meat scrap on the floor was something else again.

I incessantly preached that we were engaged in one of the most important tasks in the world—feeding people. Nothing that contributed to the quality of their food was too much trouble. Consumers might never know whether clean or dirty hands handled their food, whether knives, tubs, floors and utensils were scrubbed and clean-smelling, but we knew. Although we had to make a profit to stay in business, we were going to earn it, not by turning out vast quantities of poor products, but by the excellence in what we did.

In such a business, there were no unimportant workmen or opera-tions since everything contributed toward the final result. A blurred stencil on a package was important, for people naturally identified its contents with its appearance. Fresh, unused containers were assumed to be clean, but an assumption was by no means a certainty; hence the rule that every container must be inspected before it was filled. These things might seem small, but perfection was always an aggregate of small things, and perfection was no small thing.

As the business grew and others took over supervisory jobs, two rules were laid down for their guidance: their function was to look over the work the employees were doing and not to "overlook" it. An assistant foreman didn't get tough in the way he managed; he couldn't get tough and keep his job—not even with the newest recruit in his department. We were engaged in processing animals for food and not in killing off our human talent. We couldn't know, until he'd been given the opportunity to show us, each recruit's possibilities; it was his foreman's job to help us find out what they might be.

Applicants for the "clean jobs" in the business were generally invited to lug beef for awhile, or they went into the hide cellar, the fertilizer plant, the smokehouse, or the lard room. I saw no advantage in giving a man a place in the business, with perhaps authority over others, who hadn't gotten some grease, blood, and dirt on his hands and gone home at night with aching muscles, since every "clean" job rested on the man who had a "dirty" one. This rubbed out any illusions a man had about being "better" because he had different capacities or had gone away to school. And it gave the bright, young men we were trying to attract into the business a wholesome respect for the manual labor on which it rested and a speaking acquaintance with the men who make it possible.

Which brings me to Austin.

When I first made its acquaintance, it wasn't much of a place—if judged by numbers or wealth. It was just a little crossroads country town as seen from the depot by travelers on their way to the Twin Cities—and not very impressive, I'm afraid. But what it lacked in size, it made up in spirit. It was as cocky and bumptious as Chicago. Its citizens and the editors of its three weekly newspapers talked of its future in the most glittering word pictures. Before we had adequate water and sewage systems, we were told that "Austin ought to have a college, a park, telephones, and an electric street railway." When somebody tried to sell the town horsecars, people snorted in indignation. "The very idea is offensive," said the *Democrat*'s editor, Hunkins. "Let them sell horsecars to Albert Lea. Austin is going to be the brightest jewel in Minnesota's crown next to the Twin Cities. Such a city demands the best. Our transportation system will be electric."

Albert Lea, the county seat of neighboring Freeborn County, was the chief target of editorial spleen. For it, too, according to its citizens and the *Albert Lea Enterprise*, was the "gem of Southern Minnesota, the center of a contented, progressive community, the home of resistless energy, inexhaustible resources, and unparalleled advantages."

When it was reported that a well digger near Albert Lea had struck natural gas, Austin was stricken to the heart. The editor of the *Austin Register* tore off to see for himself. The editor of the *Albert Lea Enterprise* went along to gloat. The Austin man held a lighted match to the end of the pipe, and an unmistakable blue blaze appeared. "Ah ha!" crowed the *Enterprise*'s editor. "Now what do you say? I never expect to hear of you blowing Austin to the skies again!"

The Austin editor raced back home and, without stopping for breath, began raising funds for a test well in our town. "For," said he, with irrefutable logic, "if God put gas in the earth at Albert Lea, He probably put it here in Austin. Its discovery would make our cup run over. We should attract industry and save thousands spent for fuel."

His fellow editor, Hunkins, of the *Democrat*, was not to be stampeded, however. Although admitting that he couldn't "explain the blaze at the end of the pipe," he suspected a trick and suggested that "the only natural gas found at Albert Lea was generated in the office of the *Enterprise*."

A great deal of what went on in our town had its inspiration in the fertile brains of our newspaper editors, who were continually admonishing, urging, and needling the community spirit. As in ten thousand other American crossroads, no factor was so potent in building faith in the future and pride in the present. The newspapers were the tradition builders and the community cement. They lent their support to the time-tried and the new, and worked unceasingly to bring to "the greatest little city on God's green footstool" the benefits of the world beyond its borders.

No local enterprise was too small to be beneath an editor's notice. "Are we a city?" Hunkins would ask. We certainly were! And he would quote statistics to prove it:

"Puccini & Co. sold in one week ninety-six bunches of bananas, a thousand dozen, at retail. P. H. Zender made and sold in one day, just an ordinary day's sale, two hundred and seventy-six loaves of bread, eighty-three dozen assorted rolls, rusks, fried cakes and cookies, and twenty-six fruit cakes! Shupe, the barber, had four chairs and a central marble fountain, while Bailey's

barbershop had just installed the first rotating barber chair in
Southern Minnesota. Why shop elsewhere when the Austin
Secondhand Store carried everything in stock except cold pan-
cakes? Dr. Avery had extracted three teeth and had placed gold
fillings in seventeen others for Mrs. Ahlons. Dr. Lewis' patients
could now take advantage of a wonderful new dental chair with
a fountain cuspidor and a running water attachment for the
removal of saliva from the mouth while the patient was in a
recumbent position. Dr. Allen's new offices were magnificently
carpeted in green velvet Brussels."

In closing, the editor pointed out, "As a matter of fact, Austin has all
the enchantments that lure men onward and upward."

Needless to say, when I read in the *Democrat* that "George Hormel has tastefully decorated his Provision Market with sausages
wrapped in red, white and blue against a background of evergreens,"
or that Hunkins credited the Market with selling "one hundred fatted calves as veal last week," I might wonder where the editor got
his figures on those "fatted calves," but I, like Puccini and Zender,
would feel almost as good as if we had sold one hundred veal or one
thousand dozen bananas or twenty-six fruitcakes. Furthermore, we
might try to match Hunkins' optimistic estimates of our ability as
merchants by running a little advertising copy in his paper. And
once Hunkins pointed it out to them, people felt considerable pride
in their professional and businessmen's attempts to keep abreast
of the times, which further spurred us on—such is the power of the
press.

But the editors did more than spur private enterprise. They
were the custodians of the public's rights. While they never tired

of forecasting that "Austin will have twelve thousand population by the next census; it is the coming great city between the mighty Mississippi and the great Missouri," they were equally insistent that "the public has some rights upon the sidewalks opposite their own premises." In a great metropolis such as ours was soon to be, "owners of horses and cattle must abandon the practice of hitching livestock to lampposts to save a few cents worth of feed." Though they might chortle when "a man from Albert Lea arrived in town today who is thinking of establishing a broom factory; says he prefers Austin for investing his money," they were equally capable of tearing our civic pride to shreds by reminding us that "the citizens of Albert Lea voted to tax themselves for a new road grader," and we wouldn't. If Albert Lea's schoolrooms were better lighted than ours, we heard about that too. When "business and industrial leaders, one hundred strong, sat down to a banquet in the hotel where the walls were covered with banners, each having a merchant's name, and rare cactus plants were used in making a picture which, under the blaze of electric lights, was simply magnificent," Hunkins might piously hope that the purpose of this distinguished gathering might have something to do with "those rotting sidewalks and loose planks on Main Street."

Hunkins lived long enough to see his faith in Austin vindicated in a degree and himself the proud possessor of a flourishing, daily paper printed on a fine web press from machine-set type. His weekly *Democrat* became today's *Daily Herald*.

When I first made "the gem of Southern Minnesota's" acquaintance, it was not long removed from the caravans of creaking wagons, drawn by oxen harnessed in rawhide, I had seen pass through Toledo as a boy. In the late 1880's, prairie schooners heading toward the

Dakotas and the Canadian border still passed through town. Sometimes, lured by stories of the "inexhaustible resources and unparalleled advantages" to be had in Austin, these fortune seekers went no further but stayed to "locate." Their new home town, whose population did not reach five thousand until 1900—ten years after Hunkins' prophecy of "twelve thousand by the next census"—was a typical American melting pot blend. Germans and Scandinavians—many of them recent arrivals from Europe—predominated, with Holland Dutch, Bohemians, English, Irish, Scotch, and a scattering of Jews and Italians adding an international flavor to its basically old American pattern. For New Englanders, Southerners, and Midwesterners were present in sufficient numbers to fuse the old with the new.

Although most people had migrated here to farm, there were opportunities for the artisans among them. The Milwaukee railroad shops provided the town's largest monthly payroll—twenty thousand dollars—until their removal in 1900, but fine clay and cement beds provided material for such local industries as brick and tile, terra cotta ornamental pottery of fine quality, and cement. Possibly three hundred workers were employed in these activities and in flax fiber processing, vegetable canning and meat packing. When diversified farming supplanted the old one-crop system, the surrounding districts became increasingly productive. And, since both farmers and townsfolk were thrifty and industrious, Austin was able to support a surprisingly large number of social, cultural and business enterprises.

Against a background of people who were sturdy and independent, democratic and cooperative, it was not possible for industry to produce the sad results I had seen it produce for the workers of the big cities. There was a job for every willing worker and there was no reservoir of hungry unemployed who had to put up with anything the employer chose to dish out. Men wouldn't work for a job tyrant; they didn't have to. Nobody was destitute and no one more than well-to-do. Most people owned their own homes. The ones who didn't were saving toward that end. Public opinion—as it always should be—was here a potent factor to aid or curb the individual.

In the early 1890's, the retail clerks decided their hours of work were too long to give them any time with their families; they called upon their employers "not to make any compulsory demand but to take the matter up with businessmen and to cooperate with them." Among the twenty merchants in town, only one declined to consider his employees' point of view, the others agreeing that their clerks had a case. The dissenter's clerks got other jobs and he lost trade. The public agreed with the clerks that from eight a.m. until six-thirty p.m. was a long enough workday.

Citizens of our town took their community responsibilities seriously. Every business and professional man of my acquaintance devoted both time and money to an active part in municipal affairs—mostly as a "labor of love," for few city jobs had salaries attached to them, nor were taxpayers always grateful either. They often wanted public funds spent for projects that were not needed and, again, sometimes refused to pay for things they needed but mistakenly felt they could do without. For example, the importance of pure water and an adequate sewage system for protection of public health was little understood.

When my turn came to serve the city as alderman in 1894, I took up the problem of water supply as my special province, for its importance had been impressed upon me when Friedrich's market burned in 1887. A water system of sorts was installed, drawing its supply from shallow wells to fill a one hundred thousand gallon reservoir from which it ran into the city mains. But people now felt they wanted a pressure system, thinking more of protection against fire than of domestic water supply. They insisted that the city install fifty-two fire hydrants to four and a half miles of water mains—and never mind about water meters; each user would pay a flat rate. Since there was no object in saving water, they wasted it. Leaking faucets and conservation meant nothing to a householder whose pocketbook was not penalized for waste of a vital utility.

When the water level fell in summer and the wells began to dry up, water from the Cedar River was pumped into the mains and a serious epidemic followed, quelled only after six weeks' quarantine. Now people were as hysterically insistent upon a better water supply as before they had been stubbornly resistant. The council was deluged with proposals to buy up all the springs within miles of Austin, regardless of expense. It is at such times of public hysteria that officials must learn to keep their heads.

My fellow councilman, John L. Gulden, and I, who had been entrusted with the water problem, decided first to make a thorough survey of the geological formation of our section before doing anything. We consulted the state geologists and investigated the water supply of neighboring cities while the rest of the council and most of the townspeople fumed.

What we learned was that our wells needed only to be thrust deeper in order to draw on the ample water supply, which others were utilizing, from under the thick layer of St. Peter sandstone. By plugging our wells down to the sandstone and dynamiting the casing that was shutting off the water from the lime rock, and after installing meters to prevent careless waste, we were able to get all the water we needed from the wells we had. It was so simple a solution that we had a hard time making people believe that nothing more had to be done.

The establishment of a municipal power and light system was another project which presented civic problems. In order to make the city's investment a paying one, I urged that commercial rates be set up to encourage industrial use of electricity, since the current generated in the daytime before the householder turned on his lights must be used then or lost. What is accepted practice today, however, raised a storm of protest forty odd years ago. Why, people demanded, should we pay less for current used at the plant than they paid for lighting their homes?

From their point of view, my proposal was both discriminatory and self-serving. Since I was convinced to the contrary, I resigned from the Power Commission on which I had been serving. As a private citizen, I could promote, without adverse criticism, the fullest industrial use of power to the end that the city's increased income through its sale would in time reduce rates to the small householder—and this eventually came about.

I learned some important personal lessons from these adventures into public service: for one thing, not to be thin-skinned when facts were on my side but to keep on working toward a desired end no matter what adverse criticism might be encountered; and, for another, not to be deterred by public inertia from spending funds for needed improvement nor stampeded by public furor into unnecessary spending. I learned that, in making democracy work, it was just as important for the man who was exercising a public function to base his acts on what was right as it was for him to be guided by what the public thought it wanted. If he were merely a weather vane,

the public interest suffered as much as though he ignored it altogether. He couldn't always wait for "sentiment" to crystalize either.
It was as much his job to create public sentiment as to respond to
it. Whoever would be a leader in democracy had to be willing to put
his popularity to the test whenever his best judgment and that of the
taxpayers conflicted. They had a right to put him out of office, but
he had no right to pussyfoot because they might do so.

The paving of Main Street was a case in point. From the time I
arrived in Austin, permanent street and sidewalk paving had been
an issue. The council was always settling claims for accidents due
to loose planks in the wooden sidewalks. The street needed to be
widened and straightened as well as paved. But every time the council voted to undertake this work, a committee of outraged taxpayers, bearing long lists of names, would wait upon the city fathers
and the motion would be reconsidered. Many businessmen were as
shortsighted as the small homeowners. To all pleas for a real street
program, a large and vocal minority had one parrotlike answer,
"Reduce taxes."

Finally, some of us on the council decided we were going to pave
the streets for the greatest good of the greatest number regardless.
This news brought the usual "taxpayers' committee" running. I
agreed to bear the brunt of their arguments. By now I was used to
fighting for what I believed—and beginning to like it.

The *Herald*, which prided itself on being a family paper, reported
that historic fracas in these tempered words: "Mr. Hormel waxed
eloquent, pouring hot shots into the objectors. 'You show me a town
out of debt,' he cried, 'and I'll show you a dead town!'"

Main Street was paved that year.

And although we didn't know it, not a minute too soon. A year later, people crowded to the new cement curbs to watch the first "horseless carriage" seen in our town roll down its first paved street. Soon, even the objectors agreed that, with things like that about, we should have to begin to haul gravel for the roads.

But while Austin taxpayers were often reluctant to make other public improvements, this was not true of their attitude toward schools. When the town had a population of less than three thousand in 1869, they built a forty thousand dollar high school. This burned to the ground in 1890, but the day after the fire, pupils were attending classes in temporary quarters and the school board met and agreed to commence work at once on a bigger and better school. The problem of providing adequate facilities for every schoolchild was a town issue for years. When the census of 1900 gave Austin a population of five thousand, its school enrollment was one thousand and three hundred. People began agitating for a college before we had paved streets and sewers.

This attitude toward education in the Northwest was in marked contrast to that prevailing in some other sections of the country until well toward the close of the nineteenth century. I do not know when Minnesota adopted a compulsory school attendance law, but public opinion rather than compulsion was the leaven at work in our town. The largest part of our foreign population came from Northern European countries where illiteracy had long been considered a disgrace. Thus, while only five and a half million children, out of a total school age population of three times that number, received daily instruction in each term, according to the census of 1880, no such mass neglect of the young was true in Minnesota. As a consequence, the intense and savage dullness among the working classes in the great cities had no counterpart with us. Our schools, instead of being the rudest and least convenient buildings in the community, were the finest.

Education begat education. Parents in our town who could read and write, no matter how poor they might be, rarely removed a child from school before it had finished the grammar grades, as was customary when I was a boy. These were not the idle and the avaricious, nor the poverty-stricken slum dwellers who opposed compulsory education elsewhere on the grounds that it deprived them of their children's earnings.

The same kind of parental responsibility that kept children in school kept them off the streets in their free time. And I doubt if children anywhere had a happier time than they had in Austin in the days when, to quote the distinguished historian, Charles Beard, our unenlightened young "had not yet been weaned from the restricted living room of their urban homes" by the delights of movies, juke joints, and roadside taverns. The social life was homely, but built as it was around the activities of sports and music-loving Germans and Scandinavians—to say nothing of the gay and enterprising peoples of other cultures who composed its citizenry—the child or adult who could not find some niche or group in which to play was strange indeed.

In the days before people depended upon commercial amusements and spectator sports to provide them with entertainment, they seemed amazingly well able to organize barbecue suppers, strawberry festivals, sleigh and hayrides, bicycle excursions, amateur theatricals, baseball, football and hockey teams, and an infinite variety of fraternal lodges, patriotic and civic organizations, and self-improvement clubs. And they still found time to work ten hours a day on weekdays and go to church on Sundays.

We did all these things and, looking back from a softer age, I wonder how.

In summer, the *Belle of Austin* chugged up and down the Cedar River carrying boatloads of merrymakers to strawberry festivals in Columbia Park, where the young people waltzed in the rustic pavilion to the music of Tische's orchestra. The Park was the favorite site of roast suckling pig suppers given by the young blades of the town who handsomely entertained their girls at feasts prepared by themselves.

These young fellows at the "sparking age," like my brothers, belonged to the "Terpsichorean Society" which sponsored "grand balls" for members of "The Young Ladies' Social Club," who, in turn, entertained the boys at what Hunkins called "elaborate functions." Together they produced *Pinafore* and other light operas and sometimes "home talent" plays at the Opera House.

Summer also brought Saturday evening band concerts—and the circus. The whole countryside flocked into town to see Ringlings' or Forepaugh's spangled elephants majestically swing down Main Street. And every boy in Mower County was on hand when Stearn's Wild West Show made its annual appearance. Big-eyed, they watched painted Sioux braves in war bonnets and long-haired Indian scouts on prancing buckskins relive the not so old days their grandfathers had helped to make history.

The Kickapoo Indian Medicine Show was another of our prized summer visitors until one of the noble red men of the company, after imbibing too freely of the white man's firewater, put on an unscheduled show of his own. Under the expert guidance of old Indian fighters, he was relieved of his tomahawk and lodged in jail until he cooled off. Then, in the interests of public safety, the company was ordered to leave town and forbidden to return. After that sad occurrence, Austin's sufferers had to get along as best they could without Kickapoo's "secret, invaluable, and never-failing boon to mankind."

It is only fair to Kickapoo to say, however, that when the "grip" seized the town the following winter and the *Austin Register*'s editor solicited the advice of the laity and the profession on what to do about it, many staunch supporters of the Indian remedy decided to get their next winter's supply—if they lived until summer—even if they had to catch up with the show in Albert Lea to do it!

Their determination becomes easier to understand after a look at what the doctors ordered. Dr. Hollister advised the sufferers to "put a fifty-pound piece of ice on the head, the feet in boiling water, and keep them there until the ice melts." Dr. Allen said, "Keep the head cool, the feet hot, eyes open and mouth shut. This good, all-around remedy will keep you out of trouble." A member of the laity, Con Weisel, reported, "Eat nothing but salt mackerel and black coffee; they cured me in three weeks." Besides these drastic and uncertain means, Kickapoo's positive promise, "Relief for grip within one half hour or your money back," looked like a sure thing.

There were other things on which to take chances besides the doctors' opinions. The town and countryside boasted some fast thoroughbreds. Horse shows with Roman chariot races, trotting, pacing, and saddle events, offered further scope for red-blooded citizens, as did a small professional baseball club backed by them.

For those who preferred the drama to the sport of kings, the Austin Opera House offered frequent fare, since companies playing out of New York en route to the Twin Cities generally stopped off at our town to give a performance. People flocked to see Walker Whiteside in *Shylock* or a notable cast perform *Richelieu* or *Faust*. Celebrities such as Mrs. General Tom Thumb played to "standing room only." *East Lynne, The Old Homestead* and *Way Down East* were still good, although we had grown a bit beyond *Uncle Tom's Cabin*. On its last appearance in the 1890's, Hunkins dismissed it: "The same old chestnuts, only a little more decayed."

Music was a living thing of the people—and some very good music too. The Scandinavians and the Germans had their *saengerfests*, and other singing societies also did a great deal to foster a love of music and to develop such community talent as existed. There was a popular Ladies' Double Quartet and Tische's Orchestra—both in great demand at home and public functions. More than one of the church choral groups was under the direction of men who had been trained to Europe's exacting standards. St. Olaf's Lutheran Church and other congregations were justly proud of their fine choirs.

The activities embraced by the word "culture" were as generously supported and as enthusiastically pursued as open sports and entertainment. The Ladies' Floral Club, founded in 1867, did much to improve the town's yards and gardens and, as a sideline, managed the library in those pre-Carnegie days. When the club celebrated its twenty-fifth anniversary in 1892, the ladies announced that they had accumulated two thousand, five hundred volumes in the library and that five thousand membership cards had been issued to readers throughout the county—two cards to a volume!

Another group of busy housewives, the Ladies' Cemetery Association, announced as their purpose that "every grave would have a plant by Decoration Day." The Ladies took care of building fences, restoring tumbledown tombstones, keeping records of the last resting places of the old pioneers; they chased out the gophers, planted trees and flowers, and generally kept the desecrating hand of time at bay. And if this were not enough, they organized a winter lecture course to gather funds for support of their good work.

There was a Ladies' Literary Club and a University Club, which vied with each other in bringing celebrities from the Twin Cities or Chicago. Professor Maria Sanford came down from the State University to launch Shakespeare and Browning classes, traveling by the night freight in order to spend the evening in Austin and meet her morning classes next day. The lady doctor of the town, Dr. Corneveaux, organized a Phrenological Club. Among other "advance social and literary features," as the *Herald* phrased it, were a Whist Club and a Physical Culture Society, with a large and enthusiastic membership dedicated to Indian clubs and croquet.

Church was an important factor in our lives. Here too there was a place for everyone. Freedom of worship embraced the newest and the oldest Christian concepts. Catholics, Christian Scientists, Lutherans, Universalists, Methodists, Baptists, Episcopalians, Congregationalists, and Presbyterians were active among us. Our pastors were fervent men who worked as hard on behalf of the community as they did for their particular groups.

My brother Henry, who relinquished his settlement work in the slums of Chicago to join us in 1894, organized the Central Presbyterian Church which remained in his charge until 1900. This church, like most of the others in town, was the joint product of its members' handiwork. After our day at the plant, Frank Hummel and I, with a small hand press, helped turn out cement bricks which were as perfect as any pressed brick on the market. During forty years they have hardened and today have a soft, grey tone which is very attractive.

The workaday Christian humanism of my brother and his fellow ministers reminded us—on the one day we could be reached above the din of the marketplace—that we were here to serve larger ends than our own. That indeed we could not serve this end profitably unless we conceived ourselves to be one and indivisible with the whole of humanity. Henry, especially, never tired of pointing out that political democracy was basically an aspect of the Golden Rule in action.

It has always been interesting to me to see how treating the other fellow as you would like to be treated works out in a specific instance. In these days, when we hear so much about what will and won't work in the Old World, when all the hates, prejudices and antagonisms which separate men are trotted out as justification for barbaric treatment and discrimination, the great American art of fusing all the elements in its citizenry into workable social instruments, as I saw it at work in the town of Austin as a social laboratory of the American frontier, assumes new significance.

Whenever I think of life in these United States, I think of the life in its little towns as I have known them. Surely, above all, they have been a haven for the nurture of the American dream and the tempering of the American spirit.

CHAPTER NINE

"Him That Thinketh He Standeth"

Although I was the apparently prosperous leader of a flourishing business, not until 1929—when Hormel stock was placed on the Chicago Stock Exchange—were my circumstances such that I could really feel I owned a surplus dollar. Most of the time, there was a mortgage on our home and my life insurance was in hock. Such hostages to fortune tend to reduce any tendency toward the big head and they are apt to produce an uncertain disposition.

These were busy years, sometimes fraught with near catastrophe, but they were also rewarding. Where the business was concerned, it seemed from time to time that we had reached the point where we could ease up a bit. Its equipment and facilities were sufficiently modern and extensive to take care of its needs for years to come, I would tell myself. Now I would have the opportunity to garner some of the rewards of hard work—maybe leisure in which to see the world or at least to take a long anticipated vacation.

Walking through the plant with George Peterson one day in 1903, I said, "Well, George, this is enough. We won't build anymore."

"We've come a long way," he commented, "in eleven years."

We had. The Milwaukee Railroad had at last been persuaded to build a spur to the plant. We no longer needed to drive livestock through the streets from the railroad yards. Much new equipment had been installed. We were catching up with the times. A machine shop, an engine room, an ammonia compressor, electricity, and a steam hoist were some of our new aids to progress. And we were now doing a million dollars worth of business a year. Who could ask for more?

Farmers were getting the largest piece of the money, and such a large ready cash market for their livestock did much to spur their interest in animal husbandry. The fat stock exhibit at the Mower County Fair, with special cash premiums offered by Geo. A. Hormel & Co., attracted farmers from miles around. Since fine hogs, cattle and sheep meant a better product for us and better prices for the farmers, the upgrading of herds and flocks was of mutual benefit and the numbers of such animals available rapidly increased. About this time we registered the name "Dairy Brand" with the U.S. Patent Office, by which we designated our finest milk-fed pork products.

The year following my walk with Peterson found us in the midst of a bigger plant expansion than before.

My brother Henry, who had left Austin to become pastor of another "packinghouse church" in Ottumwa, Iowa, was primarily responsible for this change in our affairs. One of his parishioners, Thomas D. Foster, was the local head of John Morrell & Co., a branch of an old established English concern which had a large European outlet for packinghouse products—more than the Ottumwa plant could provide. On a visit to my brother, I met Mr. Foster and, after learning about my business, he thought that some mutually profitable arrangement might be worked out between us—and he was right. The Morrell company needed production and we needed money. We increased our capital structure to five hundred thousand dollars and our board of directors to nine. Morrell bought seven hundred and fifty preferred shares for seventy-five thousand dollars and named four directors of the enlarged board. Almost overnight, the business was off to a new and different future.

The volume doubled in one year and tripled in three. All our facilities were inadequate to the demands made upon them. We needed more men and money, more water, power, and refrigeration. Every dollar we earned went back into the plant. We advertised "men wanted." We tore down buildings almost as fast as we built them—they were never big enough. A five-story curing house rose in a newly acquired cow pasture. I made a trip to England with Mr. Foster to improve my understanding of the export trade.

For the past several years, it had been our custom to close down for a day and go on a picnic to Litchfield Park. In the parade to our annual holiday that year (1905), five hundred people walked. The lady clerks rode in carriages. The traveling salesmen made quite a section by themselves. I had been so busy that not until I saw all the organization together did I realize how large it had grown in so short a time.

My surprise was nothing compared to that of my fellow townsman, the editor of the *Herald*. He wrote, "The parade came as a big surprise to many who had a general idea of the number, but it was not until they saw the army of men in a body that the real truth came out. There were more than two hundred and fifty well-dressed women and children in the parade in addition to the employees."

His last sentence gave me a real thrill! I mentioned it to my wife. "Yes," she said, "it really means something—'well-dressed women and children.' People as well-fed and well-dressed as you and I. You can be proud of your part in that."

I was also proud that the business offered increasing opportunity to ambitious farmers, more of whom were coming into town to work for us in their slack season, winter, our busiest time. Many who had been handicapped for lack of labor-saving tools were now able to acquire them. One farmer, whose son and three young brothers worked for us and lived at home, was able to lift the mortgage from his farm through their contributions. The constant stream of money pouring into the countryside as wages or from livestock sales worked wonders in the increased well-being of the farming community. Farmwives had better clothes and equipment too, and more farm children went away to school. Some farmers invested their savings in Hormel preferred stock, thus establishing another relationship.

As the business increased in size and importance, new relationships were established, notably in finance. Where formerly I had had to beg for a line of credit, now such banks as the Security National of Minneapolis and the Corn Exchange Bank of Chicago offered working funds without solicitation. As I had foreseen, when a man demonstrated ability to put money profitably to use, owners of money sought that man.

A red letter year was 1906. I bought myself the first expensive plaything I had ever owned—a White Steamer automobile. Also, the Pure Food and Drug Act became the law of the land.

We were not among those food processors who opposed the passage of this act on the grounds of its constitutionality. In the first place, conditions in many packinghouses were bad. The workers lacked sanitary facilities necessary to health and cleanliness. Wooden tables, carts, tubs, floors and walls were greasy and water-soaked—perfect dirt collectors. Buildings were dark vaults without light and ventilation. Refuse was allowed to collect and meat was handled without regard to the most elementary health conditions. What I knew to be true from firsthand observation in the meat industry was equally true in the plants of other food processors. Inferior fruits and vegetables found their way into jams and catsup, just as inferior meat became sausage. Food purveyors, properly conducting their businesses, had nothing to fear from public regulation. Indeed, they stood to gain. In my opinion, everybody stood to gain.

Honest goods would no longer have to compete with products cheapened with adulterants. Efficiency in management and not chiseling on quality would decide who should stay in business. Regulation would end this kind of unfair competition. Consumers, once assured that commercially processed foods were produced under conditions both sanitary and decent, would become buyers of such products on a scale hitherto undreamed of. The workers in such industries, as well as the consumer public, would no longer be subjected to unnecessary health hazards, with a resultant increase in plant efficiency which would more than make up for the added expense of improving conditions.

Incidentally, those of us who were conscious of our public responsibility were getting mighty tired of being under constant attack for the sins of others. After the appearance of Upton Sinclair's *The Jungle*, with its exaggeration and misplacement of incidents, the articles of Charles Edward Russell in *Everybody's Magazine*, in which he charged all packers with graft, corruption, and uncleanliness, and similar attacks in the *Outlook,* it would have been a tough packer, indeed, whose head wasn't several sizes too small for his hat.

Louis F. Swift, speaking for Swift & Company, attempted to answer these charges—emphatically denying many—but the public was in no mood to listen or be fair. The big packers had not been overly sensitive to the public's interests. Now the shoe was on the other foot. The public had them on the run and has kept them running ever since.

There was one provision of the new Meat Inspection Act which I did consider most unfair. The purpose of the law was to safeguard the public health—a purpose with which no one can quarrel—and the cost of its administration should have been provided for out of public funds.

A packer buys animals from the stockman in good faith. If they look to be healthy, he has no way of determining that they are not. The government inspector examines each animal as it passes before him on the killing rail. Before slaughtering, he is no better able to judge its conditions than we are. If the inspector finds evidence of infection no bigger than the point of a lead pencil in the neck glands, then the animal is tagged. If, further on, the viscera shows infection, the animal is dropped in the fertilizer tank.

The country slaughterer's operations did not come within the province of the Act. This, among others, is one good reason for not buying meat which does not bear the familiar blue "U.S. Inspected" stamp. You may be sure that meat lacking the stamp has neither been inspected nor produced on premises subject to government regulations. Besides health, the great waste of valuable byproducts needed in both peace and war are further reasons why the public should not encourage country slaughtering beyond a farmer's own needs. The use value lost to medicine alone through country slaughtering is tremendous, since many lifesaving drugs are only obtainable from animal tissues ordinarily thrown away. And the public should always keep in mind that, once those telltale neck glands and viscera are removed, nobody knows just by looking at a piece of meat whether the animal it came from was healthy or not. Black markets can be dangerous in more ways than one.

The coming of the government inspectors to Austin found us already conforming to the new laws. Dr. M. O. Anderson and W. H. Ritman, permanently assigned to the plant, and the traveling inspectors who went over it, inch by inch, were most complimentary. Tile, brick, and rustproof metal had long been our specified building and equipment materials. Our consumption of caustic soda and soap was prodigious. We did not establish our own laundry for another year, but a clean smock every day was another standing rule. There was plenty of air and light. I wanted to prevent careless dropping of meat scraps on the floor—those little scraps that meant a profit at the year's end if they went into sausage and lard and not into fertilizer.

When news of the inspectors' presence got around town, our local news hawks came over to interview them and watch them at work. Judging from their comments, they had all read *The Jungle*.

"It is indeed comforting," said the *Herald*, "to learn from the traveling inspectors that our packinghouse ranks among the most perfect in the entire country, from a sanitary standpoint."

And we were particularly pleased when some of our practices were incorporated into government regulations for all similar enterprises. Our workers' morale had always been good, but this public recognition gave them increased pride in the part they played in the organization.

Visiting city packers going through the plant often commented on our people's fine appearance—how superior they looked to the general run of packinghouse employees. They were superior, partly, I believe, because they felt differently about themselves. In consequence, our production per man was much greater than in the average plant at stockyard centers. Living under better social conditions, they produced more and earned more. We insisted upon discipline, but men like discipline where it is fairly and impartially administered. It has been my experience that when men know how to do what is expected of them, they prefer to meet high standards of performance.

As the business reached proportions where it is very easy for management to lose contact with the production end, I was careful to see that I was not engulfed with executive duties which kept me out of the plant. Other men could perform many of these duties as well as I could. Every day I made the rounds of every department. Management, for the worker, isn't the front office; it's the foreman. I met with them daily. Since the foreman is the hub of most labor trouble, and no department is more efficient than the man directly in charge of its operations, I never let anything else interfere with the training and counseling of these men. They were always the best I could find. We kept a sharp lookout among the workmen for supervisory material. When we found a likely prospect, we tapped him on the shoulder just as soon as he was ready for more responsibility. A senior foreman who couldn't produce competent assistant foremen in his department had to tell us why. Free enterprise can't be free for the men at the top and hogtied for those at the bottom and get along. Advancement and promotion is the only way to operate such a system without stripping its gears—the only way I know to identify a workman's interests as being consistent with those of management.

Since Morrell & Co. had in mind the building of a new plant in Sioux Falls, South Dakota, the arrangement with them, which had served both firms well, was terminated in 1907. We reacquired the stock held by them and once again became a local enterprise, beginning our seventeenth year "out of hock," so to speak. Since the profits were kept at home, more money was available for plant expansion and improvements. Some of it was spent for five acres of new cement hog pens roofed over, each pen connected with piped water for cleansing and drinking. This added to the comfort of the animals and reduced flies and odors, which benefited the community as well as ourselves. Although we had a large and flourishing poultry and egg business, we abandoned handling poultry at the plant because we could not control the dirt. A great deal of our time and money was consumed, like the housekeeper's, in chasing dirt and in keeping up what we had after we got it.

By the time the momentous year, 1914, arrived, we were still a little business, but much had happened in between. We had survived corn crop failures, the depression of 1907, severe hog cholera epidemics, and disastrous floods. After each crisis passed, I used to wonder how we had managed to meet it without greater loss than we suffered. But the organization was always adequate, somehow, to the demands of circumstances and that was what really mattered. There were gains to offset losses. We even carried coals to Newcastle.[10]

In 1913, the Interstate Commerce Commission issued an order reducing freight rates on fresh and cured meats shipped from Northwestern points to the East. For the first time, we could compete

---

10 Something brought or sent to a place where it is already plentiful.

with Chicago packers on something like equal terms. Our location, which heretofore had disadvantages, was now an asset. Doing business next door to livestock producers eliminated shipping charges on live weights hauled long distances, brokers' commissions and stockyard feeding charges, all of which were added to Chicago packers' costs.

At the same time that the I.C.C. reduced Northwestern rates to Chicago, it also changed the rate schedules from Mississippi points to the East. We could now also compete on even terms with Iowa packers, who had formerly enjoyed preferential treatment. But when we announced that we were going to open a selling branch in Chicago, many people thought we were crazy, that success had gone to our heads. They were sure of it when they learned that our bid for the Chicago market was to be based upon quality alone. As a matter of fact, this was all we could offer.

Three days was the minimum time between our receipt of an order and its delivery in Chicago. Since we couldn't compete with Chicago packers on price alone, only one thing remained—quality. Our salesmen sold merchandise on the basis that, if the product was not superior to anything obtainable elsewhere, the goods were still ours. All we asked the butcher to do was to let his customers judge the superiority of our merchandise—his most particular customers. If, in their opinion, it did not live up to all we claimed for it, the risk was not his. Anything we sold him, he could sell on a money-back guarantee.

It was slow going at first. But we kept on hammering away until one day somebody had an inspiration. "Why don't we place a ten-pound pail of fresh, farmer-style pork sausage on consignment with every butcher in Chicago? Sure, the butchers and the Chicago packers utilize their trimmings in this way, but we know that people buy ours by preference. They say it is the best they ever ate. Let's tell this to Chicago."

We did. They believed us. So, some forty odd years after I began life as a bit player in Chicago's "Drama of the Hog," I was back competing with the "Titans of Pork" in their own bailiwick, selling Hormel to the most discriminating meat buyers in this country.

By then we had sold many millions of pounds of meat in Europe—a third of our business was export—and we had opened successful branch houses in Minneapolis, Saint Paul, Duluth, and in San Antonio, Texas. But none of these accomplishments gave me quite as much satisfaction as sending those first refrigerator cars to Chicago with "Hormel, Austin, Minnesota" emblazoned on their sides. The fact that we could send those cars at all said a lot for the country's determination to keep the door open for all private enterprise regardless of size; it was, to me, another evidence that the machine age could be brought under social control without invalidating the rules governing freedom of choice. While food processors were held to minimum standards of quality, every one of us was equally free to make anything we chose of finer quality than any similar product. Now we were all equally free to sell it where and to whom we could.

But events soon took my mind off Chicago. Overnight, we were swamped with demands from our overseas customers. Within a few weeks after receiving the cables ordering vast amounts of cured meats, the reason was plain. Europe was on the march again. And again we were short of men and facilities, for in the midst of our round-the-clock efforts to meet Europe's need for food, Company G was ordered to the Mexican border, taking a number of our scarce and valuable men. To prevent any undue hardship to the families of the men suddenly called to duty, we arranged for wage compensation to be paid to them during the men's absence. I found time to act as a member of a civic committee named to raise funds for the relief of other soldiers' families abruptly left without their breadwinners. Then and since, I have often wondered why it wasn't possible for society to plan for these situations in advance of their coming. As long as society relies upon guns to solve its problems, it ought to be able to make provision for the families of the men it asks to use the guns.

We had a week of hard rain that spring. The Cedar River became a rushing torrent. Early on a Sunday afternoon, I was called to the telephone. "The Water Street dam is out," said my brother John.

This was a major catastrophe. When the water ran out of the mill-pond, we would have no source of water for the ammonia condenser. With the machinery shut off, millions of pounds of meat would spoil for lack of refrigeration. The city also depended upon the water flowing over the dam to operate its turbine. There would be no electric lights and no power. We were now helpless without the genii of the dynamo we had come to depend on.

John rushed off to Minneapolis to find an oversized pump and gasoline powered motor. Another of our men, Chuck O'Berg, went with him to arrange with the railroad for an extra train to bring the equipment to Austin. Men at the plant and every able-bodied man in town worked feverishly, day and night, without sleep, to build a sump in the river and lay an oversized pipeline to the water and light plant. Racing against the disappearing flood tide, we managed to install the new equipment almost at the hour the river dropped below the level of the city's intake pump. While it was being tested, the whole town held its breath. Would it work? It did! Tired men sought their beds for the first time in days. Once again, we had surmounted a crisis worse than a smallpox epidemic in the old days.

Those of us who understood what failure in this instance would have meant gained a new appreciation of the profound change which had taken place in society with the coming of electric power. We had formerly thought of it as a good servant. It was now revealed as something else. A community dependent on its tireless energy faced a breakdown in its vital lifelines on a scale virtually impossible under the old order—any interruption in its ceaseless flow spelled wholesale disaster. I really understood, for the first time, another fact: whoever controlled the master switch in the powerhouse controlled communal life in all its phases. We had witnessed an illuminating and frightening demonstration of what could happen to men in this new age of power. Through its use we had gained freedom from much backbreaking toil—but at a price.

To protect the business against a repetition of this disaster, we bought the Water Street and McAfee dam sites and commenced to build reinforced concrete dams sufficiently sturdy to hold back the Mississippi. We also acquired a small, one hundred and fifty barrel a day flour mill along with the Water Street dam site. By the time this dam was completed, the United States was at war and the old mill had been converted into a one thousand barrel mill, working twenty-four hours a day to supply a fraction of the demand for food.

Many of our valuable men from the office and the plant left for the Army and for jobs where profit was figured on ten percent of costs, the costs payable out of unlimited public funds. The leading men who remained in our employ, as well as branch managers, were continually being offered higher pay, which we had to meet. While we were constantly urged to keep down the cost and to produce more food—"food will win the war"—our manpower was being drained away through wasteful and discriminatory practices favoring one group of producers at the expense of all others and the public purse. I vowed that, if another war occurred during my active business career, I would choose to shoulder a gun and fight in the trenches, rather than conduct a business.

To help keep down the soaring cost of living for our own people, we put on a garden campaign. The company provided eighty acres, manured and plowed, and the services of an experienced gardener-instructor. Many of the two hundred men who joined the Hormel Garden Club, in addition to their caring for their plots in the eighty acres, also planted gardens in many vacant lots around town. The members planted whatever they pleased in their plots in the main garden and were free to exchange produce with each other or to give it away; their only restriction was that the plantings should conform to a plan so that horse-drawn cultivators could be used. As a result of this carefully planned cooperative venture, a large yield of first quality vegetables was obtained at an expenditure of time and energy within the means of men working long hours.

The company also made it possible for the men to purchase Liberty Bonds on terms advantageous to themselves. We bought the bonds outright. They could be paid for on installments of as little as fifty cents a week. The eventual owner got the interest which accrued to the bonds while in our possession, and paid no interest to us for the accommodation. Consequently, when we urged our people to add to their capital through purchasing bonds, the ones without ready cash were not penalized by being forced to borrow money from the bank at six percent to pay for a bond bearing four percent interest, and the small wage deduction made it possible for workers in the low income bracket to own at least one bond. We never had to plead with anyone to do his duty in the bond drives. On this basis people were glad to mortgage their future earnings.

I had watched my son growing more restive every day after the declaration of war but kept hoping, in spite of evidence to the contrary, that he could be induced to continue with his part in the indispensable job of producing food. From the time he was a little fellow, he had worked in the plant after school and during vacations. Jay thoroughly understood the business and shared with the men the responsibility of management. If he went into the Army, it would be all but impossible for me to find anyone able and willing to take over his work as an experienced packinghouse executive. But knowing his disposition, I was doubtful that he would consent to stay at home no matter how important a contribution he could make as a civilian. When I sounded him out, he confirmed my opinion.

"Deferment is out of the question, Dad," he said. "Perhaps I could be more useful here, but what would people say if you had me deferred? Why, simply that you don't want to risk your son's neck. I know that this would be more unfair to you than leaving you in the lurch would be. And to ask me to stay home when every able-bodied, young fellow my age is expected to join up is hardly fair to me."

He was right. I could see that, for the best reason in the world, it was unfair to place him in a position where people could question his motive or to deprive him of a share in the risks of his generation.

He had gone to school at Shattuck where he had received military training. While waiting to be called, he organized a company of young men and busied himself initiating them into the mysteries of "squad right."[11] To his great joy, his number was among the first

_____

11 A military drill instruction.

to be called. He was told to await orders to report to Camp Dodge at Des Moines, Iowa. But the days passed and no order came. Impatient of further waiting, he went to Camp Dodge without orders. The officers, busy with the paperwork of organizing the 351st Infantry, 88th Division, refused to admit him. He refused to go away. Finally, tired of his importunities, they swore him in on September 5th, 1917, and put him to work scrubbing tables and floors around the cantonment. Without a doubt, Jay had gotten his wish; he was in the army now!

His insistence gained for him the distinction of being the first enlisted man in the 351st Infantry and the first Minnesotan to report for duty at the camp. Once in, Jay made up for lost time. Nine days after he enlisted he was made a corporal and, by the end of the month, had been promoted to regimental sergeant major. Commissioned second lieutenant in October, he was sent to France in January where he put his packinghouse know-how to good use.

He was assigned to the chief quartermaster at Tours, who had charge of the distribution of meat to the A. E. F.—American Expeditionary Forces. The number of refrigerator cars at the disposal of the quartermaster's department were far too few for the enormous task of supplying the many camps throughout France with fresh beef and pork. The beef was sent from the United States frozen in quarters. It was up to the men in charge of its routing to know when and where this frozen meat could safely be transported without additional refrigeration, and to see that the few available cars were used to the best advantage in supplying troops farthest from the base.

As the number of American soldiers in France increased, cargo space on land and sea became wholly inadequate. How to feed more men with no increase in transport facilities became a quartermaster's headache. To meet the situation, Jay pursued the idea of boning the beef and shipping the frozen meat in tightly packed boxes. This would increase cargo capacity by forty percent, since it would eliminate inedible waste by that amount. He was requested to write out a courier cable outlining the plan to Washington. General Pershing sent the cable over his signature. As a result, Jay was detailed to the quartermaster general's office in Washington to take charge of putting his plan into operation. There he worked out rules and specifications so that different packers filling war orders would uniformly bone and pack their products.

When news of Jay's activities came back to Austin, I was more than glad that he had followed his inclinations even though, as I had feared, we were unable to find a trained man to replace him. The Army had called up one hundred and seventy other Hormel men but, despite a shortage in personnel, we were breaking all former records in getting out food. Ninety-three million pounds of fresh and cured meats left our shipping dock in 1918.

Under the tremendous inflationary pressures of wartime demand and wartime wages, prices spiraled at a rate impossible to control or anticipate. At one time, large purchasers of our products were able to offer hams at twenty-four cents a pound which they had bought six weeks before, while we were quoting forty cents a pound for the same quality ham. Profiteering? No. Packers were bidding against each other. Farmers were holding back for higher prices and the rapid advance in cost of hogs increased the cost of hams.

The temptation to speculate by withholding goods or piling up inventories was irresistible to most people. But, from the beginning of the business, I had firmly resolved that price speculation was one pitfall we could avoid. This policy saved us after November 11, 1918. Almost overnight, hog prices reversed and dropped from an expected twenty cents a pound live weight to twelve cents, and packers with big inventories took a licking. We were forced to take a sizable loss on goods on hand but, in the face of the most ruinous decline in the history of the packing industry, we earned a small profit in 1919. If a large deficit through inventory losses had been added at this time to the catastrophe waiting for us around the corner, we could not have survived them both.

Up until now, I had always thought of myself as being a fairly forward-looking businessman, not too far behind the times on social questions, but some postwar trends found me convinced that American business was headed for the skids. I had foreseen that the war would release energies and ideas which would profoundly affect American life and had delivered myself of the opinion, at our annual plant holiday in 1918, that "the men who are to conduct the great enterprises of the future are the boys who are now fighting shoulder to shoulder in Europe. There they are all equal and they will see that less inequality exists after the war. . . . A purer and more comprehensive democracy will be developed." But face to face with the postwar world, I was unable to see that it was feasible to introduce wage and hour reforms at a time when postwar economics had forced down prices, thrown men out of work, and generally demoralized the business picture.

For the life of me, I couldn't figure how business could grant an eight-hour day with no reduction in wages. Although I had grown up in an era when men worked fourteen hours a day, and I had seen that working day reduced to twelve and then to ten hours with no decrease in productivity and at ascending wage scales; still, to my way of thinking, an eight-hour day at a ten-hour wage scale coming now would put the nation out of competition for foreign business and would increase the cost of production to where the domestic consumer could no longer afford to buy. Goods would pile up faster than consumed, and more men would be without jobs.

I was so dead wrong that now I wonder why I couldn't see the obvious. But like most businessmen of my generation who had been conditioned to long hours and hard work in an era when success could be achieved only through such means, I only partially understood the true nature and function of a machine age society. Even though we used machines, we didn't think machines—we still unconsciously reacted to old, industrial habit patterns—and while we were saying "machines," we were thinking of them in terms of human muscle, not mechanical horsepower. I lived in a power age for a third of a century before I learned to think in its terms.

After the war, there was no unemployment in Austin. To that extent, our problem differed from that of our competitors in the great centers of population. There was such a shortage of local manpower that we went to great lengths to induce men to come to Austin. But Eastern packers were cutting wages. The Big Six had lost much of their overseas trade, had taken huge inventory losses, and as a result posted two sharp wage reductions in one year, wage cuts amounting to as much as twelve percent. Each time Eastern packers posted wage cuts, we hesitated—between the devil and the deep blue sea. In a highly competitive business where profit is figured on fractions of a cent, to buck the trend of lower operating costs and prices meant eventually losing our markets. If we followed suit and cut wages, labor trouble was sure to result.

I was learning something else, too. As long as our business field of operation was more or less restricted, we could do things we couldn't do when we attempted to go after volume. Longtime customers in

Minneapolis might buy Hormel products at a price slightly over competition, but we couldn't sell Chicago when the gap between our prices and those of our competitors widened conspicuously.

We had always found it profitable to pay better than prevailing wages. Even though we had not been able to avoid a wage cut, our rates were still substantially above Chicago's when Chicago packers announced the second cut. Soon, every packing center in the United States was operating under strike conditions. Labor was in arms. Thousands of employees were idle and all plants operated on a reduced scale.

It was in the midst of all this turmoil that President Harding called Judge E. H. Gary to Washington in an effort to avoid another disastrous steel strike. Steel workers had gone on strike in 1919 for shorter hours and lost. Steelmakers contended that conditions in their industry demanded a twelve hour working day. They had been forced to reduce the hours in some departments to ten, but a general eight-hour day was out of the question, they said. Three eight-hour shifts instead of two twelve-hour shifts would ruin them, since mills must operate around the clock—certainly if labor received the same wages for the shorter shift.

The judge was on the spot. Many of the rest of us felt that we were on the spot with him. Men worked long hours in our industries too. If Big Steel yielded, public opinion, which was on the side of the shorter working day, would force acceptance elsewhere. Combined pressures from government, organized labor, and the public could not be resisted. As a human being I felt one thing, as a businessman another. Eight hours was long enough, but what would happen to business if it were forced to meet higher operating costs in a downswing?

We soon found out. Gary, under hard protest, established the eight-hour workday in Big Steel. Other industries, ours among them, followed steel. Within six months, increased buying power through reemployment increased mass consumption to the point where prices and wages could be stabilized. Men working shorter hours were fresher and the output per man hour greatly increased. Employers were forced to use high-priced labor more efficiently. This meant replacing obsolete machines and techniques. Most plant managers found, after they had given their establishments a good overhaul, that they could increase production past the stage where the higher wages were a burden. We did. The better feeling between employers and workers alone was an asset worth money to any business enterprise.

As the scales began to fall from my eyes, I suddenly realized that the machine, once its function and possibilities were properly understood by industry, offered the American manufacturer the greatest mass market in the world—his home market. He had the means of production; the age-old problem of how to produce enough was solved. From here on, the problem was wholly one of distribution, not of goods but of income—the spreading of wealth into the pockets of consumers automatically created the demand for his goods.

I could see that, in the future, benevolent paternalism on the part of employers was not going to be enough. Industrial peace and prosperity depended upon a real understanding of the relationship between men and machines, of production and the circulation of money through all the arteries of trade. Furthermore, I could see that, whether we liked it or not, the times had sounded the death knell to the old industrial individualism. Few manufacturers confined their activities to particular localities. We sold our products in all forty-eight states, in competition with similar products produced under varying local conditions. Well-paid labor in one area could not afford to compete with poorly-paid labor in another. Identity of interest would force the former to aid the latter or lose its gains. More labor leaders were coming to see this and they would soon see that underconsumption, because of low purchasing power in part of the country, was as great a loss to labor as it was to commerce and industry.

While I underwent no change of heart which made me more willing than I had ever been to subject our business to outside control, either through government or organized labor, I became increasingly sure that, unless I could develop the same kind of leadership in this situation as I had during the formative years of the business, such interference was inevitable. Higher wages and shorter hours were here to stay, and full employment was part of the industrial formula as much as skill and production know-how. From now on, if they wished to retain independence of action, it was up to the leaders of industry to recognize the overall nature of the new business picture and to use their abilities toward the end that full production became a means to collective well-being; which, for them, meant increased possibilities of personal wealth and lessened risks. Business was in a position where, if it would, it could eliminate industrial strife and much of its old anxiety over markets and its fear of periodic economic collapse through overproduction.

But it was also apparent that before many businesses could take advantage of the increased possibilities of the home market, the men at the top would have to restyle their approach to the market. Big changes were taking place in distribution, especially of consumer goods. The population shift to cities, married women in industry, smaller families living in apartments around the corner from sources of supply, were affecting buying habits generally. People bought in small quantities and were beginning to be trademark conscious. Since they were willing to pay more for branded merchandise of uniform quality than for bulk goods of unknown merit, more food was being packaged. And more packaged food was of the ready-to-eat variety; women hadn't time or didn't want to spend it in the kitchen. There were other changes in diet and taste. Fried foods were less popular than they had been, even in the South where the big lard business of former times was fast disappearing. With more money to spend for food, Southerners too were eating differently; wholesale grocers in the South, as elsewhere, were abandoning the sowbelly salt pork.

As I saw the wave of the American business future back in 1921, it seemed to depend on two recognitions: first, an increased realization on the part of all business of its great possibilities through wider distribution of income; and second, the need for individual enterprise to get closer to the consumer. If business collectively failed to recognize the only true basis for continuous prosperity in a machine age or individually failed to identify itself with the buying public's tastes and needs, it was courting disaster and missing the chance of a lifetime. American business, alert to its opportunities, could now play for stakes which made the prizes of the past look like peanuts.

I had time for a little intensive thinking about these things that year; Jay was back in harness and my wife and I took a needed two months' vacation in California. The war years had taken a lot out of me and a lot out of the organization. Profits had come comparatively easy during those years, and there was a growing tendency, I felt, on the part of the older men in the business to rest on their laurels. Somehow, as an organization, it was losing the aggressive spirit which had built the business in the face of so many difficulties. Seemingly, we were going ahead; but were we looking ahead? I doubted it. An executive rarely came into my office in the morning with that look in his eye—"Say, I just had an idea last night. Why don't we . . . ?" And for some reason, we were always short of money. Something was wrong. But what, I didn't know.

I was inclined to blame the war. It had released speculative fevers in the countryside quite as virulent as the variety common to Wall Street and boards of trade. Fortunes had been made in buying and selling farmlands. A few of our company executives were up to their necks in these trades during the boom years. But with the coming of peace, I had hoped that the fever had run its course and that, once again, they would redirect their energies toward the business. As a onetime—and cured—poker player, I had come to distrust gambling in any form. It seemed to me more insidiously to destroy judgment and character than any other folly a man could embrace. Once a man began relying on the Goddess of Fortune to take care of him, he became a thin reed for anyone else to rely on.

But nothing prepared me for the blow my son, Jay, delivered late one Saturday night after our return from the Coast. It was about bedtime when he walked in, looking unbelievably tired.

"I've bad news for you, Dad." he said abruptly. "I came across some figures several days ago in the accounting department that I didn't understand. I decided not to ask any questions at the plant, but called in Dick Banfield at the bank to spend the evening with me in the office. We found a sizable discrepancy in Thomson's accounts."

This could be. I had never been satisfied with our assistant comptroller's story of the rich aunt who had left him a fortune to manage.

"I wouldn't be surprised," I said, "to hear that the fellow had made away with a hundred thousand dollars."

Jay looked at me pityingly. "Dad, it's well over a million," he said. "I—I think we're broke."

"Why, we don't own a million dollars in cash—how could he steal it?" I asked, astonished.

"Borrowed money, our working capital, from the banks. He covered up by kiting checks," Jay explained.

Then I understood.

Jay's "I think we're broke" was a magnificent piece of understatement. The money of Geo. A. Hormel & Co.—our family's and our neighbor's money—was invested in brick and mortar—in branches, buildings, and equipment. In one sense, we never had had any money of our own. Every dollar the business earned had been put back into facilities which would bring less at a forced sale than the "over a million" they were now liable for. More than a thousand people—ten percent of the town's population—were employed in the plant; their families depended on it for their daily bread. Many of them were old men, like myself, who had given the best years of their lives in its service. Their savings, too, were in brick and mortar. They had trusted George A. Hormel. My three brothers, John, Ben and Herman, would now have little or nothing to show for all their years of hard and faithful work.

There are no words for such crises; we both stood silent. Then, since there was nothing I could do at this hour and I should need a good night's sleep to fortify me for the ordeal tomorrow would bring, I said to Jay, "My boy, give me the details in the morning. I'm going to bed now."

The next thing I knew, it was morning.

CHAPTER TEN

A Blessing in Disguise

In the early days of the business, back in the 1890's, a young man named Cy Thomson who worked in the plant, came to me and said, "I'd like to work in the office, Mr. Hormel. I want a chance at something better than a workingman's job."

Under questioning, he admitted that he had had very little schooling and no other training to fit him for an office position. I pointed out to him that some knowledge of business procedure was a necessary qualification for the kind of job he wanted, whereupon he left the plant and disappeared.

I had hated to turn him down, for he was a nice young fellow, clean-cut and well-spoken despite his lack of education. I knew all about his background, for he was born and raised near Austin and lived in a house built by his grandparents, old pioneers who had settled in Southern Minnesota many years before. His family was highly respected in the community and Cy was the kind of boy I should have liked to keep in the business.

A year passed before I saw him again. Then he came to the plant one day, wearing the smile of a conqueror.

"I'd like to talk to you about that job again," he said.

In the year he had been away, he explained, he had gone to both day and night school and had brought along his diploma from a business college to prove it.

I was filled with admiration for a youngster who would make this kind of an effort to fit himself for a chance in life. Cy got the job he wanted, and over a period of years was pushed ahead as rapidly as his ability and circumstances permitted. He had a good head for figures and for some years had occupied the important post of assistant comptroller, whose duties included handling the company's thirty bank accounts.

Our working capital was drawn from many sources. The First National Bank of Chicago was our largest lender, but banks all over the country had invested their depositors' money in million-dollar and five million-dollar notes of Geo. A. Hormel & Co., with the consequence that the company owed these banks better than four million dollars on the hot Sunday afternoon in August that I sat listening to Cy Thomson's story of how he had stolen nearly a third of that sum.

After hearing Jay's account in the morning of what he and Banfield had discovered, Thomson had been brought in and confronted with the evidence. He denied nothing, readily admitting a total theft of one million, one hundred and eighty-seven thousand dollars over a period of six years.

Apparently, it had been easy to do. Around thirty million dollars passed through our bank accounts each year. The bulk of our sales was made in the South, the East and abroad. Money for the purchase of livestock in the Northwest was transferred to banks in that area from banks in the principal market areas which handled our deposits from sales. There were many transfers of funds each day. When Thomson removed a chunk of money for his own use, he covered the withdrawal by issuing checks which he shuttled back and forth between these banks.

Although only a longtime and trusted associate would have been given the responsibility of such an important task, nevertheless we had exercised every precaution, we believed, to check his operations and to safeguard our interests. Our books were audited annually by an accounting firm of national reputation usually recommended by our leading banks. We employed an efficiency expert at fifty dollars a day to go over our system of accounting and records. The auditors gave Thomson a clean bill of health and the expert had few changes to recommend.

Where then had we failed? As I began examining the evidence, I could see that in one sense we had done the best we knew how, but in another we had not and this failure was a bitter pill to swallow. I had put my trust in systems, forgetting that no system is ever any more foolproof than the man who operates it. I knew that eternal vigilance was the price of success in the plant and had never taken it for granted that a casual overlooking of its operations was the same thing as a good, daily looking-over. The smallest detail had received my personal scrutiny and the men I had trained to act as my eyes and ears had been drilled to question, the instant it appeared, any deviation in expected results or procedures. Now the ruin of the business had been brought about because I had not questioned sufficiently what I had not understood in another department of its activities. And I had furthermore failed to evaluate, in terms of my associates, what I knew to be true of human nature in general.

In chasing my particular pot of gold at the end of the rainbow, I had been willing to go to any lengths to achieve what I wanted—always allowing that I could do so within the compass of my beliefs of what was fair and right. I noticed that other men who achieved their ends did so, not because they were more talented than their fellows, but because of a singleness of purpose—which is more uncommon than talent. I had tried throughout my business career to attract men who, like Thomson, knew what they wanted and would pay the price of working hard enough to get it. And I had tried, as best I knew how, to focus their whole interest on the business by making it worthwhile for them to do so. I should have been suspicious of such a man's change of focus. That I had not been sufficiently so was now evident.

As far back as 1915, I had noticed that Thomson was becoming engrossed in land speculation and the breeding of purebred poultry. He had established the Oakdale Farms at Leroy, Minnesota, where his poultry was housed on a scale befitting royalty. Nothing in the way of breeding stock was too high priced or fancy for him. He specialized in single comb, white leghorns. We later discovered that, at one time, he had paid ten thousand dollars for a rooster at the New York poultry show at Madison Square Garden. His Oakdale Holstein and Duroc Hog Farms at Blooming Prairie were stocked with equal care and managed by the most scientific methods known.

Apparently these farms were making money hand over fist, for from relatively modest beginnings they developed rapidly. According to Thomson, expansion was out of profits.

I didn't like it and had Thomson in for a talk.

"Don't you think," I said, "it would be better for you to give up your job and devote yourself exclusively to poultry and livestock?

Hobbies are good things, but when breeders' pamphlets and magazines take the place of office reports and price lists on your desk, I think it's time you made up your mind whether the packing business is the hobby, or the leghorns."

"Is there anything that isn't satisfactory about my work?" he countered.

"No," I said, "there isn't, but there will be if you keep this up."

"Of course, you know," he said, "my job is far more important to me than anything else in the world. It's true that I'm interested in the Oakdale enterprise, but I am only one of a number of stockholders. My cousin actually operates the farms. The management is entirely in his hands. Consequently, there is no reason for me to spend time on them which belongs to the business."

"How are they financed?" I asked.

"One of my aunts is well-to-do," he answered. "Some time ago, she had some idle money which she asked me to invest for her. I recommended livestock raising. With prices the way they are now, she can't lose. Naturally, I look out for her interests."

While it sounded fair enough, still I wasn't altogether satisfied. Thomson had certainly led people to believe that his interest in the farms was far greater than a minor stockholder's or a dutiful nephew looking out for his aunt's interests. He talked of little else and, until our conversation, I had been under the impression, along with others, that the farms belonged to him individually. On the other hand, it was also possible that he had bragged a bit as to the true ownership—it was something in a farming community to be the proprietor of establishments like the Oakdale Farms.

At this interview, Thomson's eyes never left my face while we were talking and I had the feeling that he was speculating about

me quite as much as I was about him. He was probably wondering
how gullible I really was, for at that time he had already embezzled
a quarter of a million.

I was hesitating when he said, "Mr. Hormel, why should I be
treated differently than Eberhart? He is interested in farming and
owns fancy livestock too. Has this kept him from doing a good job
for the company?"

It had. But I was in blissful ignorance at the moment of just how
far Eberhart's interests in his farming ventures was affecting his
judgment in company matters. One of Eberhart's duties was to
check the weekly bank statements and the daily bank reports. He
was Thomson's superior and, like him, a longtime trusted associate.
And, though he was a good friend of Thomson's, sharing with him an
enthusiasm for fine livestock—he at one time owned the world champion milk-record cow—it was hard for me to imagine that this would
cause him to overlook any irregularities in Thomson's accounts or
lack of attention to his duties. Eberhart had joined the business in
1900. Upon its incorporation, he became its first secretary and had
served continuously as a director and company officer. Much of our
subsequent success after he joined the organization had been due
to his great sales ability and dynamic personality. I certainly had no
reason for believing that, with Eberhart on the job in the office, there
could be anything seriously wrong. And, as Thomson had pointed
out, I could not fairly object to one man's private interests and make
an exception of another's with no better reason than I had for so
doing. So Thomson remained the assistant comptroller.

However, when the next outside audit took place, I questioned
the accounting firm's Northwest manager. I wanted to be relieved
of a gnawing doubt about Thomson for my own sake as well as his.

I was personally fond of him and it annoyed me to be suspicious of a man on no better grounds than a hunch.

"If there should be anything wrong, are you going to find it?" I asked.

"We certainly are," he answered. "And in our business, we don't take anybody's word for anything. We always consider a man a horse thief until we find him honest."

We paid the auditing company's handsome fee in return for their assurance that their eagle-eyed accountants had found "nothing wrong" with the conduct of the business.

By then, Thomson had already embezzled something over half a million.

He had nerves of steel and never lost his head, for on one occasion, we found out later, Nemesis almost caught up with him; quick thinking on his part confused a man of less subtle wits.

An auditor from one of our Minneapolis banking connections came to Austin—there were discrepancies between the bank's records of certain transactions and ours. The visitor asked permission to go over the books, which was readily granted. When he asked Thomson to explain one glaring dissimilarity, Thomson, as cool as a cucumber, suggested that we go to the First National Bank in town and check the item there; perhaps they had made the error. During the Minneapolis man's absence, Thomson altered his records. When the auditor returned, Thomson glibly pointed out that an overlooked transaction explained everything. The auditor became confused and left. Later, he said that he had become suspicious things were not as they seemed, but since he could prove nothing he kept his suspicions to himself.

Whereupon, to celebrate his good fortune, Thomson abstracted another hundred and fifty thousand dollars.

But he really went to town after I left for the California vacation. In the two months I was gone, he bought a magnificent farm property, equipped it with the finest barn in the state, and stocked it with the best herd of Holsteins money could buy. The governor of Minnesota and other state dignitaries were his guests at the opening party which, according to descriptions, was quite the most lavish affair ever seen in these parts.

If Jay had not inadvertently stumbled onto a transaction he could not trace through the books and if, after finding it, he had gone to Thomson for an explanation or had dropped the matter, we should probably have been out another million in short order. Thomson's delusions of grandeur were growing. Just as he had fixed his mind on the kind of a job he wanted as a boy, now he was equally determined on being the greatest livestock breeder and land speculator in the country, and nothing short of discovery and the penitentiary would have stopped him.

But Thomson had met his match in Jay Hormel. Although he knew nothing of accounting—he was only twenty-six and had spent his time, since leaving college and the Army, in the plant—he was as tenacious as a bulldog. Once his suspicions were aroused, the fact that three different nationally known auditing firms had given Thomson a clean bill of health meant nothing to him. He was neither overly impressed by the fact that systems of checking devised by experts had formerly failed to reveal discrepancies, nor was he deterred by his own lack of experience. From the time he was a baby, his mother and I had been confronted with an individual who knew exactly what he wanted and who, moreover, was determined to get it. Our task had been to shape his character toward the end that his objectives should be worthy of the fixity of purpose with which he would seek to realize them.

So, thanks to Jay, Thomson's long career of speculation came to an end—but much too late, it seemed, to save the business. After he finished his confession, I telephoned our bankers in Chicago and told them what had happened. They would immediately call a meeting, they said, at which the firm's fate would be decided and I was asked to be present.

To make matters more difficult, I knew that I should have to tell the bankers that our year's operations would produce a deficit of at least half a million. We had not taken time by the forelock in our old, aggressive manner by developing new ways of turning our product into consumers' specialties—two thirds of our output was still being sold in bulk, which meant that we had had to meet the stiffest kind of price competition from the big Eastern packers in the domestic and foreign markets. Our labor policy had prevented strikes, but it had also been expensive. Only an organization on its toes could have successfully met these issues, and I had realized on my vacation that we had lately been anything but that. Now faced with this additional catastrophe, how could we ride out the storm?

By Sunday night when, following his arrest, news of Thomson's defalcation became generally known, all Austin asked the same question. I had no answer to give, for I didn't know the answer. All I could say was that I was going to Chicago to plead with the bankers that the business might live and, if I could, to save the town from disaster.

"Why, it's almost as bad, George," said one old friend with tears in his eyes, "as if we had been invaded by an enemy."

"We have been," I said, "and it's going to take ammunition a lot harder to come by than bullets to get the better of him. We've all been a little too proud and cocksure or this wouldn't have happened. I thought I was a good judge of men and, perhaps because I picked them, I've been soft when I should have insisted upon performance and proof. Men who are responsible for the safety and well-being of others can't afford the luxury of taking anything for granted, least of all the infallibility of their own judgments. That scriptural text, 'Him that thinketh he standeth, take heed lest he fall,' exactly fits my case."

It did, too. The growth of the business the past few years had been so spectacular and had seemed to be built on such solid foundations that I had felt I could relax a bit. As it had grown bigger, it had been easier to rely on systems or to accept an office executive's smooth explanation of why this or that activity was losing money than it had been to dig in and find out for myself what was wrong and to correct it. In the plant, where I had kept a large measure of control, no such letdown had occurred. If, by any miracle, the business could be saved, it would be because the production end had made an enviable record sufficiently impressive to warrant our bankers' continued faith and support in its future profit-producing possibilities.

The night before I went to Chicago was a bad time for all of us. But I was immeasurably strengthened by the knowledge that the prayers of the community were added to my family's and my own. I thought I had known my friends in prosperity—our lives had touched at many points and out of our united efforts had come past successes—but in adversity I was gaining knowledge of them and of myself I had never had before. In this test of our characters and of our friendship, nothing gave me so much courage as to know that they were fervently asking that I be given the wisdom and guidance I so needed. The knowledge that they were standing shoulder to shoulder with me in this crisis was a mighty comfort.

On our way to the depot the next morning, little knots of farmers and townspeople gathered on Main Street and watched us pass—Jay went with me. They were silent and downcast. Again, it came home to me that success or failure in this world is no individual matter. It was literally impossible for a man to say, "This concerns me alone," and to speak the truth. I had thought of and called the business "mine," but the only thing about it that couldn't be shared today was responsibility. I had helped create the thing on which these people now depended. But, from the moment it had been translated from idea to action, it had ceased to be personal and, by the very nature of its function, had become communal. I understood, as never before, the moral implications and responsibilities inherent in the control of goods-producing mechanisms—what went with the power and privilege of industrial leadership and being called "first citizen of Austin." The initial impetus and driving force which had created the business had been personal, but the results could never be. Indeed, there would be no results for the one without the many. And once the community of interest had been set up, it was no longer possible for me or any other man to say with any truth, "This is an individual enterprise with which I may do as I like." If I failed in Chicago, it meant that not only the men at the plant but the businessmen on Main Street as well would share in the misfortune.

I vowed that, if the Lord would see me through, I would never forget as long as I lived what I owed to others in return for the support and help which they had given to me. I have more than my share of egotism, but one gets a very different concept of its legitimate exercise on an occasion such as this, which tends to cut a man down to size.

I thought on these things all the way to Chicago, across the fat corn lands of Southern Minnesota, Iowa and Illinois, carpeted with

heavy-eared grain which the August sun would soon ready for harvest, past familiar farms and little towns linked to me by some tie
or association—places where I had traveled for Oberne and Hosick,
where John had bicycled in the old days to sell a few pounds of
sausage, or Gid Smith and Sam Moe had gone to buy livestock or
open accounts. Here, a bank, part of whose assets was invested in
Geo. A. Hormel & Co.'s notes; there, a producer or a livestock feeder
or a customer. The business and the countryside, like the town and
the business, were bound together by a hundred past and present
mutualities of interest. The sudden snapping of some of these ties
in a postwar farm slump would bring uncertainty to many another
Main Street besides Austin's. I asked myself, for the thousandth
time, how Cy Thomson could have forgotten this; he knew it so well
since through his hands passed the stream of paper tokens which
daily evidenced the connection.

The bankers' committee was in session in the directors' room of
the First National Bank of Chicago when Jay and I arrived. I quickly
gathered from their faces and general attitude that many of the men
present thought the company should be liquidated in an effort to
get back out of brick and mortar their million odd dollars. This was
understandable. Thomson, plus the current year's losses added to
the business downswing, was not an encouraging picture from a
banker's viewpoint. Furthermore, to continue we should need the
loan of another million dollars' working capital to take the place of
the stolen money. Reversing our positions, it was easy to read their
minds.

Now it was up to me to make them change their minds. Somehow,
I had to make those men see that they were not foolishly risking their
depositors' welfare by allowing the business to live. I had to find

words to sell them the idea that we still had to offer the one thing on which they could afford to take the risk.

When the chairman asked me to speak, I tried to put into words what Geo. A. Hormel & Co. had tried to put into practice for thirty years. I told them how we had double checked live weights to make sure that the shippers and the farmers who brought in their livestock would receive, to the penny, the money due them; how we double checked all outgoing orders to customers the same way. Invoices were checked twice. We had left nothing to chance in our business dealings. I told them how we had guarded the reputation of our product; how we had striven for quality and uniformity in the days when our facilities consisted of a few small makeshift buildings and secondhand equipment and the office work had been carried on in the kitchen at home after the day ended at the plant—the only room in the house with a stove.

I told them about our sales organization. How it had grown from my brothers scouting the countryside on bicycles and my excursions on branch line trains to a group of men who could sell thirty million dollars' worth of goods at a credit loss of under three thousand dollars; men who could be trusted, not only to sell goods, but to sell them to customers who paid for what they bought. On the record, our accounts receivable represented as nearly one hundred cents on the dollar as we knew how to make it.

I told them what the closing of the plant would mean to Austin; our people and many others would have to sell their homes and businesses to start life somewhere else. Farmers and stock feeders, for a time at least, would lose a dependable source of income.

"Gentlemen, if you will grant us this extension," I concluded, "I will make over my home, my life insurance, and every dollar of real and personal property I possess. I believe we can make up the loss in two years' time, and I give you my word that nothing will be left undone to justify your continued confidence in the company."

I had done the best I could; it was now up to the bankers.

The room was so quiet for an instant that I could hear my heartbeat.

Then E. E. Brown, now president, then vice president of the Chicago First National and head of its legal department, rose to his feet. The die was cast.

"Gentlemen," he said, "I move that we grant Mr. Hormel the extension he has asked for, and that we put the affairs of his company in the charge of a committee chosen from the members present. All in favor of the motion, say 'Aye.'"

It was carried by unanimous vote.

The bankers smiled and Jay and I smiled back. They were almost as relieved to be able to say "yes" as we were to hear them.

In many ways, it was the proudest day of my life as a businessman. They were hardheaded businessmen too, and they were kind enough to say what I well knew—they were not lending money on the assets of the business but on the characters of its personnel and management. They were risking over four million dollars on the soundness of the organization. And even though the creditors' committee, which the bankers proposed to set up for the duration of the indebtedness, would deprive us of much of our former freedom and mobility of action, nevertheless it was a small price to pay for the chance I had asked for. The road of opportunity was still open, and we weren't the men I hoped we were if we couldn't take a few more hurdles on the way.

I went home to clean house.

When we arrived, the news of Chicago had preceded us via Associated Press dispatches. I was touched by the relief expressed on every hand.

Down at the *Herald* office, they said, "You ought to have been here when the news came—why, you'd have thought the town was under siege and relief forces were nearing Blooming Prairie. Hormel means a lot to us, George. Folks would have sure hated to see outsiders take over the plant. It would have been almost as bad as closing down and, next to an earthquake, that's the worst thing that could happen."

But many townspeople didn't like the next thing which had to be done. The doing of it caused me more grief and unhappiness than any previous act of my business career. I asked for the resignation of Al Eberhart and other longtime company executives.

Our sales manager was easily the most popular man in town. His winning and magnetic personality had won for him a place in the community's esteem almost from the day he came to live in Austin. And it would be hard to estimate his contribution to the business during the years he so ably represented its interests. He was one of the best known packinghouse executives in the country, with more warm friends than is the good fortune of most men to possess. He radiated energy and enthusiasm and, like Thomson, had been not only a powerhouse in the business but a warm personal friend.

Eberhart had brought into the business a type of experience that until his coming it had lacked. A former car route manager for Swift & Company in Saint Paul, he knew all there was to know about refrigerator car selling and, had he wanted to, could have sold iceboxes to Eskimos. However, as the business grew he proved to be a poor manager, though he had few equals as a personal salesman. Alibis from his branch managers who showed a statement in the red at the end of the month seemed to satisfy him.

Like many men of his temperament, as time went on he began to rely more on charm and inspiration than on work to carry him through. This was perhaps inevitable. During the war, the morale of the men in his department went haywire. They were being offered higher pay than they were receiving, he among them. He didn't seem to appreciate the value of his position or the possibilities of the future of the business and his department went ragged.

In due course, he began to lean more heavily on past accomplishments than on present performance. And, in little ways, it became apparent that he considered his great contributions of yesterday ample justification for what it didn't please him to bother with today. And the more he thought about the past, the more certain he became that the company's success was solely the result of his efforts. He began to impress this "fact" heavily upon our banking connections and his fellow executives.

But when the war came and the business required hypervigilance from all department heads, he failed me. I was either busy from morning till night with production problems or attending food conferences in Chicago and Washington. For the most part, I was simply unaware of much that came to light later. So, although I realized that his center of interest had shifted and that his pedigreed Holsteins now caused his eyes to light up the way sales reports had once lighted them, I was by no means prepared for the general neglect of affairs with which he was charged until the day the true nature of Thomson's activities was at last disclosed.

Thomson, on the other hand, had been well aware of his chief's growing absorption in the Holsteins and his growing inattention to detail. He, like other subordinates, knew how to take advantage of Eberhart's desire not to let his reputation for affability be impaired by imposing discipline, and he was also clever enough to take advantage of my ignorance of the true state of affairs. For just as long as I believed that Eberhart was on the job scrutinizing those daily bank reports, just so long would it seem unlikely that anything was being put over on a man as smart as he was.

Thomson was exactly right. This was just how I had reacted to the situation. On the several occasions when company directors discussed the possible source of his affluence, Eberhart, alone of those present, evinced not the slightest worry. Everything was all right. He went over Thomson's figures; he understood the transactions they represented; he checked them each day while they were fresh in his mind.

But what he didn't tell us was that he was hardly in a position to scrutinize his subordinate's work—he had borrowed fifteen thousand dollars on his personal note from Thomson.

And so, as I saw it, there was nothing to do but to ask Eberhart to go. Eastern bankers whom Eberhart impressed as being the brains of the business immediately wrote protesting letters. How could we possibly recover without his brains and ability? In reply, I informed them that most of the other executives in the business had been asked to resign, and that we were doing so in order that we might make a good showing at the end of the year. Eberhart's friends considered him harshly treated, but I believed the organization came first. It had come to grief through divided loyalties and interests; it could only regain its onetime effectiveness by putting men in charge of its affairs who were willing to put twice the energy and thought into its building than we expected from men in the ranks.

As an aftermath of the Thomson affair, I had another decision to make.

"Morally and legally," Catherwood advised, "the company has a clear case against certain banks and public accounting firms. The bankers admit that, notwithstanding their suspicions, they failed to notify the company of what they believed was going on. The accountants haven't a leg to stand on, either. They admit that, by analyzing some of that senseless switching back and forth of funds between banks, they could have found out the reason, too."

Company officers, some stockholders, and the creditors' committee held opinions similar to our chief attorney.

I thought it over. The publicity of a suit would certainly hurt, if not wreck, the accounting firms involved. The payment of damages would seriously cripple the banks. While we carried expensive litigation through the courts, the business would stand still. My strength and time and thought, as well as that of others, would be consumed in an essentially non-creative activity. Reexamining my beliefs toward money, I concluded that nothing in my recent experience had basically changed my concepts: it could be either a useful tool or a source of evil; in no case was it a true source of wealth. Depending on the man, it could aid or corrupt, but it couldn't produce. A year's effort invested in the business, on the contrary, might go a long way toward paying off the money loss, produce results for years to come, and at no harm to anybody.

"We'll work a little harder and get it back in our own business," I told Catherwood and others.

Some thought I was foolish and said so. But time proved what I was beginning to suspect—our million dollar loss was a blessing in disguise. Because of it, every executive who remained put on his thinking cap and buckled down to the best job of which he was capable. Near disaster made us all do what comparative success had failed to make us do—take stock of our possibilities. In the light of dire necessity, we reexamined sales and production techniques. We economized on such little luxuries as red ink in the accounting department. Men who held the viewpoint that there would always be some losses in their departments or in the branches they managed—and that viewpoint generally goes with a marked capacity for losing money—were replaced by men allergic to red.

As early as 1912, we had begun to build up an exclusive dealer arrangement for the distribution of our products. By selling the trade on the advantage of handling only quality merchandise for which there was a consumer demand and by enabling one dealer in a given locality to capitalize on the demand for our goods, we had developed a market which we now proceeded to cultivate intensively. New products were added, old ones improved. More attractive packaging, better delivery service, and tastier flavors gave our salesmen something new to talk about that meant volume and profit to the dealer and to ourselves. In city after city, Hormel salesmen developed sizable accounts which six months before they didn't know existed.

To prove what could be done, Jay organized a crew of crack salesmen who put on a sales campaign in areas served by branches long in the red. When money losers became moneymakers, the news of how this was done was passed on to other branch managers who were adjured to go out and do likewise. If they didn't, a smart salesman who did supplanted them.

We had sensed the need for new blood in the organization after Jay's return from the army. Nothing short of the shaking up I received as a result of the Thomson affair could have convinced me that Jay was as right as he thought he was. The average age of the company's officers was only thirty-four, which at sixty-four seemed young to me. At first I couldn't see what troubled him—and that was that we were so pleased with what we had accomplished, we failed to see how much more we could do. Yesterday, and not tomorrow, was the yardstick by which we measured achievement. I had been ahead of my time—as had other men in the organization—but, according to Jay, we were now not abreast of the times. Mass circulation magazines for advertising, more efficient use of trucks in combined sales delivery operations, the development of a sales organization that knew how to merchandise to replace the old type of order taker—men able to assist our customers to sell more goods—were all present day aids to volume we were not using to the best advantage. Young men who thought in terms of these things should be brought into the business, Jay insisted.

In an effort to find the kind of young men he believed we needed, he prepared a little booklet called, "Where Do We Go From Here?" aimed at college men. Copies of it were sent to colleges and universities throughout the country. Its gist was: which of three career possibilities—a vocation, profession, or business—offered a young man most? Where could he render the greatest service to society? If he chose business, which business was most essential? How about food? And how about a food business which was big enough to offer full scope for a man's talents and small enough so that a good man was not lost sight of by management? Why not try Hormel? It was big but not too big. For the young man of more than average intelligence and training, it offered possibilities worth investigating.

Jay didn't catch as many fish in his net as he had hoped for. Some of his young men thought that they should step into big jobs without any preliminary plant training. But a few were smart enough to serve an apprenticeship in the ranks so that they might fit themselves for executive positions on an adequate base of personal experience. One such young fellow was E. N. Sturman, a former divinity student. Attracted by Jay's brochure, he came to Austin and went to work as a common laborer in the plant. Later, he became a salesman. It was Sturman who led one of Jay's shock troop units into action against branch house red ink. He was so good that when Eberhart left he became the new sales manager, a position he filled with great credit.

Others among the young men stepped into equally important jobs when the need became vital for executives in 1922. I, for one, was amazed at the speed with which these boys, none of them long out of school, learned to assume responsibility. It was a valuable lesson for me to watch the trained mind address itself to the new and unfamiliar; to see the fresh approach which such minds brought to the problems of business. These young minds were not shackled to precedent and routine nor satisfied to leave what worked well enough alone. They questioned everything, offered suggestions, tried out innovations.

I learned from listening to these young fry that we weren't going to run an old style packinghouse anymore; Geo. A. Hormel & Co. would become food specialists. A fleet of Chevrolet trucks was put on the road in charge of salesmen who sold, delivered, and collected on the spot. These trucks provided quick outlets for dozens of high-priced specialties which we could produce but which heretofore had accounted for little volume. Energetic young fellows in charge of these branch houses on wheels sold as much as two and a half tons a week of fine sausage and luncheon meats, introducing our products

into stores where they were formerly unknown. Two hundred and
fifty of these trucks, with special refrigerator bodies built in Austin,
were soon touring the country.

We expanded distribution by rail, but abandoned the time-
honored method of selling from "peddler cars." Under the new plan,
salesmen sent their orders to the nearest supply base to be filled.
The invoices were mailed to a trucking company which took over
from there. When the car containing the order arrived, the trucker
met it and delivered the goods called for on the invoice to the customer. The salesmen collected when they covered the territory a
week later. This freed our car route men from the drudgery of deliv-
ering the merchandise they sold and increased their opportunity
to deliver something in which we were far more interested—orders.
The refrigerator cars, like the salesmen, could cover more territory
in the same length of time under this system. Sometimes, within less
than an hour, a car would be met, unloaded, and on its way again.

In order to give our new men the freedom of action necessary
to carry out these innovations, it became apparent to me that we
should have to place ourselves in a position where the policies to
be established did not have to run the gauntlet of a creditors' committee. No purchases could be made without the approval of the
chairman of that committee. He also had the power to veto policies not to his liking. To progress, we should have to take risks, and
creditors' committees are notoriously poor risk takers. On the other
hand, there would be the hazard of what might happen if any of the
conditions set up in the grant of credit were not met on the dot.

I was not prepared to take any chances with the latter or to ham-
per the success of the former, so I began casting about for other
sources of money. One of my business axioms had been to expand

from earnings and not to burden the business with debts and interest; in my opinion, nothing so choked initiative while simultaneously draining off the fruits of effort as debt. A business free from debt is a business able to take advantage of every good wind that blows. But now it seemed wiser to transfer the bankers' debt to first mortgage bonds, payable over a ten-year period.

The transaction was handled through a longtime believer in the company—a boy by the name of Lyman Wakefield who had worked as a handyman in the First National Bank of Austin back in 1902 when we first tried to raise money by selling a few hundred preferred shares. He had invested his small savings in five shares. Since Lyman now occupied a responsible position with a large bond house, Wells-Dickey Company of Minneapolis, I went to him with the problem of how to raise money through a bond issue. This was the year following Thomson's exposure. How it might affect company credit was an open question.

Wakefield believed it was no particular handicap. "With your promise to pay on those bonds, we'll sell 'em," he predicted, confidently.

But his firm was by no means as enthusiastic as he was. The postwar slump had not made bonds too easy to sell and they were not overly optimistic about the issue's selling possibilities; although, they did finally agree to sponsor the bonds.

"Bring the boys to Austin who are going to sell the bonds," Wakefield advised. "Take them through the plant; have them meet the young fellows whose efforts are behind the value of the paper. Tell them what you've done and plan to do."

The bond salesmen came, looked, and listened, and went off to sell the entire issue of first mortgage bonds the day they were offered. So the creditors' committee was no more, four years later the bonds followed it into retirement, and we began our thirty-fourth year once more "out of hock"—a convincing demonstration of what could be done in a business where teamwork and ideas had free rein. A very great deal of the credit belonged to my son and his young coworkers, for they had really known how to put the spirit of the times to work.

But it was not always easy for me to let them have free rein. Jay went to Europe in 1922 to marry Germaine Dubois of La Vernelle, France, whom he had met while soldiering there. He came back with a bride and an idea—canned ham. In Europe, he had met a man named Paul Joern who operated a small packinghouse. Herr Joern packed ham in cans. Jay was so impressed with the possibilities that he persuaded Herr Joern to come to Austin and work with us in developing a successful method of canning hams at the plant.

For the next several years, Herr Joern and the executive personnel devoted themselves to the problem of how best to process and promote canned ham. Finally, in 1926, they had ironed out the kinks and arrived at the answers to what kind of a can was suitable, through whom—butchers, grocers, or both—should the new product be distributed, how much ham to a can—quarters, halves, a whole ham, or all three sizes—and a name had been selected: "Flavor-Sealed."

Selling tests began in Seattle. Institutions, hotels, restaurants, delicatessen shops, and sandwich counters were the first purchasers of the hams. Our Seattle representative also sold a considerable quantity for export to Alaska and the Orient.

Then other Western cities were sampled. In Denver, a Hormel salesman sold one mercantile company a carload of "Flavor-Sealed." Jay brought in the reports of these samplings, waited for my reaction, and then said, in an offhand manner, "I've just signed contracts for five hundred thousand dollars worth of advertising on 'Flavor-Sealed,' Dad."

"You did what!?"

Jay repeated his announcement.

Back in 1910, I had succumbed to an advertising agency to the extent of taking a minuscule advertisement in *The Ladies' Home Journal* which cost, for the year, seventy-five hundred dollars. We had renewed the contract each succeeding year in order to support our specialty men, who established an exclusive agency for our "Dairy Brand" products with the leading merchants in towns of over five thousand inhabitants. The idea helped the merchants establish the brand. He would say, "It is advertised in *The Ladies' Home Journal.*"

"A half million dollars!" I exploded. "Why, that's a handsome year's net profit. I can't imagine myself spending my father's money in any such fashion."

"I'm sure you couldn't," said the grinning Jay, "but you're forgetting something; you didn't have a rich dad like me."

I was burned to a crisp by his levity. Here I had worked like a galley slave for thirty-odd years, only to have a half million dollars tossed out the window on "advertising." "Had the business been built by squandering money on knick knacks like colored pictures in the papers?" I demanded. "What would our bankers think? They'll think we're crazy," I snorted.

I could just see and hear some of the conservative old bankers from whom I had squeezed a sufficient line of credit to carry on operations "against their better judgment," they were fond of saying, raise their eyebrows and call in their loans over this.

But Jay persisted in treating my indignation over his waste of hard-earned money as though it were a funny joke. I had made him

acting president of the company in 1927 and, as such, he was empow-
ered to sign contracts. He reminded me that I had given him control
of operations. If he were the manager, he was going to manage.

This was a characteristic attitude. When he was thirteen, Jay got
himself a job as janitor of the church we attended. One evening he
came home with tears in his eyes, but he looked more angry than
sorrowful.

"What's wrong, Son?" I asked.

"So-and-so is butting into my job," he said angrily. "Tomorrow I'm
going to get this business straightened out. If I'm going to be janitor
of that church, I'm going to janit it and nobody else!"

Of course, he was right. I had told him then what I knew to be
true now—no responsibility without authority. And while the success of his "Flavor-Sealed" promotion was not profitable the first
few years, his five hundred thousand dollar advertising not only
established a market for his canned ham but, in addition, acquainted
millions of consumers with the name "Hormel." At the year's end
when the figures were in, I had to admit the results were better than
I expected, and I couldn't very well object to another expenditure
of a half million dollars the following year for the same purpose.
Aggressive selling and advertising had extended distribution all
over the world. The sales organization had doubled in size. Canned
whole chickens and canned spiced ham were about to be added
to the "Flavor-Sealed" line. They too would be shipped to places
like Guam, Puerto Rico, Samoa, and the Philippines. A new world of
business had come into being. I envied the younger men the opportunities it offered. But it was no place for me. Reluctantly, I accepted
the fact that I should have to go.

It was not an easy decision to make. Building a business had been a romantic adventure to me. At sixty-seven, I was still hard as nails and quite able to keep up in work or play with men many years my junior. I wasn't weary or tired of my job. On the contrary, I had never been so fascinated and interested in what was going on at the plant as I was now. But the habit of years was strong. No matter to whom I delegated authority, when their ways of doing things differed too much from my own, I wanted to interfere. Just, as given the chance, I would have vetoed the advertising.

I remembered my father's startled, "Boy, oh, boy, what are you going to do with all that space?" when he had first glimpsed my new two-story brick. He was not without courage and daring in his own way, but he was always apprehensive at the kinds of risks I felt impelled to take. I had visualized a greater undertaking than my father would have dreamed of attempting and it had surpassed all my expectations. My son's conception of what the future offered him was built, like my own had been, upon an appreciation of the factors present and anticipated which were peculiar to his time. And I could well understand the necessity that men who thought in today's terms be allowed to deal with the present without hindrance from the past. But it is one thing to recognize a fact and another to feel it—and act upon it.

There was also something I wanted to know which could only be found out by leaving the new management to its own devices. How good a foundation had I built? This was a matter of men's characters quite as much as established business principles. I had tried to establish principles based upon something more enduring than expediency and profit. The business had survived its bad times because men, in their hearts, pinned their faith more upon sincere effort and integrity than they did money in the bank. On occasion, they had been willing to trust the rule and ignore the exception. How would my son and his bright young men stand up to the bad times? How would they stand prosperity? Sometimes men could measure up to one and not the other; observation and experience had taught me that the capacity to bravely endure and to struggle against adversity did not mean an equal ability to withstand the impact of prosperity. As someone has truly said, "If adversity has killed its thousands, prosperity has killed its tens of thousands." Only time and freedom of opportunity would provide the answers. And furthermore, not until I stepped out of the picture would our bankers have the chance to make up their minds as to what they thought of the new management's ability. They wouldn't be giving me credit I hadn't earned for successes and innovations, or distrusting Jay when the time came that circumstances removed me from the scene whether I would or no.

He was thirty-four and raring to go. In fact, he had been "raring" almost from the day he got out of short pants. I hadn't wanted him to be a packer. I had hoped that he would choose a profession, preferably law. My friends, Catherwood and Shepherd, whom I greatly admired for the many useful ends to which they put their knowledge of men and institutions, were trained in the law. The packing business was exacting, treacherous, and confining. Profits and losses were figured in fractions of a cent per pound. A slight miscalculation, an easing up on the eternal fight against waste to say nothing of drought, disease, market declines and business depressions, swept away profits and capital almost overnight. He had the chance to step into a field which I could never hope to reach, and I urged him to take advantage of his opportunities.

But although I had wanted an easier life for him than my own, I had wanted him to know at firsthand how money was earned.

Spending money wasn't given to him; he mowed lawns, raked leaves, and cut wood for his dimes and nickels.

In order to point up the lesson of thrift, both in business and at home, I showed him one day how many pennies went down the kitchen sink in the little particles of grease the average housewife didn't think worth saving. Together, we made a fifty-pound lard can into a grease trap into which greasy water could be poured. The water escaped down the sewer but the grease remained in the can. He was all attention at the demonstration.

"Now," I said, "I'll pay you four cents a pound for all the grease you bring to the plant which you collect in this can. You'll be surprised at how much money goes down people's sinks. When I was a boy, we saved grease and made soap—good soap—enough to do all the washing and keep the house clean. By not wasting what we could use, we were often able to own things we wouldn't have had otherwise. This is the whole point of saving. Money is a form of energy—its exchange value. Smart people don't waste energy; they use it to get what they want out of life."

Nothing more was said about the matter, but shortly thereafter an astonishing amount of grease seemed to have been going down our sink, judging from the amount Jay salvaged. I made inquiries; it was the neighbors' grease. Jay had sold the idea to a number of housewives, paying them half the amount I paid him. His argument to them, however, had nothing to do with thrift—unless large plumbers' bills fell into that classification. He warned them that if they let the grease go down the sink, it would stick to the walls of the pipe and clog the sewer. By saving grease for him, they were saving themselves great expense and inconvenience. Furthermore, he had a partner, Ralph Daigneau, one of his schoolmates, now Hormel vice president in charge of the provision department. By the time I discovered what was going on, these energetic young enterprisers had already built up a sizable grease business and had great plans for the future.

A short time after this episode, I saw him trying to remove from his clothes what looked to be red paint. In response to questioning, I learned that he had been taking advantage of a recently passed city ordinance which required all gasoline cans and drums to be painted red. This was in the days before filling stations, when automobile owners purchased gasoline for their cars in five-gallon cans at the Standard Oil tank on the outskirts of town or had drums in their garages which were filled by peddlers. Every car owner—there were perhaps fifty in Austin—owned a number of these cans, and the Fire Department wanted to be able to spot them in a hurry in case of fire. Jay secured a can of red paint, a brush and a list of car owners. His fee was fifteen cents per can—more for drums. Capitalizing on the cheapness and quickness of his service in contrast to the large fine for non-compliance with the ordinance, he secured a monopoly on this bonanza, literally painting the town and himself red.

Believing he would benefit from a change of scene, I sent him off to Shattuck Military Academy for part of his schooling and finally to Princeton University. But not without protests. He didn't want to enter a profession; he had set his heart on being a businessman. A university was no place to find out what he wanted to know, he insisted; the place was under my tutorship at the plant. Since he had no basis for comparing one kind of life to another, I said emphatically, "No!" He went to Princeton.

I made him what I considered an adequate allowance. But shortly after he arrived at college, he began writing home for more. His reasons for needing large additional sums were distressingly vague, particularly in view of his well-known canniness where money was concerned and his usual gift for concise statement. What had he gotten into? His mother and I were greatly disturbed. I wrote to the Dean.

The Dean informed us that our son had taken over the laundry business at Princeton. According to Jay, said the Dean, the laundry system was antiquated and inadequate. He was now installing new machinery and bringing the soiled clothes business in Princeton up-to-date. The Dean warned us, however, that at the end of his four-year term Jay would have a fine laundry and a poor class record. I got on the next train headed for Princeton.

Once there, when I got through with the unhappy Jay, he was no longer in the laundry business and we were equally furious at each other. He thought I was the most tyrannical father and I thought he was the most headstrong boy in the world.

When he finished his junior year, I gave up and allowed him to return to Austin and go to work in the plant.

But we had our differences over this as well. On the morning he started work, he came down dressed in what the young college man turned business executive should wear. I looked him over and asked what he was going to do.

"Oh, learn from you what's to be done and then carry on," he replied airily.

"So that's your idea," I said. "Well, it won't work at all. Sit down and let's talk it over."

For the next hour, I impressed it upon him that no one ever learned a business sitting in a swivel chair. And in a business like ours, a little knowledge was a dangerous thing.

"You can be a good business executive, a diplomat with the workmen and the public, and the best salesman in the world, but you'll be a flop as a packer if you can't tell from personal inspection whether a product is right or wrong," I said. "You can't run this business by relying on the opinions of Tom, Dick, and Harry. If you yourself don't know more about standards of quality and the processes by which they are achieved than any other man on the payroll, this is no place for you to start playing the executive.

"How are you, with your present knowledge," I asked, "going to originate and develop new products instead of imitating competitors? How are you going to achieve uniformity in the finished product despite raw material variations? When you've 'taken over,' who besides yourself is going to strive continually for higher and higher standards of quality? These are the cornerstones of this business. Can you learn what they are by sitting at a desk—by just asking a few questions?"

He listened without comment and rubbed his head a couple of times. When I finished, he got up and walked out of the office. The next morning, he showed up at the plant in brand new overalls.

Before he started out, I gave him a few instructions. "Don't take anything for granted," I charged. "If a man picks up a piece of meat here and puts it there, know the reason why. Watch efficient men at work. Then ask yourself, can the same result be had with greater economy of movement? Could the same man accomplish more with better equipment? By changing the setup? Would a division of the operation step up production without a speedup? What constitutes a fair day's work for a man performing this operation under ideal conditions?"

The next I saw of Jay, he was unloading cars and trucks of hogs and cattle. On this job, he noticed that the hog drovers carried heavy canes with which they prodded the animals to hurry them along. Sometimes, when the hogs refused to move fast enough, these men lost their tempers and kicked them. He had seen carcasses in the cutting rooms with bruises and discolorations which had to be cut out. He immediately put a stop to the practice of kicking or prodding animals and posted "No Swearing" signs in the pens. It was both bad business and inhumane to frighten and abuse the animals, he told the men responsible for their care and treatment. In place of canes, the drovers were given short handles with three-foot loops of four-inch canvas tacked on one end. The noise of the smacking canvas hurried the animals along more effectively than pounding them had done. And the cattle drovers found that, while it had relieved their pent-up feelings, swearing was no aid to soothing a frightened steer. Visitors to the plant familiar with stockyard practices were more impressed by the absence of angry yelling and maltreatment in the animal pens than by anything else we had to show them. Farmers would look at those "No Swearing" signs with their mouths open, sometimes hanging around with their ears cocked for the blue streak which should logically follow some balky steer's performance—sign or no sign.

As Jay went through the plant during the next two years, he made notes on everything he observed while it was fresh in his mind. He didn't tell me about this practice until he had finished the rounds. By then, he had compiled a ready reference book on what to do and why, which later became the textbook for the organization. When I read what he had written, I knew that Jay Hormel's overall knowledge of packinghouse operations and procedure exceeded any other man's in the organization.

As I prepared to turn over to him the control of my life's work and the livelihood of several thousands of people, there was no question in my mind but that he knew the business. How well he would acquit himself toward his responsibilities was not a matter of know-how but of judgment and character. Neither of us could find out how good he was until time provided the tests. The year of my retirement was 1927. The test was nearer than we thought.

CHAPTER ELEVEN

Trees Die First at the Top

One of the first things to be considered as plans for retirement from active business unfolded was the disposition of our home. In 1901, we had bought the first and only home we ever owned in Austin. Built many years before, in 1871, it was known when we took it over as "the old Cook house." During the years of our occupancy, we remodeled and furnished its spacious rooms to our liking. By the time we were ready to leave it, much of Austin's, as well as our own personal history, was associated with this fine, old, pioneer landmark. Since people had been coming together for a long time under the hospitality of its sheltering roof, my wife and I decided that it should continue in use as a place for social gatherings in the community. We wanted it to mean as much to others as it had meant to us. After removing a few personal belongings, we turned it over, completely furnished, to the Y.W.C.A. to be used as a meeting place for the town—a community home within whose friendly atmosphere people could gather for social and community purposes.

Before leaving for California, we also provided the Girl Scouts with adequate headquarters in town. Sometime before, I had built a camp for the Boy Scouts on the ground given by Mr. Everett of Waseca —a place called Everett-Hormel Camp where youngsters could rediscover Nature's ancient lore in a natural, wooded park.

My wife and I felt that no better disposition could be made of these properties than by making them available to young people. Out of our own experience, we knew that the twentieth century's trappings—jalopies, juke boxes, and moving shadows (movies)— were no substitute for the kinship between growing things and the earth. A child who identified his leisure with nothing but these contraptions could hardly be expected to identify himself later with the fundamentals on which life on this planet rested. He'd never see the trees for the road signs, or his ears pick up the music of the little voices for the blare of "Pistol Pacin'." It also seemed likely that when his notion of his country's "rocks and rills and templed hills" were only seen as backgrounds for Hollywood's version of life in America, it would be as equally difficult to engage his interest in their preservation as in their enjoyment. How could he appreciate what he didn't know?

Another project near to my heart was to provide adequate pensions for longtime associates in the business. Discreet inquiry soon disclosed that few men had accumulated enough capital, notwithstanding years of steady work at fair wages, to be able to retire in dignity and comfort. Family men around my age usually owned their own homes, a modest insurance policy and a bank account. But as long as they could work, they were naturally reluctant to draw upon these slender backlogs against a rainy day and equally reluctant to become pensioners upon their children's earnings. Many of them had been burdened with the care of their own elderly relatives and knew at firsthand how unsatisfactory these arrangements usually are from each party's point of view. As one old friend put it, "Of course, my boys would do anything in the world for their mother and me. That isn't the point. We don't want to change our way of life to suit them anymore than they want to accommodate their way to ours."

When I left, there were those past the age of sixty who had been with me more than twenty years who were provided with a one hundred-dollar monthly pension as long as they lived. I would like to provide such a pension for all our workmen, but no industry could undertake such a program if their competitors shirked a like responsibility. I have suggested to business leaders that a federal pension should be enacted into law by Congress providing a one hundred-dollar monthly pension for all persons past the age of sixty, to be financed by a two percent gross income tax, to be paid monthly. Industry would add such a tax to the cost of doing business, same as any other item of expense. In our business, it was figured that three tenths of one percent per pound added to the tonnage shipped last year would have met this cost. This isn't much of a tariff to add to the cost of a pound of meat in return for the assurance it would give to the worker of being able to enjoy the same kind of dignity and comfort past sixty that, in his shoes, each of us would want for himself.

The company was reincorporated under a Delaware charter and its shares listed on the Chicago Stock Exchange. Holders of employees' shares received one share of the new common stock in exchange for each share they owned. This added quickly negotiable capital to many an oldtimer's nest egg. If, like me, he chose to translate some of his holdings into United States Government gold bonds, he could then free himself from further preoccupation with money. Or so it seemed for a little while in the late 1920's.

But the rumblings of the approaching storm could be heard, even though there were no clouds in the sky discernible to most people as yet. Several events occurring between 1925 and 1928 made me sometimes wonder if things were as basically serene as they seemed to be. I had no worries about the business; it was in capable hands, out of debt, and in possession of enough capital—obtained through the sale of sixty thousand shares of common stock—to finance eight new structures without recourse to bankers. And furthermore, we had taken time by the forelock before we had been harmed by the shrinking export market. Our concentration on domestic distribution had begun just in the nick of time. By 1926, when the "Flavor-Sealed" line was launched, quota and tariff restrictions had already made sharp inroads into American industry's foreign business. I realized, in retrospect, how fortunate we had been. But it was no less a matter for speculation as to just how others would fare who had not developed an alternative policy to make up for lost business abroad. I had lived long enough to know that one swallow didn't herald summer. Because we had successfully extricated ourselves from one piece of flypaper, it didn't mean we couldn't be caught on another. If goods—anybody's—piled up in American warehouses, Americans would lose their jobs; when they lost jobs, we lost customers.

About this time, in the winter of 1926 while I was in California, I had an urgent long distance telephone call from my son, Jay. The Austin National Bank was about to fail. The bank examiners had summoned him to a conference. A quarter of a million dollars was needed. Something had to be done and at once. The bank's assets were tied up in farm mortgages, and ...

"Wait a minute," I said, "I can't be separated from that much money without a little time to consider the matter. After all, I've worked hard for it. I'm not too anxious to exchange cash for worthless paper."

"If you don't," said Jay, "it will mean hardship and misery to the community. Many old folks will lose their all."

I promised to call him later and hung up.

With that phone call, I knew that the speculative fever in farmlands had run its course. I wondered how many other Mid- and Northwestern banks were going to be in the same fix before long. Farmers had stretched their credit to the limit to buy high-priced land under the illusion that two-dollar wheat and eighteen-cent hogs were here to stay. And ever since the Armistice, they and their mortgage holders had been hoping for a miracle to bail them out. I wondered if throwing good money after bad was any solution. And what was my moral responsibility in the matter? One hundred and twenty-five thousand dollars might be just a temporary plug in the leaking dam.

While making up my mind as to the wise and useful course to pursue, I picked up the morning paper. The big news of the day was the scrape a rich man's son had gotten into which would cost his father more money than the sum Jay asked for. I began contrasting my good fortune to his. This decided me. If my son was willing to undergo the hard work, to assume the risk of failure and the drain upon his energy and time, I was a poor sport if I didn't back up his attempt to rescue the defunct bank, whether he lost the money or not. In any case, his was the sacrifice. I had wanted to know how he would discharge his social responsibilities. I had the answer.

I immediately called him up and told him to "shoot."

"You won't regret it," he said.

And I didn't. Jay assumed the presidency of the bank, and nine outstanding businessmen agreed to serve with him as directors for five years. They met weekly and passed on all loans. Each of them invested money in the bank's stock, standing to lose twice the amount through the double liability clause if the bank should fail despite their efforts. By teamwork and good management, they pulled the institution through to where it could be merged with the First National Bank of Austin—and once again proving what I really knew in my heart—that men are usually equal to any situation they are determined to master. A smart, young bank manager, Park Dougherty, who had been brought in to aid the directors, shared the credit for saving its depositors a million dollars—a lot of money for a little town to lose.

But for one little country bank that survived, hundreds failed. Since these banks were in difficulties long before 1929, I have never been able to understand why some official cognizance was not taken of the danger in this situation before panic on Wall Street brought down the speculative house of cards around the country's ears.

Perhaps because I have always regarded the false optimisms of the boom periods as being more dangerous to real progress and security than lack of faith, the prevalent disregard of perilous factors in the business structure of the times enhanced my native distrust of a future built on the hope that tangible wealth and inflated values were one and the same thing. From boyhood through the years, I had watched the speculators, the gamblers and their dupes bring periodic disaster to the country and its institutions. Now, with leisure for once in my life to read and think about issues other than my personal concerns, the reams of propaganda issuing from government and business alike, proclaiming that prosperity and Wall

Street had something to do with each other, made no sense. In my experience, inspired values had always turned out to be impaired values. The important things were the permanence of capital, the stability of production and consumption, and not the markup of shares and land. In 1928, the curve of production and consumption turned downward. To me, the figures said, "Look out!" Because they suspected I had money, people were continually coming to me with schemes which they guaranteed would make me as rich as Croesus, and they were never able to honestly understand why I either didn't want to be as rich as that or distrusted their ability to make me so. In their eyes, I lacked "vision."

When the hurricane struck in the fall of the following year, the first question I asked myself was, "What will Hoover do?"

I had a very great respect for Mr. Hoover's ability as an administrator, based upon firsthand acquaintance with him during the war. When he outlined his program and policies to the assembled food producers in Washington, his grasp of detail of all phases of food production was nothing short of astonishing. Meat packing and canning processes, as well as cold storage and distributing problems, were at his fingertips. He really knew the answers. Men who were specialists in these fields came away impressed by his knowledge and his dynamism, for he also knew how to get things done. Persuasive and enthusiastic, he convinced us that nothing was too difficult to accomplish or solve. Now, as President of the United States, it seemed probable that he would exercise the same talents and capacity in a situation as fraught with social dynamite as defeat in war.

But the day by day revelations of unwise promotions and demoralizing fraud which underlay a large part of the financial structure revealed a situation which was more than he could cope with successfully. Perhaps no one in his place could have saved a people so anxious to part with the results of accumulated thrift in return for paper promises backed by fairy tales. And the alternative confronting him and business, which was to stabilize mass buying by putting a floor under wages and shortening the working day, was too big a change in the old way of doing things for either of them to accept. It took courage for the President to propose this and to appeal to the people, over the heads of business, to bring it about through their elected representatives—more nerve than I should have had in his shoes or did have when it came to our business. For it is one thing to recognize the need for a change and something else again to introduce it, if insolvency is the answer to a bad guess.

It was on the eve of the great crash of 1929 that I retired to become chairman of the board and Jay became president of the company.[12] The reader may know that the Hormel business has more than doubled in magnitude since my retirement. But frankly, that is not what has interested me most. It is the human aspects that have interested me primarily—humanity and one's obligations to it from the industrialist's standpoint. That is why I have written this book—no small job at my age for one who has been anything but a writin' man.

And so, if Jay now begins to run away with the book as well as the business, that is to me deeply satisfying. The fact that, after a fashion, I was able to pass on to my son a "silver spoon" in the shape of some thirty acres of packinghouse floor space is a comparatively minor thing. My major satisfaction is that I have watched my son

---

12 George A. began the process of his retirement in 1927 when he became CEO and Jay became acting president.

carry into practical demonstration the basic principles which my father held so dear and himself put into practice wherever opportunity offered—as I, in my way, have tried to do likewise.

Many times, in passing, I have dwelt upon the amazing advances of the past century in the matter of mechanical improvements. The years just ahead will, in their turn, I believe, be even more distinguished by improvement in methods of human relations. I recognize that human improvement is often effected by mechanical advancement. As a matter of fact, the two are interwoven. I've seen more slums improved by better construction, better plumbing, better drainage, than in any other way to date. But there must be something more fundamental.

My son's sense of social responsibility as a private enterpriser and employer has come to public notice in his advocacy of industry's obligation to adopt more dependable employment practices. This has been implemented by his organization of employment at the plant in Austin on a round-the-year basis—a steady job basis. Just now, as I write this concluding chapter in 1946, improved employment techniques are receiving national attention. To my knowledge, literally thousands of employers are considering stabilized wage plans for their workers.

I take no credit for "the Hormel Plan." In fact, I vetoed it when Jay first proposed it for our business. It was put into part operation in 1931, after I retired. But then, I hadn't thought the eight-hour day was good either. I thought it was a nice, kind idea but that it wouldn't work. My life has been a record of finding out about nice, kind things that worked even though most of the solid people said they would never work. To present that point for public contemplation is a major reason for my plodding away at this book.

Back in 1924, when our hog purchases reached a million for the first time, Jay tried to get me to consider a guaranteed yearly payment of fifty-two checks to each regular employee. No involuntary layoffs, no overtime pay, but a guaranteed wage that each worker could depend on. Our business was seasonal in the sense that farmers sent their animals to market in the fall and winter, and summer offerings were always light. This was an old habit pattern, dating back to the days when animals could only be slaughtered in cold weather without undue risk of spoilage. Jay contended that the farmers could be educated to raise and send their animals to market on a year-round basis. And by way of demonstration, he had prevailed upon enough of them to market their animals in accordance with our needs to make our purchase of a million hogs possible.

"If we can do it one year, we can do it right along," he argued. "And if we educate the farmers to send us stock on a year-round basis, where's your argument against a guaranteed weekly wage plan?"

"It's desirable," I agreed, "but there are still arguments against it. What about drought, crop failures, disease, panics? Any one of these things can slow down operations. And with a fixed overhead, then where will you have established a wage precedent?"

He was willing to take the chance if I was, he said. Then he pointed out that in the old days, before the introduction of the hourly rate, I had hired men on a year-round monthly basis and had done all right.

"Yes," I said, "but in those days every man was a jack of all trades. Now they're specialists. Furthermore, I didn't have a couple of thousand men on the payroll. When the hog run was light, men like George Peterson worked on plant construction or your uncles jumped on their bicycles and went off to sell sausage. Things are different now."

"They're no different from the standpoint of a man who depends on his wages to support his family," Jay stubbornly contended. "His problem hasn't changed. And let me tell you something: if we're going to have any real industrial peace in this business, or in this country, a guaranteed weekly wage plan is one of the answers. You admit that labor turnover and strikes cost money, don't you? Well, how are you going to make a man value a job that doesn't value him? We can't get rid of an obligation toward a building whose upkeep is a burden when bad times come along. We don't rid ourselves of contracts or debts at such times, either. We just junk the men."

"You're giving me back my own arguments," I said. "I've been saying these things for years. But still, I don't see how we can afford to do what our competitors are not forced to do and stay in business."

And there the matter rested.

After my retirement, I thought of Jay's plan often, but never with any real conviction that it could be made to work as an isolated policy in a highly competitive business. From 1912 on, Eastern packers had tried, with indifferent success, to stabilize employment in the industry. And it was true that more men had steady jobs than in the old days, but their incomes were by no means guaranteed. Incidentally, I also had my doubts that workers used to big overtime checks during the rush season would willingly part with them, even in the interests of a certain income—a bird in the hand.

Jay, however, never relinquished faith in his guaranteed work plan. He always had an argument to any objection I raised. Two years after the stock market crash and following the drought year of 1930, he put the plan into limited operation, at first with the smokehouse crews. They didn't jump at it; he had to talk them into it. Loss of overtime loomed large in their eyes. And a suspicion that perhaps the plan was, in some way, connected with a speedup, also had to be dispelled.

Although the times were most inauspicious, an incident at the plant decided him to try it out anyway. High-priced "Flavor-Sealed" hams and chicken had gone into a slump, along with cabin cruisers, chain store stocks and fancy investment trust shares, and there were many layoffs. One day, an old employee who had been laid off with many another, walked into the office.

"You can't do this to me," he said to Jay. "I've worked faithfully for your father and for you. And now—and now, what's to become of me?"

Men all over the United States were asking themselves and their bosses that question. To my son, there was only one answer: keep them on the job—make work, share the work, develop new products to take the place of the old—do everything possible to keep the wheels of industry turning. Expansion, not retrenchment, was the order of the day.

Watching all this from California, I admit I was apprehensive, even though I knew there was no other solution to licking the depression. In my thinking I went further; I admitted to myself that unless men who could, would take the risks and make it work at times like this, there was small justification for the present system of private enterprise.

So I read the reports each day of what was going on in Austin with mingled feelings of pride in the organization's imagination and daring, and apprehension lest it overreach itself. Naturally, the business was losing money, but Jay stuck to his guns. He kept insisting that it would stand by its employees to the point of insolvency, refusing to lay off several hundred men who could have comfortably been dispensed with.

"If we lay them off," he said, "we aggravate the problem we're trying to lick—unemployment. There is something cockeyed about a system which sanctions turning human beings out in the street because management finds itself unable to employ them profitably at the moment."

He argued that price cutting and wage reductions were the twin refuges of the bankrupt executive mind and, for believers in the profit system, a fatal confession of inadequacy. A business without profit was of no use to anyone and in time would perish, but profits were the result of activity, not inertia, and a business, like a tree, dies first at the top.

So Hormel made ready to launch the first of its canned soups as one of the answers to how to keep the wheels turning. This certainly looked, to most people, like a bad gamble in 1932, with millions out of work, banks closing, and public soup kitchens springing up like mushrooms. This new product, furthermore, was to sell for fifteen cents, as against Campbell's excellent concentrated soups selling for less.

"Yes, but look at the good ten-cent soups already on the market," I had protested when Jay told me ours was to sell for more.

But I was informed that our vegetable soup was not intended to compete with Campbell's. Hormel was going to sell a pint of rich beef stock, plus fifteen vegetables cooked in the can to retain mineral salts and vitamins, to people who heretofore had not been purchasers of ready-to-serve soups. Instead of stealing the business developed by someone else, we were going to do as we had in the past: aim at a new consumer market. Once again, we would originate, not imitate. The soup was to be offered to the public on a guarantee. If, in the purchaser's opinion, it wasn't the best money could buy, he had only to say so to get "double your money back." And there was to be no price cutting. In order to assure all dealers a reasonable profit, wholesalers and big distributors were warned that no subsequent sales would be made to those firms which insisted on selling the soup for less than the established price.

"We can't make a product worthy of our promise to the consumer to sell for less than fifteen cents," Jay said, "and the dealer is certainly entitled to a reasonable handling charge for his services. We'd rather sell less soup than build volume at the small dealer's expense by allowing it to be used as a loss leader. Keeping him in business is part of our job, too."

I gathered that there was considerable skepticism behind the scenes as to how this venture would turn out. Some of the company's officials were doubtful. Dealers were reluctant to invest additional capital in an unknown item. Salesmen had to buck widespread discouragement. Only the advertising men seemed certain to reap a harvest, win or lose. For a sizable fortune had been invested in advance publicity, with thousands of dollars more to follow before the company could be sure that its message had reached hoped-for buyers.

The new venture was a success from the start and Hormel was in the soup business!

I was understandably pleased. The new product's reception was a demonstration of my lifelong conviction that quality could always demand a premium at any time, and of my belief that private enterprise was equal to its responsibilities whenever businessmen had nerve instead of nerves.

Meanwhile, plant morale hit an all-time low in 1933 when the annual wage plan ran amuck and we experienced our first and only strike in plant history. Echoing countrywide restiveness of labor in those early depression years, there was agitation—originating from the outside—for organization of a union. This done, its leaders promptly raised objection to payroll deductions for a pension fund and to straight time which had been ordered for the whole plant. Despite the fact that Hormel was paying the highest wages in the industry, they also joined an industry-wide demand for more wages. The hidden issue, however, was the annual wage plan, for the suspicion persisted that this was a company device for a speedup.

My only reason for recalling this acute—though happily brief—crisis in the course of more than a half-century of untroubled labor relations is to point out the sound approach and the immediate effectiveness of the state plan then originated to deal with a situation of extreme delicacy at a critical time throughout our country. Governor Olson said he was impressed with the willingness of both sides to submit their problems to arbitration by an impartial state industrial commission, established by law and equipped to handle cases of this nature, and subject to ratification by members of the union.

While the Governor's quick and firm action was a salient factor in the prompt settlement of difficulties, community cooperation was of equal importance. No one in Austin that memorable weekend will ever forget the almost continuous succession of conferences of merchants, town's folk, union leaders, and plant executives—culminating in an all night session—with coffee and doughnuts served in the wee hours.

When the state industrial commission got into action later, one of the strikers' several demands was that the annual wage be dropped—to which the company consented. Before many months, however, the union's seniority board was confronted by the painful necessity of deciding which of their men should be laid off during the dull season. Someone reminded them of Jay's earlier effort to put the plant on an annual wage basis. The result was a union request to have the plan reinstated. A lesser man than Jay might have told them where to go in terms that would have ended all possibility of progress. Instead, he patiently went to work on a new set of schedules for which he now recognized he would have the advantage of union cooperation.

In 1935, the company also went into the building business. I do not know to whom the credit belongs for this bright idea; it seems to have generated spontaneously out of the need for keeping men at work. Why not put the men who were not needed at the plant to building homes for Hormel workers? There had always been a dearth of houses in Austin. During the war, we had built dormitories to take care of single men unable to find other shelter. There had never been enough places available for men with families.

Now was a good time to do something about it. So the company financed a prefabricated house within the means of workers in the average income brackets. The men who erected thirty-three of these houses found the purchasers. It seemed that everyone who didn't already own a house wanted to be a homeowner. Employed workers on a guaranteed yearly income could afford to assume long-range obligations and were eager to do so.

By now, the company had evolved its own form of social security so that the risks of buying a house or any piece of needed equipment on credit was, in our opinion, at about an irreducible minimum. A full-time company doctor had charge of first aid and employee health problems. Since 1917, studies in the prevention of industrial accidents had been underway in the plant. Free life insurance to the amount of five hundred dollars—the amount was later increased—was provided for every worker. Additional insurance could be purchased at low rates and financed through small payroll deductions. Employees were encouraged to make use of these benefits to protect their health and dependents. We also had a credit union and a pension system.

But more important than these things, the rules governing the discharge of a worker guaranteed him a job as long as he wanted one, assuming that he had demonstrated his sobriety, ability, and honesty. Hormel was a business organized for profit and not a philanthropy. It was no place for a social saboteur who disbelieved in the tenets on which it was founded. We accepted freely, without reservation, the principle and the fact of collective bargaining. But we insisted that we had an equal right to demand of every worker a production in keeping with the rights and dignity we accorded him. And applicants for jobs who couldn't or wouldn't give us suitable assurances that they were in sympathy with our aims were not hired.

Once on the payroll, however, a man or woman couldn't be separated from the job for any reason except failure to perform. Foremen and supervisors could neither favor their friends nor fire the people they didn't like. Only after a superior had exhausted every resource to correct poor workmanship or lack of cooperation—and he had to prove that he'd tried—could he file a complaint against the employee at fault. And he must tell the employee that this was being done. The written report was known as "first warning" and had to be filed with the employment office the day the offense occurred. It could not be a vague bill of complaint, but must contain the date, hour and exact nature of the error, together with the names of witnesses familiar with the circumstances. Then, if the employee did not effect a correction within a reasonable time, a "second warning," like the first, was filed. If, after this "second warning," the offender still gave cause for complaint, the foreman accompanied him or her to the employment manager, who handled the case from then on.

If, after hearing both sides of the case and studying the records, the employment manager was not satisfied that the employee had had sufficient time to correct the fault or that the warnings had not been made with full consideration of the employee's rights and interests, he could return the worker to the department for further opportunity or he could transfer him to other work. Whatever the manager's decision, it was not final unless the employee agreed to accept it as such. If he protested the decision, he made a claim through his department committee to the executive in charge of his particular part of the company's activities. The division executive, the employment manager, and the division supervisor then held hearings to which the employee could send representatives to appear on his behalf. Either side could call witnesses. A stenographic report of the proceedings was made. When all the evidence was in, the final decision was handed down by the division executive.

By erecting these safeguards around the employee's economic status, we hoped to increase his independence and his feeling of personal responsibility. He couldn't say, in relation to his work at least, that he was the victim of circumstances over which he had no control. Insofar as it was possible for us to help him do so, he was now in a position to discharge fully his obligations toward the business, his family, and the state. The business, of course, was equally the gainer, since insecurity and worry, frustration and failure, have never been the foundations on which good workmanship and good citizenship rests.

During the early depression years, the company was busy developing ways and means to aid the farmer, as it was concerned with the development of new products and personnel. This, again, was undertaken in the interests of intelligent self-serving. In 1932, the company brought in lambs from the West and put them out for feeding with local farmers, who were assured a price on their gain in weight which would yield them a profit. Range cattle were likewise brought in for farmers to fatten. The figures tell the story. In 1931, the company bought thirty-three thousand sheep and eighty thousand cattle. Within two years, our purchases had risen to three hundred and forty thousand sheep and one hundred and ninety thousand cattle.

The development of such new products made necessary the hiring of more workers. As dozens of new specialties from soups and cocktail sausages to chicken à la king came out of the Hormel kitchens, each in its turn broadened the farmer's market for poultry, vegetables and meat animals. For example, such items as SPAM and spiced ham—both originating with Hormel—increased the demand for and therefore the value of heavy hogs. Few consumers these days are in the market for twenty pound hams. But by converting these heavy hams into a twelve-ounce product sold in a can, it finds a ready sale and the farmer has a ready market for his big hogs.

To encourage farm children's interest in animal husbandry, the company supported the clubs by offering premium prices for their stock exhibited at county fairs throughout our buying territory. Also, a complete market information service for the farmer was organized. Radio broadcasts four times a day acquainted the farmer with pertinent market news and with our market prices for the day on all classes of animals. This kind of information is of prime importance to the farmer. It enables him to know what he will get for his stock while he is in good bargaining position with it still on the farm. He can then either take advantage of prices in his favor or hold it back for a better price. He takes no chances or losses by shipping to a distant market and he can't be swindled by a dishonest stock buyer. For further aid to him, the company published a monthly magazine, the *Hormel Farmer*, sending it to ten thousand farmers in the area. Its purpose was to tell the farmer as much as possible about economical production to the end that he not only remain in business, but profit by it. Only if he made a profit was it possible or to his interest to raise more and better animals. Since quality was our competitive ace in the hole, any aid we gave him in realizing higher standards of production enabled us to do likewise.

By a little providential foresight, the company distinguished itself throughout the so-called "bank holiday" by paying cash for all livestock purchases. To aid local trade when the banks closed, the company established its own, known as the "Wallpaper Exchange," which did a flourishing business exchanging paychecks for Hormel checks of one-, five- and ten-dollar denominations made payable to bearer and acceptable around town as currency.

I must mention in passing, also, an earlier plant publication. *The Squeal*, started in 1916, its name suggested by the traditional packinghouse boast of utilizing "every part of the hog but the squeal." In the case of Hormel, this now made utilization one hundred percent! The monthly magazine—dropped for a short time in early depression years but resumed in 1934—proved to be a fine morale builder.

Each year, when my wife and I went back home, usually during the month of June, there was always something new to be seen—perhaps an electric lift truck scampering over the plant, or new buildings and equipment; new processes and products gave evidence of continual growth and expansion.

A new system of sewage pre-treatment, developed in the Hormel laboratories, was of special interest to me. How the company solved a problem as old as our industry may be of some interest to others. It should be, for it concerns public health. In earlier chapters, I mentioned the pollution of streams and lakes through the disposal of packinghouse wastes in them. In the old days, Chicago's odorous "Bubbly Creek" was a prime example. This situation, however, was not confined to Chicago; it was present, in some degree, wherever organic matter in solution had to be disposed of. Packers and other industrialists had long ago learned how to filter suspended matter present in wastewater through the use of fine screens, but how to treat dissolved solids was a much more difficult matter. Ordinary ways of precipitating organic matter in settling tanks was of little or no value in the treatment of our wastewater. The high sugar, salt and fat content interfered with the various biological and chemical processes that were attempted. Furthermore, the best and only partially successful methods were so expensive that they constituted an excessive financial burden. We disposed of over a million gallons of water a day at that time. To treat this water chemically cost two hundred dollars a day.

In the interests of economy, we had long trapped water as it left each room in the plant, saving grease as close to the source as possible. But, in spite of our best efforts, conditions in the Cedar River were bad. There was always an odor. In the course of years, the large, quiescent pools between the river's two dams allowed sufficient settling of the organic matter so that they were septic. What had once been a lovely country stream was now covered with floating sludge. This condition troubled us, and we spent a great deal of time and money trying to find a remedy.

Chemical analysis showed that this waste contained one hundred parts of nitrogen per million of water. This suggested a new approach to the problem. If the organic matter could be reclaimed instead of being treated to hasten decomposition before it was dumped into the river, which was the usual purpose of chemical treatment, then another good reason for packers to abate a nuisance would be added to beauty and sanitation. Our chemists went to work and success finally crowned their efforts. They evolved a method of treatment by finding a way to recover the nitrogenous material through the use of chlorine and clarifiers. The moment they hit on this, the rest was easy. While their method of reclaiming nitrogen called for an expensive plant with a crew of five men to run it, this was of small consequence, for by such means we could do what had never been done before: we could recover values heretofore lost. What had been a nuisance in the river could be reclaimed as fertilizer, some five tons a day. Its market value was sufficient to pay the cost of operation as well as interest and depreciation on plant investment.

Shortly after the new reclamation plant was put into operation, all odors disappeared. The Cedar River once more became a limpid country stream whose waters were so clear they passed the state sanitation inspection. Since packinghouse waste everywhere could be similarly treated, our innovation was of nationwide importance. Chemistry, coming to the aid of industry, had turned a public liability into a commercial asset. This incident seemed to me to have far greater implications than that it enabled us to save money or abate a nuisance. It was a concrete example of the right and wrong approach to a universal problem: how to convert to useful ends what is otherwise harmful. A thing put profitably to use was a benefit; the same thing unused, a menace.

In 1941, we went back to celebrate the fiftieth anniversary of the company. Of my brothers, Ben, the youngest, was the only one still active in the business, and he was preparing to resign as senior vice president. Back in 1891, at the age of fourteen, he had all but run away from home to join me, and in the course of those fifty years had done a little of about everything there was to do in the plant and out of it. In the early days, his horse-and-buggy sales record had been outstanding. During many of the years since incorporation, he had served as treasurer of the company, more or less alternately with our brother John. Always a lover of animals, Ben was responsible for many of our advances in the care and handling of livestock. In the later years, besides supervision of livestock, the farm and public relations had been his successful concern.

John had retired to California in 1936 after resigning as secretary and director. He too had done somewhat of almost everything since he had come to Austin, in 1893, waving a high school diploma and all agog about the wonders of the World's Fair in Chicago, where he had taken a post-graduate fling. His great contribution in the early years had been as a salesman on bicycle, pedaling the fame of Hormel sausage. Perhaps his greatest service in the latter years of expansion had been as purchasing agent for the company.

My brother Herman had retired some years before when, in 1923, he had sold the local provision market—that once all-important outlet for surplus products. He had been a good merchant and made the market pay a profit that was vital to the business in those early days. He had served as vice president of the company after incorporation in 1900 and continued as a director until his resignation in 1934.

Much more might have been said about the participation of my brothers in the business, but this participation was so full and of such value that I should have had to mention them continuously.

As a part of the anniversary program, I conducted a tour of the plant with local newspaper men and longtime friends, pointing out the contrast between what we were seeing and what we would have seen in any comparable institution fifty years ago. The changes were almost unbelievable. The company had spent three and a half million dollars on new buildings and equipment since my retirement. Its new offices were now air conditioned and soundproofed. Noiseless typewriters eliminated the clatter I remembered. Orders were coming in from branch offices over the recently installed teletype; electrically typed in duplicate, they were on their way to be filled as fast as they left the machine.

In the new general office there were no partitions or walled off cubbyholes marked "private;" everybody worked out in the open. Executives' desks, including my son's, and office workers' desks, were so arranged that paperwork flowed in a straight line from beginning to end. In this quiet, well-lighted office—where you could hear a pin drop—it was possible for about the same number of people to handle twice the work in half the time it required in the old office building of my day. I had thought it was efficient, but by comparison it was overcrowded and badly arranged, and noisy as a ballpark. I could well understand why people who worked under these circumstances had energy left at the end of the day to expend on their own purposes.

Air conditioning and proper lighting were not confined to the place where "white collar" personnel worked. The new beef house, where immense window space permitted daylight operation until the sun went down, was also air-conditioned. At the time of its completion, it was the only air-conditioned abattoir in the world. The cooling system was designed to maintain an average of about fifteen percent below outside temperatures in summer. In the hottest weather, workmen could go about their business without discomfort. Floors and walls, of course, were of easily cleaned tile. This building, which in the old days would have been the dirtiest and least pleasant to work in, was now as clean and odorless as a housewife's well-kept kitchen.

The pickle cellars, where meat is flavored, no longer were the places where sweating, straining men struggled to lift the huge tierces containing meat in pickle. It used to be the duty of the "tierce gang" to pile the big barrels one on another in tiers, only to break them up and roll the tierces from one end of the room to the other in order to keep the curing ingredients uniformly mixed. Then the gang exercised by lifting them into place again. This had to be done each week for three weeks, after which the tierces remained stacked until curing was completed. It was laborious backbreaking work, which only strong men could undertake, and even they often hurt themselves. But there just wasn't any other way to get a mild, uniformly pickled product.

The thought of the backbreaking days of the not-so-long ago was still a green memory as I stood with my friends and watched an electric lift truck run a lifting jack under a monumental vat weighing a ton, lift it in an eye wink and run it back and forth across the room. In that operation the genii of the dynamo was doing what the dynamo had been created to do—to harness the genii and make it take the burden off men's backs. Should it then, I asked myself, be allowed to transfer the burden to their spirits? A thousand times, no.

Many of the devices we saw in operation as we went over the plant were my own inventions. In one workroom we stopped before a long metal trough into which was mechanically dumped load after load of hams directly from the curing vats. Here they were quickly washed by a series of revolving brushes as they moved along a conveyor which finally placed them on a moving table. There they were branded by workmen who then hung them on overhead trolleys which conveyed them to the proper room in the six story smokehouse—one of fourteen smokehouses on the premises.

Before this machine and method had been developed, the same operation required the individual handling of each ham or side of bacon, which must be taken out of the pickle and allowed to soak in fresh water, then scrubbed with a soft brush by hand. The new method saved time and labor. It was more sanitary and efficient. But if we had not found a better way to use them, more than a dozen workers would have lost their jobs because of it.

Another of my inventions was a quick method of defrosting meat with a minimum of time and handling. Meat leaving the freezers as stiff as a board goes into one end of a metal trough containing circulating hot water and comes out the other end ready for the cure. Formerly it had to be spread on racks in a room kept at ordinary temperature until it thawed out. Now, within a few minutes after leaving the freezers, it is hurried off to various departments for processing.

Everywhere in the plant, human labor was reduced to a minimum. Power machines, wherever possible, did the work. Men pushed buttons and guided levers from the curing cellar to the smokehouse. Electrically controlled thermostats regulated the temperatures. Electric trucks, conveyers, moving tables, trolleys and gravity brought goods to the workers to be processed and took them away again.

We stood watching workmen in the cutting room—an assembly line in reverse. Through the center ran a series of moving stainless steel tables. Shining white carcasses from yesterday's kill, after thorough chilling, came down the conveyor table at the rate of twelve to fifteen a minute. Expert cutters took each one and guided it against power-driven, circular band saws in passing, and the next man and the next each performed a single quick cut on what remained of the carcass before the table carried it still farther on to the next. Within a few seconds, one after another skilled knife man plied his art of separating the parts to be sorted and graded. At the far end of the table, the hams, which the first operators had cut from the carcass, were being readied for the curing vats by expert trimmers. In one moment's time, fifteen carcasses had passed through on their way to become hams, bacon, and more specialized products.

Someone commented on the incredible ease and speed of it all. "Yes," I said, "this is what can be done now with comparatively few men working as a team with power machinery to aid them. Before the division of labor into single processes, and without power, it would have taken the same number of men you see working here at least two ten-hour days to accomplish what these men do easily in one eight-hour shift."

As I walked about the plant in that anniversary year of 1941, my mind was awhirl with the contrasts the years had brought. Two million head of livestock had been processed that year and employment figures reached the all time high of close to five thousand. They were now handling six hundred to nine hundred hogs an hour in contrast to our total of six hundred and ten for the full first year of 1891!

With time at my disposal to read about what was going on in the world, I came across continual confirmations that the world's waste and weeds were just names given to things for which no use had yet been found. While critics assailed the "profit motive" as being the cause of all our evils, nevertheless, it was this continual need to transform the useless into the useful—into "something we can sell"—which was creating new means of incalculable human benefit. Soy beans transformed into glycerin, paint, varnish, linoleum, soap, plastics, rubber substitutes, printing ink, and a dozen other products detracted nothing from their earlier uses as food for men and animals; something had been added to the sum total of humanity's material gain. This process was continually taking place in the domain of science and industry whenever and wherever men intelligently sought to find a use for substance. In our own industry, hundreds of life-saving drugs and industrial aids had been developed out of waste. Our company, among many, participated in research programs with universities. Since 1934, Johns Hopkins and Hormel have collaborated in research. The Hormel Institute (for research) was established at the University of Minnesota in 1938.

These were not easy years but a period which taxed ingenuity to the utmost for survival. By 1939, however, business once more became sufficiently stabilized to introduce a joint earnings plan. Profits were not high, but were sufficient to pay stockholders a proper return for the use of their capital, which made the business and jobs possible. To dividends were allotted twenty percent of the profit; the remaining eighty percent was distributed to the employees on the basis of their salaries which, in turn, were based upon the measure of their skill and productivity. There were no hat tricks in this profit sharing. The company's books were open to inspection. Any employee was privileged to see for himself what the earnings were and how the money he helped accumulate was spent. Such a division was, as near as we knew how to make it, both good business and social justice.

The business profited because, for all reasons—old age, sickness, and death—fewer than seven people a month, out of nearly five thousand employed in Austin and elsewhere, left the company in an effort to better themselves. They received fifty-two full-time weekly paychecks a year—this figure excluded workers above the rank of foreman—of nearly thirty dollars a week (to be exact, twenty-nine dollars and ninety-three cents) which, according to figures for the national income, put a Hormel worker among the thirty-three percent of Americans who earned one thousand dollars a year or better. Perhaps two things in addition to money kept our people happy and on the job—two short rest periods a day in midmorning and midafternoon—and living in a town where there was no depression. The same people had a job in 1939 who had one ten years before. Catastrophe wasn't hanging like a sword over everyone's head.

"When the annual wage was first proposed by Jay Hormel," said a member of the union bargaining committee, "I fought it. I was wrong and I'll admit it. The proof that the annual wage is right in principle is in the new residential sections of Austin. They are made up mostly of workers' homes."

The transforming effect of all this on the city of Austin has been described in a ten page chapter, "Austin Speaks for Itself," in a recently published book, *Guaranteed Annual Wages*,[13] from which the following is quoted:

> A visitor, made aware of the city's industrial dependence by
> the size of the Hormel plant, sprawling over thirty-three acres
> just a few blocks from the business district, is struck first of all

---

13 Jack Chernick and George C. Hellickson, *Guaranteed Annual Wages* (University of Minnesota Press, 1945).

by the absence of a working class as such. Taken on a tour of old and new residential districts, he might inquire where the workers live and, to his amazement, be told he had been shown.

* * *

The change literally took place overnight and Austin still is not quite sure it isn't all a dream. For half a century, the city went about its business in the usual way of towns that grew up in the agricultural Middle West. The population in the four decades from 1890 to 1930 advanced from four thousand five hundred to twelve thousand two hundred and seventy-six, leveled off there and then suddenly in the five years from 1935 to 1940 shot up to approximately twenty thousand, an increase of roughly forty percent. Yet few 'growing pains' were suffered by the community. . . ."

The second half-century in the life of the business was begun in the looming shadow of the greatest war of all time. In a few months time, every resource at Hormel command was concentrated upon the important task of supplying food for the armed forces and for our allies. SPAM was destined for strange fame. It had been put on the market in 1937—nearly two years before its earliest twelve-ounce rival—and after two years' delay for proper testing and for want of the right name. That name was to be taken in vain the world over during the war years as a coverall for the canned meats of a dozen packers, while Hormel—at government request—was turning out two hundred and fifty thousand "K-rations" a day.

In 1944, both production and employment reached an all-time high although one thousand nine hundred and sixty-five of our regular employees were given military leave of absence from their jobs before the war's end. During those straining years, my son's greatest concern was that the company should have work for these men on their return without dismissal of the new men and women who had toiled faithfully in their places. He and others worked tirelessly on a program of postwar make-work projects. A full year before the Japanese surrender, there were ninety-four of these projects in the making on the plant list. The sales manager and the credit manager had been given the full-time job of managing this planning and worked under the title of "Vice Presidents in Charge of Tomorrow."

By August, 1944—a full year in advance of victory—company files showed that thirty-four projects had been completed which would require the full-time productivity of one thousand four hundred and thirty-eight of the one thousand eight hundred and eighteen people which the records of that time indicated we must provide for.

As I finish these pages, a copy of the *Squeal* of January, 1946, lies before me with a feature story of the "Welcome and Indoctrination" dinner the company had given in honor of a second group of returned veterans. It runs in part:

> Mr. Hormel said that the average annual wage at the Hormel company in 1945 was two thousand five hundred and forty-three dollars, and that it can be increased in the future if employees help management to an improved operation. On the other hand, the wage income will decline and the ability to keep all employed will be endangered if the quality and efficiency of the operation is not improved. . . .
>
> *   *   *
>
> 'Therefore,' said Mr. Hormel, 'under our setup, if the stockholder is to get more he first must find the means for the

employees to get more. Only as the stockholder through management gets more than enough to pay the base rate does he begin to
share. The greater the earnings above this first requirement, the
more the stockholder gets. Likewise, the more the employee gets.

'This also applies to members of management,' he continued. 'Before they can get extra income, they must provide extra
income to the employees. In order to increase their own income,
they first must increase that of the employees.

* * *

'Not all the assets of the company, if sold at good value,
would realize enough money to meet the payroll for more than
fourteen months. The real assurance of employment,' he said,
'must come from the willingness of the employee to work and
the ability of management to manage.'

A great deal more money would have been available for the
employees' share of the earnings had it not been for the monumental taxes which, locust-like, ate away well over half a million dollars
annually. But business itself was to blame for this situation, for when
it could, it failed to reinvest in its own prosperity what it now paid
out in taxes for an army of social workers and their so-called clients.
There is nothing to be done about it until such a time as the leaders
of industry decide to be masters in their own house.

Despite those tax figures, the mounting national debt made me
realize how truly my life had spanned an era. These tax amounts
had no precedent in peacetime American history. And as long as
conditions represented by those figures continued, it was no longer
possible for the penniless young man, such as I had once been, to
carve for himself a niche in the industrial structure. No matter how

ingenious, hard-working, or thrifty he might be, he had two strikes against him before he came to bat. Without accumulated capital, he could not purchase the costly tools of a powered machine age. And, if by any chance he overcame this handicap and entered business on a shoestring, he could not expand, as I had done, by reinvesting all his earnings in better tools and facilities because so large a proportion must go for taxes. The same expansion today would mean that he must hang a millstone of debt around his neck—if he could find a lender. This age offered little incentive to the ambitious youngster who preferred the risks of setting up shop for himself to wearing another man's collar for life. The tax gatherers stripped him of both the means and the desires to build for himself and the future.

How disastrous that future could be for the creator of an enterprise was sharply pointed up for me when I underwent a major operation a few years ago. After it was over, my son said to me, "Dad, if you hadn't come through, I wouldn't have known how to raise money for the inheritance tax. Your stock in the company could not have been turned into cash—the market is inactive. The real estate you own and value at over a million dollars would have brought in very little; there are no buyers. The government would have had to take the business."

"I know," I said, "and the pity of it is that this particular goose wouldn't lay any more golden eggs if that happened." The fact that my wealth exists only in the nominal control of production-for-use tools whose continuous operation concerns the livelihood of thousands of people and benefits my heirs only so long as they intelligently use them, doesn't mean a thing to the men who think that this kind of a tax means social progress. It can just as easily mean social disaster. The answer is not in what a man owns; it's in what he does with what he has. We are more interested in this business and the community it serves than the most competent outside managerial talent the government could hire. But the government wouldn't be concerned to the extent of hiring talent to maintain it. Just as some bankers once wanted to do, Hormel would be turned over to the first bidder who furnished money enough to meet the government's claim. What happened after that would be nobody's business. A soulless corporation or a soulless bureaucracy, what's the difference so long as both are only interested in their pound of flesh?

All of which is just another way of saying that I believe popular concepts of what constitutes real wealth in a modern industrial order are all wrong. Wealth in such a society depends on more than the ownership of the tools of production. A modern industrial enterprise depends for its success on factors which are never contained in any catalogue of its physical assets. The Midas touch is not in them but in the intangibles having to do with the nature and creative capacity of men. This is a spring which flows no higher than its source. The best tools in the hands of the best workmen will neither keep them employed today nor provide them with an adequate return on their effort without a management behind them able to discern genuine opportunities for the use of their skills. The physical assets of a business are about the only thing which can safely remain static for even a short time. The minds of its managers must be ever alert and receptive to new wealth-producing possibilities. They must be men willing and able to undertake the risks and responsibilities of pioneering new fields—men able to coordinate other men's activities, to organize the production and, above all, the distribution of goods. And if all the manifold activities which they originate and supervise are, in the end, to fulfill the true purpose of human effort, they must be men with conscience as well as brains.

And because this country has produced, and will continue to produce, such resourceful men, I trust to them the future I shall not live to see. For they alone, in concert with the men of specialized knowledge, are able to explore the infinite possibilities of this wealth-producing earth, in the terms of their time, toward the end of the greatest good to the greatest number. No nation is ever richer than the numbers of such men it produces. To deny this by crippling their capacity to function is equivalent to trying to prove that standing a triangle on its apex provides the best support for its base. Which does not mean, however, that the base of society's triangle is not within its rights in everlastingly reminding the men at its top that their private interest ceases at that precise point where they forget the foundation upon which the apex rests.

How thoroughly men of different classes, races and nationalities had forgotten the common human base upon which their particular pyramids had been erected, the twentieth century was now to demonstrate abundantly.

Had I never believed before that Christ's commandments were a simple statement of law—that they are "the mortar that binds society together; the granite pedestal of (all men's) liberty; the strong backbone of the social system"—I should have had to believe it in the light of coming events,[14] for nothing else was evident.

---

14 Probably World War II.

Epilogue

George A. Hormel's poignant comment about "coming events" was very likely a reference to the Nazi concentration camps, the atomic bomb, and the other horrors of World War II. It does not appear that he was finished writing with this last paragraph.

In March, 1946, George A.'s wife, Lillian Belle Hormel, passed away. George A. mourned the loss of his wife and his health suffered. Though he still played golf just days before, George A. Hormel died three months after her passing, on June 5, 1946, in Los Angeles, California.

Jay C. Hormel became chairman of the board. With his commitment to his workers and to his community, he continued a family legacy of social conscience and innovation. He introduced new packaging and distribution technology, as well as additional product lines. His creative marketing was epitomized by the Hormel Girls, a traveling troupe of former servicewomen. These musical sales representatives visited grocery stores and performed stage shows which were recorded and broadcast weekly over national network radio. The Hormel Girls were the first all-female drum and bugle corps to take part in The American Legion competitions, twice winning their local contests and making it to the national finals (1947 and 1948).

In 1949, Jay opened the first, large-scale meat packing plant in the United States (in Fremont, Nebraska) which did not use elevators and chutes, but operated all on one level. In 1952, he also introduced what is believed to have been the first humane killing lines for hogs in U.S. packinghouse history. By use of a carbon dioxide chamber, the animals entered kicking and squealing but came out sleeping, avoiding injury and trauma to both them and the workers. Hormel became the first meat packer to receive the Humane Society Seal of Approval (in 1959), for anesthetizing animals prior to slaughter.

Jay C. Hormel died of a heart attack on August 30, 1954, at his home in Austin, Minnesota.

All three of Jay's children, George, Thomas and James, worked summer vacations within the company, but with military service, schooling and other distractions, none of the three boys remained with the company. (James, however, in 1960, was elected to the board of directors of what is now known as Hormel Foods Corporation, and served on the board until 1975.)

George A. Hormel II ("Geordie") was an artist, musician and performer. He owned the iconic recording studio, The Village Recorder, which produced many gold and platinum records. Among the notables who recorded there were Frank Sinatra, Johnny Cash, Ray Charles, Dolly Parton, Bob Dylan, John Lennon, George Harrison, The Doors, The Rolling Stones, The Beach Boys, Sly & the Family Stone, and Steely Dan. Numerous film soundtracks were also created there. Geordie's label, Zephyr Records, morphed into the first record library which became standardized in later years as a model for other companies, and established master use recording rights for film and TV. Geordie released his own vocal and jazz piano recordings, and composed most of Zephyr's cue music (used in about half of all filmed TV shows of the 1950's and 1960's, including Hanna-Barbera cartoons).

Geordie shied away from taking credit or receiving recognition, but his talents in art, music and comedy were the source of ingenious cartoons, literary spoofs and satiric songs. He developed an original political philosophy and wrote his own unpublished version of the Constitution. His eccentric character was part of his charm. Geordie passed away in 2006, prior to this publication.

Thomas D. Hormel (Tom) received a B.A. in sociology from Occidental College. Early on, he pursued various projects in business and real estate, although art and music have always been his passions. His artistic achievements include many paintings and musical compositions, continuing to this day as the driving force in his life. After opening a restaurant and organic farm in Hawaii, Tom moved to Idaho, where he became committed to protecting the environment. He is a recipient of the United Nations Environmental 500 Award, and was the founder and principal donor of the Global Environment Project Institute, Global Action Network, Eastern Africa Environmental Network (co-founder), and the Environmental Resource Center. Tom also created a program that put the first environmental textbooks in many high schools throughout the United States.

Much of Tom's art has been reproduced in a dynamic presentation that was printed in 2015. His music ranges in style from tropical Latin jazz to contemporary and orchestral. Tom has compiled several CDs of original music. His "Go For Baroque," premiered at the Wilshire Theatre in Beverly Hills and was subsequently performed by the Cape Cod Symphony. Tom's symphonic composition, *The*

Legend of Bird Mountain, was recorded by the Prague Symphony Orchestra in 2015 and was premiered in January, 2017, by the South Florida Symphony Orchestra. This ballet is also scheduled to be choreographed and danced by the Martha Graham Company in January, 2018. Tom continues to write music and is focused on reorganizing several older compositions to be orchestrated and/or choreographed.

James C. Hormel (Jim) has devoted his life to the advocacy of basic human rights and social justice. While serving as dean of students at the University of Chicago Law School (1961–1967), he focused on improving the diversity of the academic student body. He encouraged a policy to help women graduates obtain law jobs, and the number of women enrolled in the school tripled during his tenure. In 1986, Jim innovated a financial aid program at the University of Chicago Law School to facilitate its students to go into public service. Later in his professional career, Jim was a United States delegate to the 51st United Nations Human Rights Commission, which met in Geneva, and served in the U.S. delegation to the 51st U.N. General Assembly in New York. Jim served as United States ambassador to Luxembourg from June, 1999, to December, 2000, and authored a book about becoming the first openly gay U.S. ambassador called *Fit to Serve.*

Jim was one of the founders of the Human Rights Campaign, the largest LGBT civil rights advocacy group and lobbying organization in the United States. He established the James C. Hormel LGBTQIA Center of the San Francisco Public Library. Prior to obtaining his law degree, Jim received a B.A. in history from Swarthmore, and currently serves on its board of directors. Jim and his spouse, Michael P. Nguyen, are funding the construction of a new intercultural center on the Swarthmore College campus, which will serve at least twenty-one student organizations. Jim has been honored with numerous awards in recognition of his philanthropic achievements.

The company, started by George A. Hormel in 1891 with one employee and little capital, today (2016) functions as an independent corporation with over 20,000 employees, and has continued to maintain the highest operational standards in the food industry. In 2015, Hormel Foods made *Corporate Responsibility Magazine*'s annual list of the 100 Best Corporate Citizens for the 7th consecutive year.

After 125 years, Hormel Foods is still headquartered in the small town of Austin, Minnesota. With an increasingly diverse population estimated to be around 25,000, Austin is also home to the Hormel Institute, the SPAM Museum, the Hormel Historic Home, and the Jay C. Hormel Nature Center. Hormel Foods remains Austin's largest employer, and exemplifies what can happen when the management of a company stays connected to its community, as was George A. Hormel's intention.

PHOTOGRAPH AND DESIGN CREDITS

Front cover, back cover and photo insert design
by Mary Ellen Krieger, Kelkē Design LLC.

Most of the photos used in this book, because of their age, are in the
public domain and not under any copyright protection. Efforts have been made
to identify possible copyright holders, and photographers, when known,
have been credited. In case of oversight and upon notification to the
publisher, corrections will be made in subsequent editions.

Unless otherwise noted in the photo captions here or under the photos in the photo insert section, all photos are from the personal collection of Thomas D. Hormel.

COVER PHOTO CAPTIONS:

Front outside cover: George A. Hormel, circa 1905.

Back outside cover: Geo. A. Hormel & Co. plant on the Cedar River. Photo from souvenir postcard, circa 1935.

Front inside cover: Geo. A. Hormel & Co. plant, 1894. The two-story brick building in the back was the first addition to the former creamery turned meat packing plant, with staff and delivery carts. (Hardcover only.)

Back inside cover: Geo. A. Hormel & Co. plant, circa 1940. Photo courtesy of Hormel Foods Archives. (Hardcover only.)

Interior design and formatting by Lawna Patterson Oldfield.